THE WAR FOR AMERICA'S NATURAL RESOURCES

Also by William R. Nester

AMERICAN INDUSTRIAL POLICY: Free or Managed Markets?
AMERICAN POWER, THE NEW WORLD ORDER, AND THE
 JAPANESE CHALLENGE
ENDS OF THE EARTH
EUROPEAN POWER AND THE JAPANESE CHALLENGE
INTERNATIONAL RELATIONS: Geopolitical and Geoeconomic
 Conflict and Cooperation
JAPAN AND THE THIRD WORLD: Patterns, Power, Prospects
JAPANESE INDUSTRIAL TARGETING: The Neomercantilist Path
 to Economic Superpower
JAPAN'S GROWING POWER OVER EAST ASIA AND THE
 WORLD ECONOMY: Ends and Means
POWER ACROSS THE PACIFIC: A Diplomatic History of
 American Relations with Japan
THE FOUNDATION OF JAPANESE POWER: Continuities,
 Changes, Challenges

The War for America's Natural Resources

William R. Nester
Professor of Political Science
St John's University
New York

St. Martin's Press
New York

St. Martin's Press, Scholarly and Reference Division,
175 Fifth Avenue, New York, N.Y. 10010

First published in the United States of America in 1997

This book is printed on paper suitable for recycling and
made from fully managed and sustained forest sources.

Printed in Great Britain

ISBN 0–312–16589–7 (cloth)
ISBN 0–312–16591–9 (paperback)

Library of Congress Cataloging-in-Publication Data
Nester, William R., 1956–
The war for America's natural resources / William R. Nester.
p.   cm.
Includes bibliographical references and index.
ISBN 0–312–16589–7 (cloth).— ISBN 0–312–16591–9 (pbk.)
1. Natural resources—United States.   2. Natural resources-
-Government policy—United States.   I. Title.
HC103.7.N38   1997
333.7'0973—dc20   96–35139
                                                        CIP

To Jess, Laura, and Will – three great adventures, characters, and, above all, friends!

Contents

Introduction: Philosophies, Politics, and Policies

HISTORY OF IDEAS AND POLICIES

American attitudes toward the use of natural resources, and the policies which flow from those attitudes, have changed markedly over time.[1] For most of American history, those who shaped natural resource policies were inspired by the Biblical injuncture to, "Be fruitful and multiply, and fill the earth and subdue it; and have dominion . . . over every living thing that moves upon the earth."[2] A secular version of that attitude emerged with Adam Smith's *Wealth of Nations* in 1776, and ever since has been developed by a succession of economic theorists.[3] Virtually all early Americans were "cornucopians" who saw the earth's resources as endless, and there to be exploited by humanity for its material needs. Cornucopians idealize conceptions of private property, free enterprise, and a government with powers confined to protecting Americans from internal and foreign violence.

In the mid-nineteenth century, a handful of New England philosophers and artists developed an alternative vision to cornucopianism, known then as transcendentalism. Its adherents believed that God was immanent in nature, and thus that nature should be revered and preserved as much as possible.[4] Although they had no impact on American natural resource policy, the transcendentalists became the philosophical fathers of the latter-day environmentalists. Today, although environmentalists are split over whether or not nature has a spiritual dimension, they share the belief that development must be both sustainable and able to satisfy humanity's deepest psychological as well as material hungers. A sustainable society is one which "satisfies its needs without diminishing the prospects of the next generation."[5]

A halfway perspective between cornucopians and environmentalists emerged in the late nineteenth century. Conservationists

1

reject both the "exploit today for tomorrow you shall die" outlook of cornucopians and the more esoteric beliefs of environmentalists. Like cornucopians, conservationists are essentially materialists who value a forest for its lumber, soil for its crops, the substratum for its minerals, and water for irrigation, energy, or transportation. As Gifford Pinchot put it, "the first great fact about conservation is that it stands for development."[6] Conservationism is utilitarianism applied to land, or the "use of natural resources for the greatest good to the greatest number for the longest time."[7]

Yet, cornucopians and conservationists differ sharply over the abundance and ways in which the earth's resources should be used. Over the past century, conservationists have looked closely at the ever growing demands of an ever growing population for the earth's resources, and have recognized that some resources have rapidly diminished. The culprits were private corporations, monopolized markets, and corrupt special-interest politics and policies. Thus, according to conservationists, policies should encourage the "wise use" of natural resources to sustain them for future generations.[8] Like environmentalists, conservationists believe that governments rather than markets are best suited to enhancing both the public good and private enterprise. To achieve sustained development, the government must intervene in markets and regulate industries that otherwise would exhaust one resource after another.

PROBLEMS, POLICIES, AND PHILOSOPHIES

There is a dynamic relationship among natural resource problems, policies, and philosophies. Throughout most of American history, natural resource policies reflected the dominant philosophy of cornucopianism. As conservationism and environmentalism arose to struggle with cornucopianism for mass public acceptance, so too did the policies that flowed from those respective philosophies. The result has increasingly been a range of federal policies which reflect aspects of all three conflicting philosophies.

For most of American history, the most important natural

resource problem was how to exploit the continent's riches as quickly as possible. The first European and African settlers to America's east coast stood on the edge of what appeared to be an endless continent covered by virtually impenetrable wilderness. Timber, water, pasture, and minerals all seemed limitless; the land need merely be cleared and plowed or grazed, the waters diverted, the minerals found and gouged, the trees logged. Cornucopian attitudes both reflected and shaped natural resource policies until the late nineteenth century.

It was only then, when perceptive observers recognized that the nation's natural material and scenic riches were finite and rapidly diminishing, that the conservationist and environmentalist visions and policy proposals emerged to battle both the prevailing cornucopian ethic and, increasingly, each other. Around the century's turn, conservationists wrested control over natural resource policy from the cornucopians. National forests were created to sustain the logging industry. National parks, wildlife refuges, monuments, and wilderness areas were designated to preserve the most spectacular of America's natural wonders. Throughout the twentieth century, the federal government has tried, with varying degrees of success or failure, to encourage conservation practices in farming, grazing, and logging. To manage the nation's resources, the government constructed new government bureaucracies such as the Forest Service, National Park Service, Bureau of Land Management, Bureau of Reclamation, and so on. Under the conservationist banner, the federal government constructed thousands of dams, canals, and irrigation works that have tamed and diverted most of the nation's rivers to farmers, boaters, businesses, and households.

Environmentalists did not begin really to shape natural resource policy until after World War II, and then only gradually and on a few issues. The tug-of-war among cornucopians, conservationists, and environmentalists shifted toward the latter on many issues in 1970 when the Environmental Protection Agency (EPA) was created and environmental-impact statements were required before development was allowed. Congress passed and presidents signed a series of powerful laws regulating air and water pollution that swept away earlier inadequate ones, and mandated the sustained use of the nation's natural resources.

Yet, despite these efforts, cornucopian practices still prevail in many areas. Mining remains governed by an 1872 cornucopian law which gives away public lands to prospectors, who are not required to pay royalties on the wealth they extract. Although taxpayer-subsidized water, timber, grasslands, crops, and minerals would seem to be at odds with the free market and minimal government ideals proclaimed by cornucopians, those special interests continue to enjoy them, often while denouncing similar handouts to others elsewhere in society and the economy. Upon recapturing Congress in 1994, the Republican Party has tried to gut the nation's environmental and conservation laws. They have only partially succeeded; President Bill Clinton vetoed the most extreme of the measures and public opinion has rallied overwhelmingly against the cornucopian revival. Today, a power balance exists among the three natural-resource philosophies; the relative dominance of any of those three varies from one issue, congress, and president to the next.

What accounts for these shifts in policy and power? Powerful political or intellectual leaders can tip the power dynamic and thus policies. At the century's turn, men like Theodore Roosevelt and Gifford Pinchott shifted the nation's consciousness and resource policies toward conservation. During the 1960s and 1970s, articulate leaders such as David Brower, Paul Erlich, or Rachel Carson, echoing the thoughts of Henry David Thoreau and John Muir, shifted a majority of Americans toward environmentalism. More recently, cornucopians like Ronald Reagan, James Watt, and Newt Gingrich have tried to turn the clock back to nature's unregulated exploitation.

Other changes were more gradual but no less profound. The environmental movement evolved over nearly a century. As its numbers and organizational strengths increased, it achieved significant policy shifts across a vast spectrum of issues by "decades of patient lobbying, by grass-roots political mobilization, by public education, and by research involving a multitude of organized groups operating at all levels of government,"[9]

Technology and affluence also dramatically affect natural resource policy. During America's first several hundred years, cornucopianism prevailed in part because the nation remained largely poor, agrarian, and relatively underpopulated. Then, from the mid-nineteenth century onward, industrialization created a new range of socioeconomic problems as well as improvements. America's industrialization and urbanization exploded together, dragging in their wake increasingly severe sewage, garbage, water contamination, and health crises. Not surprisingly, most of the first regulatory policies were intended to arrest and, hopefully, reverse these urban problems, which were the most obvious and which affected the most people, rather than rural or wilderness decay. As most Americans became wealthier, increasing numbers supported reinvesting some of the nation's newly created wealth in addressing some of the environmental disasters that industrialization had spawned.

The fickleness and often conflicting values of most American voters is another major obstacle preventing any one philosophy from dominating. While most Americans claim environmental values, they seem to hold other values higher. For example, in 1981 only 45 percent of Americans polled believed that environmental protection should come before economic growth; by 1989 the percentage had jumped to 80 percent. This burgeoning mass environmental consciousness was stimulated by both the Reagan Administration's systematic cornucopian assault on the environment and the mass-media reports of ever worsening environmental crises like the greenhouse effect, ozone-layer depletion, population explosion, and so on. Yet, while four out of five Americans deplored Reagan's environmental record, six out of ten voted for him in 1984, and nearly as many voted for his successor George Bush in 1988. So awareness is not enough to shift the political landscape. Pocketbook concerns such as employment, taxes, crime, and schools continue to take precedence in most American minds over more abstract environmental issues.

CULTURAL CONTRADICTIONS, MYTHS, AND REALITIES

The tendency of most Americans to support both environmental beliefs and cornucopian policies points toward deeper contradictions in American cultural values. Every society faces a potential conflict between the public good (however defined) and individual rights. Not only did nearly every society traditionally hold that the public good was far more important than individual rights, the very notion of individualism was and remains alien to those peoples.

The United States is an exception. Although the first colonists did tend to weigh the public good as more important, the concept of individual rights gradually strengthened until by the time of independence from Britain it had become the dominant value in American culture. Shortly after achieving independence, the founders debated two visions of American political and economic development. Alexander Hamilton advocated a strong central government that would guide economic development by building infrastructure and protecting industries from foreign competition. Thomas Jefferson disdained a powerful central government, industrial policies, and industrialization; American democracy, according to Jefferson, rested on a nation of small farmers, shopkeepers, and decentralized political power.

For the following century, private property rights rather than the public good was the most important value to most Americans and the policies which governed them. American civilization is built upon Jeffersonian myths of individualism and self-reliance, no region more so than the West. According to legend, the continent was tamed by rugged individuals and free enterprise. Scornful and mistrustful of government, Americans turned their back on it as they marched steadily westward. Throughout American history, radicals from Samuel Adams to Newt Gingrich have rebelled against regulations and taxes – no matter what essential or nonessential services they provided – as a violation of private property rights.

The reality of the development of American civilization differs starkly from the myth. While American values are Jeffersonian, the government's policies have become increasingly Hamiltonian. From America's Declaration of Independence, the federal government has been central to the conquest and transformation of the land from wilderness to civilization. Public and private interests have cooperated to exploit all of America's natural resources – minerals, soil, water, air, trees, grasslands.

No region cherishes the myth of individualism and free enterprise more than the West. Ironically, no region is more dependent on government handouts – welfare if you will. Yearly, tens of billions of taxpayer dollars subsidize the building and maintaining of dams, irrigation systems, logging roads, mines, oil fields, farms, ranches, military bases, laboratories, and sparkling cities in the desert. Cut the West off completely from government welfare and that vast civilization built upon sand would shrivel and crumble. Had the government never underwritten the West's development, it would never have occurred as we now know it. Yet, myths rather than realities guide most people's lives; the welfare West remains cornucopianism's most fervent citadel.

POLICY AND ITS DISCONTENTS

Policy is both what governments do and what they do not do. The impact of a government not deciding can be as powerful as its deciding what to do with a problem. Politics determine policy, and politics are shaped by the multistranded and inevitably unequal war among special-interest groups, politicians, and government bureaucracies, against the background of shifting public opinions. In the conflict between special and national interests the former usually win: "There is a bias toward politics with immediate, highly visible benefits – the myopic politics for myopic voters. Special interests induce coalition building politicians to impose small costs on the many to achieve large benefits for the few."[10]

Natural resource policy directly or indirectly affects every American. All of our lives are shaped by the ever thickening web of regulations, laws, subsidies, and programs which determine how the nation's resources will be used. But just because natural resource policies affect all, it does not mean they benefit all. Some special-interest groups reap enormous benefits from various natural resource policies, while most Americans pay through higher taxes, diminished qualities of life, and forgone opportunities to support them.

Natural resource policies are shaped by political iron triangles among politicians, bureaucrats, and corporate interests, largely independent of prevailing public opinion. The policy details governing America's mineral, forest, water, grassland, and soil resources mostly emerge from the appropriate congressional committees and subcommittees in both Houses, which in turn are dominated by politicians who represent powerful mining, grazing, logging, and farming interests. The aim of those special interests is to exploit America's natural resources for immediate profit rather than to conserve them to sustain the nation's socioeconomic development for endless future generations. Ironically, those special interests have decreased in importance within America's economy. The combined production of farming, ranching, mining, and logging contributes less than 5 percent of GNP and 3 percent of the labor force. Two hundred years ago, they composed almost the entire economy. How have those special cornucopian interests sustained their power? Political action committees (PACs) directly hand cash to sympathetic politicians and indirectly buy their votes by spending hundreds of millions of dollars on direct mailings and mass advertising to shape elections and public opinion.

Although Washington's natural resource policies affect public and private lands alike, the largest criticism is leveled against the use or abuse of the former. As historian Bernard Shanks eloquently put it:

> the history of the public lands is a tale of waste and corruption ... the public lands do not yet fully serve the American people; they serve special interests. Reforms that began as conservation a hundred years ago were never completed. While the federal lands remain in public ownership, their valuable products have largely become privately-controlled commodities. Grass, timber, water, and minerals including oil and gas are still controlled by a handful of people. This problem is aggravated by federal subsidies for every commercial product removed from the public lands. Private enterprise has used the political process to

control the market and prevent the owners of the federal lands from earning an honest profit from their resources. Inefficiency, wasted resources, overuse of the land, and unfair competition are a few of the by-products. The American taxpayer, whose land and wealth are harvested by private developers, is still cheated by every mine, and every dam.[11]

Are government programs and subsidies "investments" or "pork"? It depends. Groups and individuals tend to consider their own government handouts essential "investments" in the nation's future, while labeling the handouts to other groups and individuals "pork." Those that receive government handouts – whether deserved or not – become dependent on them. The nation's farmers, ranchers, loggers, and miners who pride themselves on their "independence" are thoroughly dependent for their economic livelihood on a vast array of government subsidies, programs, and other advantages.

Policy victories in a democracy are rarely absolute; compromise is inevitable, reversals frequent. The most important reason that no one paradigm had dominated natural resource policies in the past century is the ability of powerful special interests like logging, mining, farming, and ranching to stifle most conservation and environmental initiatives at the federal, state, and local level.

THE INSTITUTIONAL AND REGULATORY SYSTEM

About twenty different federal agencies have jurisdictions over the public's lands; many of those jurisdictions overlap or the laws regulating the use of those lands conflict. This collection of institutions evolved over time in response to new problems and new political forces which created new demands for the management of those problems.

Each bureaucracy has its own special interests which it regulates or supports. Institutions often compete for and share the same clients. Bureaucratic and political battles for the regulation and exploitation of public lands are incessant. Of course, many of the subsequent policies conflict with each other, even those implemented by the same bureaucracy. For example, laws restricting the discharge of pollution into the nation's air, soil, subsoil, and water clash with other policies which encourage the exploitation of those very resources.

Free markets are largely a myth – governments regulate more or less every industry. Washington can determine the fate of entire industries through regulations, tax hikes or abatements, subsidies, enforcing or neglecting antitrust laws, and so on. There are few ways in which the federal government can more directly shape an industry than through its public land-use policies. After all, the federal government owns one out of every three acres in the United States, and most of those acres are rich in at least one and sometimes many sought-after resources. The market value of natural resources on the 740 million acres of public lands were recently estimated to be worth $1.3 trillion; that market value appreciates yearly. Of course, the aesthetic and spiritual value of those lands to environmentalists is priceless and immeasureable. The nation's supply of natural resources located on public lands varies from 98 percent of its silver, to grazing land for only 3 percent of its cattle.[12]

There are no uniform laws regulating the exploitation of public lands. Some lands which are designated as wilderness or national park are more protected than, say, the 310 million acres of Bureau of Land Management lands. In 1960, Congress passed laws which required federal agencies to manage the lands in their jurisdiction under the principles of multiple use and sustained yield of resources, unless those lands had been designated for some specific use such as wilderness protection. These principles were strengthened by the 1976 National Forest Management Act and the Federal Land Policy Management Act which called for:

> a combination of balanced and diverse resource uses that takes into account the long-term needs of future generations for renewable and nonrenewable resources, including but not limited to recreation, range, timber, minerals, watershed, wildlife and fish, and scenic, scientific and historic values; and harmonious and coordinated management of the various resources without permanent impairment

of the productivity of the land and the quality of the environment.

These principles attempt to placate every possible interest group; in practice, by trying to please all, they end up disgruntling all.

The War for America's Natural Resources analyzes the dynamic among natural resource politics, policies, and philosophies. Each chapter and its sections explores in-depth the development of policies toward America's soil, wildlife, water, energy, grasslands, minerals, forests, and air.

1 Farming, Grazing, and Hunting

> *Those who labor in the earth are the chosen people of God, if ever he had a chosen people, whose breasts he has made his peculiar deposit for substantial and genuine virtue.*
>
> Thomas Jefferson, "Notes on Virginia"

When Jefferson penned those words, nearly nine out of ten Americans raised crops and livestock and hunted for their sustenance. Two centuries later, America is no more the land of yeoman farmers that Jefferson celebrated. Farming and ranching have experienced technological and productivity revolutions, plummeting the percentage of Americans in those pursuits to less than 2 percent of the population. American agribusiness is the world's most productive – so productive that the excess is either exported or stored in huge warehouses. Yet despite these revolutionary changes, the raising of crops and livestock has become peripheral to America's economy, accounting for a mere 3 percent of all economic activity.

Nonetheless, whether they are as virtuous as Jefferson believed or not, farmers and ranchers are today the chosen people of the American government if not of God. Among all of America's industrial policies, perhaps none has been more successful than the agricultural revolution it brought to the nation's farms and ranches. Taxpayers pay a hefty price to subsidize American agribusiness – $12 billion for federal handouts in 1994 alone! Add to that subsidized irrigation, state and local payments, and the higher prices consumers pay for foods the government protects from foreign competition. Although farmers and ranchers are among the most conservative of citizens, they do not hesitate to pocket the massive "workfare" subsidies ladled out by the government.

Federal agribusiness policy is shaped by a classic iron triangle among agribusiness, politicians from farm and ranch districts and states, and the Agriculture Department. Relevant laws are written in the Senate and House agricultural committees and subcommittees. Farming and ranching remain heavily subsidized industries because they are extremely well organized and financed, politically powerful, and economically connected with related industries. Agribusiness interests include farmers, ranchers, manufacturers of farm machinery, biogenetics, pesticides and herbicides, grain elevators, and those truckers, railroads, and barges which transport production. At least a half-dozen huge, powerful national organizations represent agribusiness interests, including the American Farm Bureau, American Agriculture Movement, National Farmers' Organization, National Cattlemen's Association, Association of American Plant, Pesticide and Control Feed Officers, National Association of County Agents, National Agricultural Chemical Association, National Association of State Departments of Agriculture, Christmas Tree Growers Association, and dozens of others. Given this array of national organizations flush with seemingly bottomless pockets full of cash, it's no wonder that agribusiness largely writes its own policy ticket.

From Jefferson's day to ours, farmers and ranchers have been popularly viewed as the wise stewards of the land. Unfortunately, this image has been at best an exaggeration. Farming and ranching are very hard on the land – soils erode, chemicals and excrement pollute streams and aquifers, grasslands and woods disappear. For much of American history, farmers would wander westward, exhausting along the way one patch after another of publicly provided land. When the frontier disappeared a century ago, this became no longer possible. Faced with an ever worsening crisis of increased demand for food and diminished supply of healthy soils and grasses, the government began promoting soil conservation among farmers and ranchers. Athough agribusiness today is less destructive of the land than before, the deterioration of soils and waters has merely slowed. So far technological advances in hybrid plants and chemical fertilizers have helped offset steady soil losses. But will this always be true?

Hunters and fishers, too, once enjoyed a hallowed place in American culture. No more. Ironically, those who prowl woods, stream banks, and the ocean's depths have acquired an increasingly negative image as rapacious destroyers of wildlife. Although that may have once been true, government regulations have transformed the hunting and fishing of most species into a largely sustainable activity. Unlike farmers and ranchers, hunters and fishers give back more than they take from the American people. The fees for hunting and fishing licenses fund wildlife restoration projects in every state. Most recognize that they have a vested interest in abundant game and fish, and the ecosystems in which they live. Hunters and fishers assert these interests and others through such political powerhouses as the National Rifle Association (NRA), National Muzzleloaders Association (NMLA), Issak Walton League, and Ducks Unlimited. This chapter will explore the federal policies toward farming, ranching, and the taking of wildlife.

FARMING

The United States has the world's most productive agribusiness.[1] Two centuries ago, nine out of ten Americans toiled in the fields and pastures so that everyone could eat. Today, less than 2 percent of the population produces more food than Americans can consume; the surplus is exported. Meanwhile, the nation's population has soared a hundredfold from 2.5 million in 1780 to 250 million in 1990. Until the 1930s, more farms and more productive farming kept up with all the new mouths to feed. The number of farms peaked at 6.8 million in 1935 during the Great Depression's height, and has steadily declined since. In 1992, the number of farms dropped to 1,925,300, the lowest level since 1850. A farm productivity revolution boosted by Washington policies made that possible.[2]

Nonetheless, contrary to popular belief, the family farm is not dying out; its production is simply becoming more specialized. Farmers, however, are aging. Between 1987 and 1992 alone, the average age of farmers rose from 52.0 to 53.3 years. Children are leaving the land for more lucrative and easier jobs in the towns and cities. Technology is largely responsible for that demographic shift. By greatly easing farm life, technological breakthroughs have allowed many farmers to work their land part-time while working at full-time jobs elsewhere. The growing popularity of "boutique crops" like shiitake mushrooms or blueberries has induced many with land to farm part of it for the extra income. Those farms with incomes between $1,000 and $9,000 recently increased by 300,000 in just one year alone, from 1,300,000 in 1991 to 1,600,000 in 1992. As Americans acquire an increasingly sophisticated palate, the number of boutique farms will continue to expand.

While family farms will persist, huge agribusiness corporations will produce most of the nation's crops and livestock. About 75 percent of the nation's food comes from about 300,000 of the largest farms, about 15 percent of the food comes from about 300,000 medium-sized farms, and another 1 million mostly part-time farmers compete for 10 percent of the market.[3]

Despite these successes, both agribusiness and small family farms alike are trapped in a terrible market dilemma. The more farms produce, the lower the food prices. Farmers must make up in volume what they cannot get in price, which simply increases the supply and further lowers prices. Profit margins in the best of times are razor thin. But when every farmer tries to maximize production and nature is benign, the crops exceed what can be consumed. Bumper crops lead to low prices that can bankrupt all but the largest plantations. Free markets may be great for consumers, but they are merciless for producers.

Farmers may advocate the "magic of the marketplace" for others, but bitterly reject it for themselves. Over the decades, farmers have become increasingly dependent on a widening array of government handouts – welfare if you will – to survive. Although it represents less than 2 percent of America's population, the farm lobby has enormous political power. In nearly every state, rural farm areas exceed metropolitan areas. Political districts are gerrymandered to give rural farm districts numbers and clout far beyond their populations. Even if most people in those farm districts do not, in fact, farm, their livelihoods and sentiments are often thoroughly tied to agribusiness.

Farm welfare is a sacred cow impervious to government budget cutters. At the national level, agribusiness has the power to make and break a president. Most presidents simply sign off on the policies and appropriations that enrich farmers. Even presidents like Carter and Reagan, who entered the White House determined to cut farm subsidies, inevitably increased them. In Congress, the farm lobby has just as effective a grip over nearly all senators and most representatives.

This was not always the case. Ironically, as the percentage of farmers in America's workforce has diminished and the importance of agriculture to the economy has faded to insignificance, farmers have become ever more politically powerful. From the nation's founding, the government has pursued policies favorable to farmers. The 1785 and 1787 ordinances provided favorable conditions for the sale of public lands to farmers and others. But from then until the early twentieth century that policy largely consisted of giving away land to those who desired it, and designating some land for colleges and other progressive purposes. Selling off land not only helped settle the new nation's frontiers but helped pay off the national debt.

In 1820, Congress passed a law authorizing the auctioned sale of half-section (320 acres) and quarter-section (160 acres) lots for a minimum price of $1.25 in cash per acre. The law neglected "squatters' rights" for those who had actually lived on and improved the land to be sold. It was not until the 1841 Pre-emption Act that Congress gave squatters the right to purchase the land at the minimum price. Only if they expressed no interest in buying the land would it be open to bids from anyone.

Throughout these decades, American agriculture was transformed by a series of technological advances to which the government contributed little. A relative scarcity of labor spurred inventors to create labor-saving devices in plowing, reaping, and processing. Each of these inventions sparked a productivity revolution in a segment of farming. In 1797, Charles Newhold received a patent for a single-piece cast iron plow which enabled farmers to dig deeper into the earth and farm larger areas. That same year, Eli Whitney's invention of the cotton gin allowed the spread of cotton plantations across the South. In 1831, the first patent for a mowing machine was granted to Jim Manning, who also received a patent for a steel moldboard plow two years later.

Obed Hussey and Cyrus McCormick received patents for their reapers in 1833 and 1834, respectively. Hiram and John Pitt unveiled a stationary grain-threshing machine in 1836. In 1837, John Deere's invention of the steel-edge plow made farming even more efficient. Farm productivity was further boosted by the introduction of seed drillers during the 1840s and threshing machines during the 1850s. Harvesting, however, still depended on sickles and hand-picking. With a sickle, a worker could harvest no more than an acre a day. From the 1850s into the 1880s, the McCormick harvester, which doubled a worker's productivity, became increasingly common in grain-producing regions.

The government aided these technological advances through the Patent Commission, which from 1836 through 1862 encouraged the introduction of productive crops from overseas. Most farmers were unaware then, or now, of how dependent their livelihoods are on crops which originated beyond the Atlantic Ocean's eastern shores. Few crops grown in the United States are native to the region. Aside from strawberries, blueberries, pecans, Jerusalem artichokes, sunflower seeds, and cranberries, all other crops originated elsewhere. Corns, beans, and squash came with Native Americans from Mexico. The Europeans brought with them all other crops, including those like potatoes and tomatoes which originated in South America. The Patent Commission expanded the variety by identifying, importing, and promoting the use of improved strains of crops and livestock.

America's labor scarcity was never worse than during the Civil War (1861–5). Several Lincoln Administration policies planted the seeds for a vast expansion of America's farmlands and productivity. The two most important public land laws in American history were passed in 1862, amidst the Civil War's horrors. Under the Homestead Act, the government gave away 160 acres of public lands free to anyone who farmed it for five years straight or paid a mere $1.25 an acre. The Homestead Act eventually transferred 147 million acres to 1.6 million people. The Morrill Act was almost as important. Under it, the government gave 30,000 acres of land to each new state for every representative the state sent to Congress. The states in turn had to use that land to establish land-grant colleges which promoted agriculture and mechanical arts. That same year, President Lincoln created the Department of Agriculture (USDA) and charged it with accumulating and dispersing data on farm machinery, soil science, and hybrid seeds.

When the public land giveaways were finally tallied, railroads had got much more than farmers. Enriching the railroads indirectly helped the farmers by tying together regional markets into one huge national market. The ever expanding railroad system enabled farmers to supply ever more distant markets. The government gave away huge swathes of public lands across the country to the railroad barons; the barons in turn sold some of that land to farmers and others. The railroads were particularly important in inducing farmers to settle the Great Plains.

Agriculture technology advanced steadily after the Civil War. The introduction of gas-powered tractors dragging plows and reapers in the 1880s further increased yields and eased the lot of farmers. Lands formerly used as forage for draft animals were converted to crops. In 1881, McCormick marketed the four-horse twine-binder, which allowed one worker to harvest between eight and eighteen acres a day. Inorganic fertilizers became increasingly popular from the 1880s onward. At the Tuskegee Institute in Alabama, George Washington Carver discovered hundreds of uses for crops like soybeans, peanuts and sweet potatoes. The invention of refrigeration by the late nineteenth century, extended the shelf life of numerous crops. Food prices dropped, particularly during the winter.

These inventions and expanded farmlands led to a doubling of some crops between 1870 and 1900: corn production rose from 1,094 million bushels to 2,105 million, wheat from 236 million bushels to 522 million, and cotton from 1,451 million pounds to 4,757 million. Exports soared during this era, with wheat sales rising from $68 million to $200 million and meat from $21 million to $175 million.[4]

As the scale of machinery and fertilizer production increased, prices for those products dropped thus generating more income for farmers. From 1880 to 1900, real wages for farmers increased 1.3 percent annually while machinery and fertilizer prices fell 1.5 percent and 1.8 percent annually. From 1900 to 1910, real wages increased 1.9 percent annually while machinery prices increased only 0.4 percent and fertilizer prices fell 1.2 percent annually. Land prices rose even more rapidly from a price index of 69.0 in 1900 to 105.0 in 1910.[5]

Farmers could have made even more money if they had used their land more wisely. Productivity increases by these inventions were diminished by soil depletion. The net productivity gain was actually quite small. In 1880, the total productivity ratio was 100; three decades later in 1910, it was a mere 102.[6]

Although the adverse effects of soil erosion on farm productivity had been obvious from the nation's founding, it was not until 1894 that the government first addressed the issue. That year, the Agriculture Department published the bulletin, "Washed Soils: How to Preserve and Reclaim Them." During his tenure as Agriculture Secretary from 1897 to 1913, James Wilson initiated a range of policies which promoted conservation and technological advances. Wilson created bureaus of plant industries, entomology, and chemistry which worked closely with land-grant colleges and state laboratories to stimulate scientific advances in their respective fields. In 1899, the Agriculture Department conducted and published its first soil survey. In 1910, it published an expanded soil-conservation bulletin. These government-led technologies and techniques were spread to farmers through federal and state extension services. Although these measures raised concerns about soil conservation, they had little effect on changing destructive farm practices.

Fortunately for the nation's well-being, there were still virgin lands to be plowed. From 1880 to 1930, about 98 percent of all increases in farm production depended on an expansion of acres farmed rather than increases per acre. The amount of acres farmed increased from 76 million in 1850 to 319 million in 1900 to peak at 413 million in 1930.[7]

Government policies were responsible for this vast increase in the nation's farmlands. Farmers continued to scatter across the West in pursuit of lands given away by the 1862 Homestead Act. Land promoters for the Great Plains claimed that "rain would follow the plow." In other words, after farmers settled and planted their land, precipitation would increase. During the twentieth century's second decade, Washington once again spurred development. In 1909, the Enlarged Homestead Act doubled the acreage for dry farmers. In 1916, the Stockraising Homestead Act redoubled acreage to 640 acres.

These measures coincided with soaring grain prices during the 1910s as Europe's agriculture was disrupted by World War I and weather conditions were optimal across the United States. At first, those new farmers and ranchers fencing the high plains succeeded, largely because the 1910s were the wettest phase of the long-term moisture cycle. The result was a land boom, particularly on the high plains. While between 1862 and 1900, 78 million acres were claimed under the original Homestead Act, the revised homestead laws and increased demand for crops stimulated claims for 328 million acres between 1900 and 1930.[8] Despite these dramatic increases in productivity, acreage, and transportation, food increases barely kept up with America's rapidly rising population.

Farm prosperity peaked during World War I when European demand for food pushed up prices. After the fighting stopped in 1919, crop prices plunged in the United States and stayed low until World War II sent them soaring again. Several interrelated reasons led to the farm depression during the interwar era. Gasoline-powered tractors increased farm productivity for those who owned them. The number of tractors increased from 1,000 in 1910 to 920,000 in 1930, while the price of tractors and other machinery decreased by 30 percent. As farming became increasingly mechanized, the need for draft animals, and the large fields of grass and oats to sustain them, correspondingly dropped. Between 1910 and 1940, the number of draft animals diminished from 24.9 million to 14.5 million, while the amount of acres devoted to forage dropped from 88 million to 65 million. Much of those grazing lands were converted to crops, which in turn increased total production. Federal subsidies further expanded production. The Agriculture Department budget for extension services increased from $14.6 million in 1915 to $52.9 million.[9]

Paradoxically, the more crops farmers reaped, the more money they lost. As productivity soared, farm income dropped. Prices collapsed during the 1920s as markets became inundated with American and European grains. Most farmers had trouble making payments on their land, seed, and equipment; many went bankrupt. To worsen the farmer's plight, the moisture cycle on the Great Plains spun to drought throughout the 1930s. Between 1910 and 1930, the price of farm land fell an average 30 percent.

During the early 1930s, the combination of generations of bad farming techniques and drought created the dustbowl years in which soil across the Midwest literally blew away. Between 1930 and 1940, the amount of cropland dropped from 413 million acres to 399 million acres. The worst year was 1934.

In Congress, there were several attempts to alleviate the farm crisis. Several versions of the McNary-Haugen Bill were proposed from 1924 to 1929. The bill would have established a $200 million public export corporation which would buy up crops to boost prices to "parity" or the level at which farm income equaled production costs. The excess would be sold overseas. President Coolidge vetoed those bills with the argument that they represented too much government intervention in the market.

President Hoover was more sympathetic. Although he refused to champion the McNary-Haugen Bill, he did recommended to Congress in April 1929 that they raise tariffs to protect agriculture and other industries from foreign competition. In October 1929, the New York stock market collapsed, precipitating the Great Depression. Congress responded with the Smoot-Hawley Act of 1930, which raised tariffs by 50 percent across the board. Other countries retaliated; world trade collapsed; America's depression spread worldwide. America's farmers and other workers were worse off than ever.

When Franklin Roosevelt entered the White House in March 1933, he faced a national depression in which one-quarter of the workforce was unemployed and production was half what it had been four years earlier. The farm economy was devastated by depressed prices, massive soil erosion, and the subsequent impoverishment of most farmers.

Roosevelt responded with a flurry of bills whose programs were designed to stimulate strategic economic sectors. One of his industrial targets was agriculture. Among the most important bills of his first 100 days was the Agricultural

Adjustment Act, which he signed on May 12, 1933. The Act targeted six crops – wheat, corn, cotton, rice, tobacco, and peanuts – with the nation's first agricultural price supports. These supports were based on the concept of "parity" – the difference between crop prices and the price of raising those crops. A parity of 100 meant that farm income equalled costs. The bill also provided below-market loans, debt relief, and payments to take land out of production.

Although, in 1936, the Supreme Court struck down parts of the bill as unconstitutional, these programs and others were reinforced by 1936, 1937, and 1938 farm bills. The 1936 Soil Conservation and Domestic Allotment Act included rewritten parts of the 1933 Agricultural Act rejected by the Supreme Court. The 1937 Agricultural Marketing Agreement boosted the prices of perishable products like milk, eggs, fruits, and vegetables by empowering the Agriculture Secretary to set floor prices or limit production in certain areas. The 1938 Agricultural Adjustment Act established the Agricultural Adjustment Administration, which would make low-interest loans to enable farmers to store their surplus crops during large harvests and then sell them during poor harvests. In addition to the power to buy up entire harvest surpluses, the bill allowed the Agriculture Secretary to pay farmers to curb production. These bills all tried to equalize supply with demand in order to maintain high farm incomes. From 1933 through 1941 alone, the government paid out $5.3 billion to farmers, and the program has increased ever since.

After depressed prices, the worst farm problem was soil erosion. No man was more influential in countering soil erosion and improving farm productivity during this time than Hugh Bennett, who had been championing national soil conservation ever since he joined the Federal Bureau of Soils in 1903. He first sounded the alarm in 1928 with the USDA publication "Soil Erosion – A National Menace," co-authored with W. R. Chapline. The Civilian Conservation Corps, which Roosevelt established in 1933, used Bennett's ideas on soil conservation and other projects across the nation. The Corps faced an enormous challenge. In 1934, the Agriculture Department completed a National Reconnaissance Erosion Survey led by Bennett which calculated that erosion had destroyed 35 million acres and severely damaged another

140 million acres. On the basis of Bennett's analysis and proposals, Roosevelt pushed through Congress what became the 1936 Soil Conservation and Domestic Allotment Act, which created the Soil Conservation Service. Roosevelt named Bennett as its first head.

Through the Soil Conservation Service, Bennett encouraged farmers to rotate crops, take fragile marginal lands out of production, contour plow, create artificial terraces, plant rows of trees, allow strips surrounding fields to remain fallow, and so on. The Agriculture Department's Agricultural Stabilization and Conservation Service subsidized farmers who withdrew land from production, used it for soil-conserving crops, or initiated soil-building practices. Participation was voluntary. Although we take such practices for granted today, farmers were largely ignorant of them back then. Through that ignorance farmers inadvertently destroyed their own land.

In addition, the Soil Conservation Service promoted new hybrid corns and other crops which produced higher yields and were more resistant to rust and other blights. Unfortunately, these hybrids depleted the soil even faster than older seeds, so farmers had to invest in more fertilizer.

Despite these efforts, the government could only slow soil erosion. In 1939, Bennett calculated that the:

> annual monetary cost of erosion in the United States amounts to at least $400,000,000 in terms of lost productivity alone. . . . To this would have to be added huge losses due to (1) clogging of great reservoirs and shoaling of stream channels with the sedimentary products of erosion; (2) the abandonment of irrigated areas dependent on reservoirs; (3) the virtual abandonment of large agricultural sections; (4) the economic devastation of large western areas dependent on grazing; and (5) the disintegration of rural communities and transfer of large farm populations to relief rolls or to new means of livelihood.[10]

Overall, the Roosevelt White House ended the farm crisis and launched agriculture into unprecedented growth and prosperity. By 1940, crop production had increased by 24 percent, farm acreage 4 percent, and the average farm from

138 acres to 174 acres, and inorganic fertilizers doubled and nitrogen fertilizers tripled.[11] Then, starting around 1940, most farmers entered a virtuous cycle of government subsidies, rising income, technological advances, and production increases. A synergy of technological advances in hybrid seeds, fertilizers, pesticides, and mechanical plowing and reaping sparked an explosion in farm production, which in turn generated more income with which farmers invested in yet more productivity-enhancing technologies. Between 1940 and 1985, crop production doubled while cropland diminished by about 10 percent. The real farmland price index rose from 100 in 1936–40 to 342 in 1981–5, while fertilizer applications doubled every decade.[12]

During that half-century, the percentage of farmers in the workforce dropped from 20 percent to 2.4 percent. As with the Civil War and World War I, America's participation in World War II created labor shortages on the farm, which were filled through mechanization and other productivity-enhancing measures. Between 1940 and 1944, the farm population dropped by 5.2 million from 30.5 million as men and women joined the military or factories. Meanwhile, with the increased demand, farm parity reached 105 in 1942 and was above 100 every war year. Never was farm production more regulated than during the Second World War when over 140 crops received price supports. Most of those who left the farms during World War II stayed on in their new careers in the cities and towns after the war, and the farm population continued to decline steadily thereafter.

Of all the forces stimulating this agricultural revolution, government policies were most important. Government subsidies to public and private research institutions and universities generated many of the new technologies. Government extension services, subsidies, import restrictions, and cheap loans helped farmers capitalize on these new technologies. The Army Corps of Engineers and Bureau of Reclamation constructed vast complexes of dams, canals, and irrigation that literally made deserts bloom, thus bringing huge profits to agribusiness and cheap food to the dinner tables of American consumers. Between 1945 and 1977, the amount of wetlands drained increased from 50 million to 105 million acres and irrigated lands from 20 million to 50 million acres.[13]

Despite this wealth of programs, farm parity slipped from about 90 percent between 1945 and 1954 to 75 percent from 1954 to 1960 as the Korean War and massive humanitarian food exports ended. Farm income fell in relative rather than real terms as it was outpaced by rises in urban and suburban incomes. Washington tried to deal with ever greater crop surpluses by encouraging more exports. In 1954, Congress enacted the Food for Peace Bill (PL 480), by which the United States gave away at least $1 billion of food to needy countries. That same year, the Eisenhower Administration made a slight step toward reform with passage of the Agriculture Act of 1954, which replaced the rigid parity rate of 90 percent with a flexible one ranging from 75 percent to 90 percent after 1956. Through the Agricultural Act of 1956, Washington tried to manipulate prices with stronger "soil bank" programs such as the Acreage Reduction Program and Conservation Reserve Program. To modernize rural areas, Washington passed the 1955 Rural Development Program, the 1961 Rural Area Development Program, and the 1962 Land Conversion Act, each of which tried to boost rural infrastructure. The 1959 Agricultural Act imposed stricter penalties on those farmers who exceeded their acreage production allotments.

As agriculture became more efficient, the size of farms increased and the total number fell. In 1945, there were 6,814,000 farms; in 1959 only 3,707,973. During those same years, the percentage of farmers in the workforce fell from 23.1 percent to 12 percent, while the average farm size increased from 194.8 acres to 302.4 acres. The total value of the average farm, which included both land and machinery, rose from $5,518 in 1940 to $34,825 in 1959, while the value of production assets per farm worker rose from $3,413 to $21,079.

During the 1960s, price supports remained high while farm production continued to increase and the number of farms and farmers diminished. In 1965, President Johnson pushed through a law that revised the production and subsidy programs so that American farm prices would be competitive on world markets.

The succession of farm bills from 1933 through 1965 were supposed to have targeted poor farmers with subsidies and price supports. In fact, the programs tended to push poor farmers out and support the wealthier farmers. These programs were supporting an ever smaller percentage of America's workforce – only 4.8 percent in 1970. The Agricultural Act of 1970 broke with a quarter-century of farm bills, each of which asserted more regulations and price supports. A ceiling of $55,000 was placed on the amount of subsidies any one farmer could receive. Although this figure may seem high, under the previous system at least some "farmers" had received $4 million each in government price supports in one year.

Reformers who hoped the 1970 bill would break up the farm welfare system were mistaken. In 1970, Congress passed a bill creating a food-stamp program by which all with incomes below $30 a month were given free food stamps; the program is yet another indirect farm subsidy. In 1971, Congress amended the 1948 Sugar Act to increase subsidies to sugar farmers. The 1972 Rural Development Act poured billions more taxpayer dollars into rural districts.

President Nixon once again tried to reform the farm system in 1973 when the Agriculture and Consumer Protection Act passed through Congress. The bill would last four years, during which guaranteed price supports and direct payments to farmers for taking land out of production would be phased out. Farmers responded by planting as much of their land as possible. The result was huge bumper crops which lowered farm income.

Washington tried to divert America's excess farm production to overseas markets. In 1972, President Nixon had negotiated the first of successive grain purchases by the Soviet Union. America's growing grain sales to the Soviet Union were profitable, but also made those farmers dependent on the whims of nature and policy. Bumper Soviet crops in 1976 squelched demand for American grain and thus farmers' income. In 1977, America's farmers received $1.2 billion in government compensation for their lost sales.

While exports alleviated some of the lower farm income and surplus problems, it also made American consumers increasingly vulnerable to supply disruptions. In 1973, President Nixon threatened to boycott soybean exports when crop yields dropped dangerously. Although the boycott never took place, the threat worried foreign consumers, particularly Japan, which took 98 percent of its soybean imports from the United States. Japan and other countries responded by diversifying their soybean imports. This hurt American farmers. In 1970, Americans produced 95 percent of the world's soybean exports; in 1981, only 59 percent.

This caused a dilemma for newly installed President Jimmy Carter. During the 1976 presidential campaign, Carter had promised to veto any farm bill that exceeded his spending limits. In office, Carter soon found the White House was impotent before the farm lobby. The American Agriculture Movement staged a "tractorcade" protest in Washington that encircled the White House and tied up traffic. Carter eventually signed a 1977 farm bill which boosted subsidies and other supports for wealthy and beleaguered farmers alike. In 1980, Carter did get Congress to agree to scrap the direct payments to farmers whose crops were damaged by nature, in favor of a crop insurance program.

On January 4, 1980, President Carter committed an even more unpopular act among farmers when he announced a grain embargo against the Soviet Union for its December 1979 invasion of Afghanistan. Although the embargo applied only to American farm goods to the Soviet Union, Carter encouraged other governments to impose their own embargos. No other government did so.

Like Washington's other unilateral embargos, Carter's only hurt the United States. It was American grain farmers rather than Soviet citizens, let alone the government which ruled them, that suffered. The portion of Soviet grain imports coming from the United States plummeted from 70 percent to 27 percent (a supply which they obtained via third markets). Moscow made up the difference by buying grain from other countries. The embargo simply transferred wealth that would have otherwise gone to American farmers to their Canadian, Argentinian, European, and Australian rivals.

By one estimate, the embargo cost America's economy $11.4 billion. Yet, the embargo really did not hurt American farmers badly. Throughout the 1970s, not just Soviet, but global demand for food increased. American farm exports increased along with it, from $7.3 billion in 1970 to $43.3 billion in 1981. The embargo simply prevented exports from rising faster than they otherwise would have done. Farmers, however, believed that the embargo hurt them and vented their frustration at the polls.

On the 1980 campaign trail, Ronald Reagan promised to dismantle farm "socialism" and unleash the "magic" of the agricultural marketplace. Once in the White House, Reagan broke his promise and increased farm welfare to its highest levels ever. He did so reluctantly. Those same conservative farm states whose inhabitants demanded "smaller government" also threatened political vengeance if the "big government" that supported them was dismantled.

Shortly after entering the White House, Reagan repealed the "food embargo" against the Soviet Union on April 24, 1981. The Soviets purchased 39.9 million tons of American grain in 1981–2, and 32.5 million tons the following year. In addition, the Reagan White House tried to "deregulate" agribusiness by reducing food safety standards. Reagan's July 1981 tax bill included liberalized tax depreciation allowances for farmers, allowed the tax-free transfer of farm assets between spouses by gift or will, and tripled the taxable value of gifts among family members. Finally, laying aside his free-market slogans, Reagan signed in December 1981 the Agriculture and Food Act that increased loan and price supports over the next four years.

Despite these favorable policies, the farm economy worsened. Bumper crops in 1981 and 1982 sparked yet another farm crisis of falling prices. Farm incomes plunged from $32.3 billion in 1979 to $22.1 billion in 1982, while farm debt reached $215 billion. Interest rates soared to record levels. Between 1981 and 1982, farm parity dropped from 61 to 58. Bankruptcies reached crisis proportions.

In January 1983, the White House responded by getting Congress to pass the Payment in Kind (PIK) program, in which farmers who planted only two-thirds of their cropland were rewarded with gifts of commodities from government warehouses matching up to 95 percent of that production. The program thus attempted to cut both production and government stored supplies, while boosting farm income. PIK did encourage farmers to plant less – 75.6 million acres less in return for $9.8 billion in surplus commodities atop their regular subsidies.

The Reagan White House also tried to boost farm exports through $1.25 billion in "mixed credit" schemes. To any poor country interested in buying American farm products, Washington offered loans at two percentage points below market rates. In doing so, the United States essentially dumped American farm crops on foreign markets. For example, American wheat which sold for $225 a ton in the United States was only $100 in Egypt. In October 1981, the Reagan White House signed an agreement with the Soviet Union to sell it between 9 and 12 million metric tons yearly. In January 1983, Reagan signed a bill whereby the government had to preserve "contract sanctity" by allowing any American farm exports to be delivered up to nine months after the United States imposed an embargo against any state. In July 1983, the United States and Soviet Union signed an agreement whereby Washington had to provide and Moscow had to buy between 9 and 12 million metric tons of grain yearly for the next four years.

Europeans and others protested at what they called the hypocrisy of Reagan's agricultural export policies. While Reagan revoked the grain embargo against the Soviet Union in 1981, the following year he replaced it with a technology and machinery export boycott in response to the agreement of Moscow and the European Community to build a gas and oil pipeline between their countries. The Reagan White House said this would make West Europe vulnerable to blackmail. The Europeans countered that it would reduce their dependence on Middle East oil, and anyway it did not affect the United States. The White House acted on its threat to penalize any American firms which sold to the project. Like the grain embargo, Reagan's technology embargo only hurt American producers and lowered American economic growth. The Soviets simply bought from other sources. The Europeans also protested that the White House's export subsidies to American farmers were hypocritical since Washington criticized the Community for the same practices.

But Reagan's subsidized farm exports were undercut by another of his policies – boosting the dollar's value. The Reagan White House acted on its belief that "a strong dollar equals a strong America." In reality, the United States weakened economically as the White House rocketed the dollar's value. When the dollar increases in value, it makes American products more expensive and foreign goods correspondingly cheaper in the United States and abroad. For example, by allowing the dollar to strengthen against the yen from 190 in 1980 to 265 by 1985, the Reagan White House essentially gave Japanese products a 25 percent price cut. America's trade deficit with Japan alone soared from $8 billion in 1980 to $59 billion in 1987. If 20,000 jobs are lost for every $1 billion of a trade deficit, then 1.2 million more Americans were jobless in 1987 than if there had been a trade balance between the two countries. America's total trade deficit deepened throughout the Reagan era until it peaked at $178 billion in 1987. The result was lower economic growth and tax revenues, and higher unemployment, federal budget deficits, homelessness, welfare payments, and crime.

Reagan's high-dollar policy hurt farmers. The Agriculture Department estimated that farmers lost $6 billion in exports during 1982 and 1983 alone. These problems were compounded in 1983 by the worst drought in half a century followed by flooding in parts of the Midwest that caused $7 billion worth of crop damage. Interest rates soared while farm land prices tumbled, along with the equity farmers needed to get credit for seed, tractors, machinery, pesticides, and herbicides. Farm income continued to drop. In 1983 it plummeted to $16 billion, the lowest level in real income since 1933! Altogether, farm income in Reagan's second year was half what it was in Carter's. Yet, image is more important than reality for most people; farmers continued to support Reagan overwhelmingly in opinion polls and in the 1984 election, and George Bush for president in 1988.

Between 1981 and 1990, the federal government gave away $135.5 billion in taxpayer dollars to subsidize farmers. The payments peaked in 1986 when subsidies reached $25.8 billion, an amount greater than the combined budgets of the State, Justice, and Interior departments.[14] And these, of course, were just the direct payments. Agribusiness may well have enjoyed as much as twice that when such indirect subsidies as irrigation, import restrictions, tax cuts, and so on, are included in the total.

President Bush's Agriculture Act of 1990 attempted to trim direct subsidies while encouraging farmers to take more land out of production with strengthened "sodbuster" and "wetland" provisions. The bill also strengthened the president's ability to negotiate farm cuts with other GATT members at the ongoing Uruguay Round, which had started in 1986. As Usual, European and Japanese representatives, among others, blasted the United States' subsidy programs while defending their own. When the Uruguay Round was concluded in 1993, there were no significant reductions in farm export subsidies, import barriers, or price supports.

After entering the White House in 1992, President Bill Clinton proved to be as fiscally conservative as his predecessors Reagan and Bush were fiscally irresponsible. Clinton cut the federal budget deficit to $140 billion in 1994, well below the average $200 billion deficits during the Reagan and Bush eras. The combined inflation and unemployment rates during Clinton's first four years were the lowest since the early 1960s.

Yet, Clinton had little more success in overcoming the farm lobby's power than his predecessors. Although farm subsidies in 1993 were only about $12 billion, half the 1986 record, no programs were eliminated or reformed. However, on December 6, 1994, the Agriculture Department did announce that it would close 1,274 of its 3,700 field offices, and eliminate 11,000 federal workers for a total of $3.6 billion in savings over the next decade.[15]

The Clinton White House also launched efforts to reduce government waste and fraud. In 1994, federal investigators uncovered widespread fraud and corruption with the Agriculture Department's aid program, uncovering $92.5 million in questionable payments from 1988 to 1993 alone. The real total might well be between $200 million or 8 percent, and $300 million or 16 percent of more than $2.4 billion paid out in disaster relief during that period. The largest-scale frauds occurred following the 1992 Hurricane Andrew and 1993 Midwest floods when farmers extracted millions of dollars in unwarranted disaster relief from taxpayers by exaggerating their crop losses. Why did such widespread abuses occur? The report cited penalties and supervision too light to deter such crimes. In other words, minimum government can be the problem rather than the solution to a problem.[16]

The government pays, with loans or supports, farmers who agree to take acres out of production. The program has little effect on production since farmers tend to take their marginal lands out of production while intensifying farming of the rest, which, of course, exacerbates soil erosion. Farmers also enjoy subsidized loans from several sources. The Farm Home Administration (FHA) serves as lender of last resort for farmers. Not surprisingly, it accumulates vast amounts of debt that will never be paid. About 12 percent of all farmers enjoy FHA loans. Commodity Credit Corporation (CCC) loans to farmers provide the most important price supports. In return for a loan, the farmer agrees to put a certain percentage of his crop in a government warehouse. Interest rates on loans are well below market rates. If the crop's price fails to rise, the loan becomes a payment which the farmer may keep. The government establishes target prices for crops at the average cost of producing a particular crop. If the market price falls below the target price, farmers can enjoy a "deficiency payment" equal to the difference. In 1992, farmers placed 7 million acres in these programs, down 84 percent from the 1987 height of 43 million acres.[17] The most direct subsidy goes to dairy farmers. The government will buy, at fixed prices, all of their production. President Carter established the grain reserve to cushion against domestic or foreign crop failures. Farmers store their grain for three years in return for a loan and a storage fee of 25.6 cents per bushel. If prices rise, farmers can withdraw their grain after repaying the loan. Government laboratories help boost biotechnology. America's foreign aid program uses taxpayer dollars to buy up crops and ship them to starving people overseas. Import barriers simultaneously boost farm incomes and diminish incomes for all other Americans. The tobacco industry is actually protected by a legal monopoly whereby a few designated manufacturers are allowed to buy up the nation's production.

The sugar industry alone received $1.4 billion of indirect subsidies in 1994. That is the amount the General Accounting Office (GAO) estimates that the quotas and price supports that protect American sugar producers cost American consumers and manufacturers. Sugar costs $22 cents a pound in the United States and $14 cents a pound in global markets.

A mere 1 percent of sugarcane farms receive 58 percent of these subsidies. The sugarcane and beet industry employs as many as 70,000 in fourteen states. The industry rallied its representatives in Congress to kill a 1995 attempt by a coalition of 100 representatives to eliminate its subsidies.

No government industrial policy for agribusiness is more controversial or morally bankrupt than its subsidization of the tobacco industry. Tobacco is by far the most dangerous and destructive drug abused by Americans. In addition to nicotine, cigarettes spew a range of 5,000 contaminants including arsenic, benzene, hydrogen cyanide, sulfer dioxide, nitrogen oxides, vinyl chloride, ammonia, and radionuclides. Although the tobacco industry still denies it, cigarettes are addictive and cause cancer, emphysema, strokes, and a range of other illnesses. Every year, 420,000 Americans die directly and prematurely from tobacco-related diseases, and at least 3,000 die from secondary cigarette smoke, compared with 20,000 deaths from all illegal drugs. Although the risk for those exposed to secondary tobacco smoke is only one-hundredth that of those who are addicted, even those risks may be unnecessarily high. A recent study found that the blood of children under five years old of mothers who smoke less than 10 cigarettes a day tests positive for nicotine and cancer-causing compounds.[18]

The direct annual health-care costs for tobacco addiction in the United States are $50 billion, or 7 percent of total health-care costs. Of the $50 billion, hospitals account for $26.9 billion, doctors $15.5 billion, nursing homes $4.9 billion, prescription drugs $1.8 billion, and home health care $0.9 billion. The taxpayers subsidize 43 percent or $21.6 billion of all smoking-related health costs, and 60 percent for those over 65 years old. But those are only the direct costs; the actual figure might well be nearly $100 billion if the $40 billion in premature deaths and $6 billion in lost productivity are included.[19]

Tobacco addiction is not just an exorbitant tragedy for the United States. Although, inexplicably, America's smoking rates have risen slightly in recent years, the tobacco industry's greatest profits come from exports – $4.2 billion in 1994 and rising at a' annual 10 percent rate. Smoking has become an epidemic in the Third World where 1.2 billion people are addicted; among the worst examples is China where 70 percent of men smoke. While the smoking epidemic in the Third World is a boon for the tobacco industry, it is a calamity for those countries whose development will be harmed by the massive amounts of money diverted to smoking and its health costs. A 1994 report of the Imperial Cancer Research Fund concluded that tobacco addiction annually murders about 3 million people around the world, or one person every ten seconds. The death toll is expected to rise to 10 million a year by 2020. Over 50 years, tobacco addiction will reap a carnage of 60 million dead worldwide.[20]

Washington underwrites the tobacco industry with a range of expensive policies. The government directly supports tobacco farmers through payments for not growing their crops, and the difference between the prices they receive and higher targeted prices. Washington indirectly subsidizes the tobacco industry by limiting production of the crop, setting minimum market prices for its sale, and providing low-interest loans to tobacco farmers. Since 1946, Washington has allowed tobacco farmers to form "stabilization associations" or cooperatives that set production quotas for their member – in other words, tobacco is organized into a legal cartel that gouges consumers and taxpayers alike. Those cooperatives can borrow money from the Commodity Credit Corporation at below-market interest rates, which they in turn use to buy up excess tobacco and store it until it can be sold at high prices. As if these subsidized loans were not a big enough handout, the tobacco industry succeeded in getting Congress to convert $1.1 billion of those loans into an outright gift. These "workfare" policies help make tobacco the most profitable cash crop. In 1992, the average tobacco farmer earned $3,862 an acre compared with $691 an acre for peanuts, $380 for cotton, $262 for feed corn, and $101 for wheat.[21]

The tobacco industry has successfully derailed reform efforts at the national, state, and local levels. With 1 million workers, 62,000 farmers, $47 billion in sales generating $11 billion in government revenues, and the 3 million-member National Smokers' Alliance, it has plenty of political clout. The industry is dominated by giant corporations like Philip

Morris, RJR Nabisco, American Brands, and the Loews Corporation.

Huge donations to politicians help keep the tobacco supports flowing from Congress. Meanwhile, the tobacco industry is adept at playing off bureaucracies against each other. As in so many other issues, government bureaucracies fight each other to assert the interests of their respective clients. While the Agriculture Department subsidizes tobacco growers, the Health Department and Surgeon General try to protect the public against tobacco addiction. The result is bureaucratic gridlock that interlocks with Congress's political gridlock – all to the tobacco industry's continued enrichment.

The tobacco industry has recently enjoyed some smashing victories. In 1993, the tobacco lobby turned its screws in Congress, forcing it to approve a 75 percent domestic-content requirement for all cigarettes sold in the United States. That same year, it helped kill the proposed higher taxes on cigarettes that would have brought them to $4 a pack in President Clinton's 1993 health-care bill. Because that bill threatened the special interests of so many industries, it was easy to defeat. In late 1994, the tobacco industry faced an initiative that proved more difficult to thwart. On October 4, 1994, the Coalition on Smoking and Health, which includes 75 health, consumer, religious, and environmental groups, announced a nation-wide petition drive to pressure the Food and Drug Administration (FDA) to regulate tobacco as an addictive drug. Led by former Surgeon General C. Everett Koop and including the American Lung Association, the American Cancer Association, and the American Heart Association, the coalition has marshaled powerful forces to counter the tobacco industry. The coalition concluded its petition campaign in December 1994 and presented the petition to President Clinton and Congress in January 1995. Although the petition did not demand an outright ban on tobacco, it did call for accurate measurements of the nicotine, tar, and other chemicals in cigarettes, the elimination of hazardous chemicals, the forbidding of tobacco sales to all under 21 years of age, and the banning of tobacco advertising. Led by the nation's two largest tobacco corporations, R. J. Reynolds and Philip Morris, the tobacco industry fought off this reform proposal with a massive national public-relations campaign and funding for sympathetic candidates during the 1994 election campaign.

After taking over Congress in 1994, the Republicans have killed any Clinton Administration attempts to regulate smoking, increase cigarette taxes, cut back indirect and direct tobacco subsidies, or even investigate allegations that some tobacco corporations have broken the law. For example, in 1995 the House Appropriations Committee voted for tens of billions of dollars in budget cuts on education, medicare, health, safety, science, arts, humanities, and environmental programs, yet defeated an attempt to eliminate the tobacco subsidy. When in July 1995 Food and Drug Administration head David Kessler announced that he was considering designating tobacco an addictive drug and thus subject to regulation, Republican House Speaker Newt Gingrich claimed the agency had "lost its mind."

Yet, the Clinton White House fought back. On July 25, 1995 the Justice Department announced it would convene a grand jury to determine whether tobacco corporate chiefs had lied to Congress in April 1994 about their knowledge of studies that revealed that tobacco is an addictive drug and causes disease, or whether their corporations actually manipulated nicotine levels in cigarettes to increase addiction. The Justice Department amassed considerable evidence revealing that the corporate leaders had committed perjury and fraud, crimes punishable by prison and fines. By spring 1996, the Justice Department's criminal, antitrust, civil, energy and natural resource divisions were conducting five separate investigations into the tobacco industry.

Across the nation, increasing numbers of cities and towns have restricted or tried to restrict smoking in public places. The tobacco industry has had varying degrees of success in thwarting these efforts. For example, in 1994, New York City's government considered a public smoking ban, promoted by the public health alliance, the Coalition for a Smoke Free City composed of 70 different interest groups. The Tobacco Institute and its ally the United Restaurant, Hotel, and Tavern Association fiercely lobbied the City Council's Health Committee with a barrage of letters, full-page newspaper ads, telephone calls, faxes, and requests for meetings. Philip Morris threatened to take its corporate headquarters, which employs

2,000 people, out of New York and eliminate its funding for the arts if the ban were enacted. The United Restaurant, Hotel, and Tavern Association estimated that it could lose a quarter of its business if the ban were enforced. The anti-ban alliance mailed literature to New York City's 10,000 restaurants to encourage them to join the struggle. Although 32 of the 51 Council members supported a smoking ban, the law's details were shaped by the tobacco industry's political and economic clout. The tobacco industry's lobbying blitz was successful in pressuring the Health Committee to exempt small restaurants and private offices from the ban.[22]

But the carnage wrought by the taxpayer subsidization of the tobacco industry is certainly not the only problem caused by agribusiness. For all practical purposes, soil is a nonrenewable resource. Depending on the ecosystem, it takes nature anywhere from a century to a millennium to create an inch of topsoil. A hard rain or wind can wash away that inch or more of soil within hours. Obviously, the less rich and abundant a soil, the lower its productivity.

Of America's total land area of 1.9 billion acres, less than one-third, or 600 million acres, have sufficient topsoil, rainfall, and drainage for some type of farming. Farm conditions vary greatly across the United States. America's farmlands have been losing topsoil since the first Europeans arrived. American farmlands annually lose an average two billion tons of topsoil. An additional three billion tons of soil are washed or blown away from the nation's forests and grazing lands. Soil erosion damages more than just farm productivity. When soil washes into streams, it damages or destroys fisheries. When that soil is laden with chemical pesticides and fertilizers, it damages or destroys drinking water.

Some early Americans understood that their traditional farming practices were deteriorating and sometimes outright destroying the environments upon which they depended. George Washington deplored his land's erosion; he once declared, "He is the greatest patriot who stops the most gullies." Unfortunately, it would take nearly another two centuries before the federal government began to deal with the destruction of America's soils. The Agriculture Department did not conduct its first soil survey until 1899, and the few conservation bulletins it issued over the next few decades did nothing to stem the destruction. It was not until 1935 when the Roosevelt White House created the Soil Conservation Service that the government seriously began to deal with the crisis. Since then, the government has spent over $30 billion to help farmers slow soil erosion. These programs got a big boost in 1985 with the passage of the Food Security Act. The Conservation Reserve Program (CRP) of that law encourages farmers to set aside highly erodable cropland for a decade in return for federal subsidies (rent) and half the cost of providing ground cover. By 1989, 30.6 million acres had been placed in the conservation reserve, of the 45 million acres the government hoped to include by the early 1990s. The "swampbuster" and "sodbuster" provisions of the law penalize those farmers that drain wetlands or plow delicate soils without permission. The 1990 Food, Agriculture, and Trade Act reinforces the 1985 law.

Many of the nation's farmers face not only the loss of soil, but the loss of water as well. Over one-third of the nation's annual crops come from 45 million acres of heavily irrigated lands. These lands are in highly arid regions. Some of those waters come from rivers. Population increases in these regions are putting increased pressure on those finite river sources. An infinitely worse problem comes from those farm regions which depend on aquifers for their irrigation. The demand for those underground waters vastly exceeds nature's ability to replenish them. Eventually they will run dry. Taxpayers underwrite the nation's irrigation systems, whether their waters come from rivers or aquifers. Over 50 million acres are irrigated in the 17 Western states alone. Washington pays up to 90 percent of the cost of building and operating the networks of dams, canals, and irrigation systems.

Many regions of the country, particularly across the West, face increasingly severe water shortages. How severe are these shortages? It depends. In many regions, the water shortages occur because of a misallocation of that resource. In the seventeen Western states, farmers and ranchers consume as much as 90 percent of all water, a gift subsidized by the taxes and water bills of the nation's households and other businesses. Federal subsidies allow them to pay for that water at prices sometimes one-hundredth the market rate. Many of those farmers are growing water-intensive crops like cotton, alfalfa, and rice. Most farmers, no matter what they are growing, make no attempt to conserve water because the rates are so cheap.

The short-term solution to run-off water shortages is economically simple but has proved politically impossible. If everyone paid water's "real price", there would be a greater incentive to conserve it. Obviously, the more water saved, the more available from existing sources and the less need to tap more expensive alternative sources. Likewise, the below-market interest rates charged to farmers for their government-supplied irrigation projects could be raised to market levels. Here would be yet another powerful incentive for farmers in arid regions to conserve water.

Even more water could be saved if the government offered tax rebates, subsidized loans, and technical aid to encourage farmers to use "drip irrigation," in which hoses are extended along each crop row, from which water drips from holes to the roots of plants. Drip agriculture is not a panacea. The initial investment is expensive. It is also labor-intensive. While appropriate for row crops, it does not work for grains.

The most serious and intractable water problem involves the draining and poisoning of the nation's aquifers. Once an aquifer is destroyed, it will remain so for hundreds or thousands of years. Nowhere is aquifer destruction a potentially greater problem than across the Great Plains which supply most of the nation's grains. The Ogallala Aquifer is a vast water pool beneath the Great Plains which extends an average of nearly seven hundred miles from north to south, three hundred miles from east to west, and a quarter of a mile deep. The exploitation of the Ogallala Aquifer has made the Great Plains America's bread and beef basket. Its exploitation is relatively recent. In 1930, only 1,700 wells tapped its waters. New technologies and increased demand for crops and livestock left the Ogallala Aquifer skewered by 42,225 wells by 1957. By the mid-1970s, Texas was daily drawing 11 billion gallons of water from the Ogallala, Kansas 5 billion, Nebraska 5.9 billion, Oklahoma 1.4 billion, Colorado 2.7 billion, and New Mexico 1.6 billion. By the 1990s, wells were annually pumping 6 million acre-feet out of the Ogallala Aquifer while nature restored only 185,000 acre-feet; or "some farmers draw as much as five feet of water a year, while nature puts back a quarter of an inch."[23] The further the water table falls, the more energy and thus cost it takes to bring water to the surface. Between 1972 and 1984, the water table dropped fifteen to twenty feet while the price of energy increased 700 percent. The result was much higher food prices and thousands of bankrupt farmers. This exploitation is unsustainable. At the current exploitation rates, huge stretches of the Ogallala will be exhausted within three decades and the entire aquifer within a century. What then will be the region's fate?

Chemicals are poisoning thousands of aquifers across the nation, upon which tens of millions of Americans depend for their drinking water. Agricultural chemicals yearly poison over 100,000 people, some fatally. American farmers first began using artificial chemicals in 1865 when an arsenic compound called Paris Green became popular in killing potato beetles. Throughout the late nineteenth and into the twentieth century, farmers began using such products as lead arsenate, copper sulfate, and calcium arsenate to kill pests and weeds. The use of chemicals by farmers did not become near universal until the 1940s. World War II helped unleash a bio- and petrochemical revolution with insecticides such as DDT and herbicides like 2,4–D. Since then, farmers have increasingly relied on a range of pesticides, herbicides, and fungicides to boost production.

The first federal policies affecting agricultural chemicals date to 1910 when the Agriculture Department began regulating the ingredients for these pesticides. No significant effort was made until 1947, when Congress passed the 1947 Federal Insecticide, Fungicide, and Rodenticide Act, which required the government to monitor agrichemicals. The law did little to affect the types and amounts of chemicals used. It took Rachel Carson's 1962 book *Silent Spring* to awaken the nation to the dangers of chemicals poisoning the environment, particularly those like DDT whose negative effects magnify as they work their way up the food chain finally to accumulate permanently in the fatty tissues of humans. Within a few years, Congress banned DDT and amended the 1947 Act with stronger powers to regulate the agrichemical industry.

The turning point in significantly addressing the chemical pollution problem came in 1970 when the Nixon White House switched the responsibility for regulating agricultural chemicals from the Agriculture Department to the newly created Environmental Protection Agency (EPA). Armed with increasingly powerful laws such as the 1970 Clean Water Act and 1972 Federal Environmental Pesticide Control Act, the EPA has prevented an ever larger list of chemicals from getting into the nation's ecosystems and, ultimately, human bodies.

In 1978, Congress amended the law to require manufacturers to make public their secret studies on the health and safety effects of their chemical products. Arguing that the disclosures would give away product secrets and thus would be a trade restraint, the chemical industry responded with a suit that blocked the law's enforcement for three years.

Farmers feel compelled to pour ever more chemicals on their fields because of simple laws of evolution. While chemical warfare against pests may succeed in the short term it fails over time. Those farmers who believe in a Biblical rather than a Darwinian explanation for creation are experiencing evolution in their own fields! Over 300 crop-eating insects have evolved into species resistant to chemicals. Environmentalists argue that integrated pest management (IPM) strategies not only reduce chemical poisoning of peoples and ecosystems but reduce farm costs while retaining productivity. So far, only about 2 percent of American farmers use IPM means of dealing with pests.

Biotechnology may eventually provide the most significant means of managing problems of soil erosion, water depletion, and chemical use. Future plant hybrids may subsist on little water and soil, repel pests, and flourish amidst weeds. The federal government has gradually increased its research and development in biotechnology since its first efforts in the mid-nineteenth century. Until recently, government laboratories contributed most of the biotechnology advances. Private industrial efforts to advance biotechnology were boosted by the 1970 Plant Variety Protection Act, which allowed individuals and firms to patent micro-organisms. The Supreme Court upheld that law with its 1980 decision in *Diamond* v. *Chakravarty*. A 1980 amendment, however, excluded from patent protection six vegetables – carrots, celery, cucumbers, okra, peppers, and tomatoes.

The patent protection spurred what may eventually prove to be a biotechnology revolution. During the 1980s, more than 730 varieties of fruits, vegetables, and grains were reengineered to achieve a variety of improvements. Today, we enjoy the fruits of genetically altered seeds that grow into crops which require far less water or nutrients and produce more, while genetically altered livestock produce more meat, eggs, or milk. For example, carrots have twice as many vitamins today as they did a generation ago. About 80 percent of all carrot improvements were engineered in Agriculture Department laboratories.[24]

Those who oppose patent protection for biotechnology fear that the nation's seed stocks will be dominated by a few huge pharmaceutical and petrochemical corporations. That fear is unwarranted given that patents are good for only fifteen years. Others worry that all the experimentation could unleash monster plants and animals. That, too, is unlikely to happen.

Biotechnology, however, does have its potential dangers. The more American farmers rely on fewer "super crops," the more vulnerable they become to unanticipated diseases that could destroy those crops. To guard against a disaster like that, the Agriculture Department maintains the National Seed Storage Laboratory at Colorado State University and three smaller seed banks elsewhere.

Yet another massive subsidy to agribusiness involves federal policies which allow farmers to provide pay and other benefits to workers at much lower rates than other industries. Ironically, while millions of people, particularly in the inner cities, are unemployed, farmers employ millions of foreign migrants to harvest their crops. Many of these migrant farm workers are in the United States illegally. Most subsist on substandard wages, housing, and health care, and are nonunionized.

The federal government has dealt with the migrant farm worker problem through a series of laws. From 1949, children were no longer allowed to work in the fields during school hours. In 1950, social security was extended to farm workers. The 1963 Farm Labor Contractor Registration Act required crew leaders to prove they had liability insurance for transporting workers and had no criminal record, in return for a Labor Department license. In 1966, Congress voted to allow a minimum wage for the 30 percent of laborers on the largest farms; a 1974 amendment extended the minimum wage to a further 10 percent of farm laborers. The 1983 Migrant and Seasonal Agricultural Worker Act allowed class action suits by farm workers against corporate farms but imposed a $500,000 ceiling for damages. Family farms were excluded from such suits. The 1984 Immigration and Reform Act allowed increased legal migration to the United States and offered an amnesty for illegal immigrants who could prove they arrived before January 1, 1982.

These measures have had little effect on farm profits or operations. Although California passed a law in 1975 allowing farm laborers to organize, the federal 1935 National Labor Relations Act which legalized unions still does not extend to farm workers. The reason is that unlike other goods, crops are perishable and essential for life. If farm laborers were allowed to organize and strike, they would enjoy enormous power not just over the farm economy, but over the nation. But the lack of unions means that workers can be hired and fired at will. By doing little to stem the flow of illegal immigrants into the country, the federal government helps keep farm wages and thus crop prices low. No matter what the issue, somehow agribusiness manages politically to twist the policies to its own advantage.

Farm policy seemed to be revolutionized on April 4, 1996, when President Clinton signed into law the Freedom to Farm Act, that replaced government subsidies with steadily declining transition payments over seven years. A coalition of fiscal conservatives in both Houses were able to push the bill past the farm lobby. In all, the law would carve $2 billion from the projected $48.8 billion in government farm spending over those years. Thus until 2002, farmers will continue to enjoy massive direct and indirect subsidies via a vast range of government and taxpayer handouts. Even after 2002, America's farmers will enjoy government protection and nurturing from a range of sources including import barriers, biotechnology promotion, water rights, and low-interest loans.

RANCHING

To most Americans, grazing is what they do at salad bars. At the same restaurant, before devouring the sizzling steak or porkchop set before them, some Americans might recall briefly that the meat was once a steer or pig that had been fattened for the gourmand's behalf on some far-away range or feedlot.

Most of the nation's livestock are raised on private lands – about 86 percent of all animal-unit-months (AUM, the monthly amount of forage needed to maintain a cow and calf, horse, or five sheep or goats) is supplied by grazing on private lands, while fodder from farmlands supplies an additional 7 percent. Federal and state lands supply only about 7 percent of the nation's livestock needs.

Although only about 2 percent or 23,000 of all ranchers graze their stock on public lands, they enjoy access to an immense territory – 256 million acres, which include 89 percent of Bureau of Land Management (BLM) land, 69 percent of Forest Service lands, and even millions of acres in national parks, wildlife refuges, and wilderness areas. The national forests and rangelands are grazed by 70 million cattle and 8 million sheep, which in turn compete with 55,000 wild horses, 20 million deer, 400,000 elk, and 600,000 antelope.[25]

The government's grazing policy is faulted for setting fees well below market rates and allowing ranchers to overgraze and thus destroy the grasslands. Although the AUM rose from five cents in 1936 to $2.36 in 1980, it then dropped to $1.86 by 1993. The Reagan White House repaid the livestock lobby for its political support with the passage of the Public Rangelands Improvement Act, which set fees through an elaborate formula that includes beef prices and production costs. The existing fees are a pittance compared with the average $9.22 AUM for access to private lands. Critics blast the low public fees as a massive giveaway of national resources to a small but powerful special interest, derisively called "welfare ranchers."

As if the government subsidies to the livestock industry were not controversial enough, the BLM has allowed ranchers to overgraze public lands, turning once rich ecosystems into dustbowls of eroded lands, dried up creeks, and decimated wildlife. In 1988, the GAO found that grazing wipes out or endangers more plant species than any other cause. That same report concluded that "the BLM is not managing the permittees, rather the permittees are managing the BLM."[26]

Yet another government handout to ranchers is the emergency feed program administered by the Department of Agriculture. In those years when a drought withers grazing lands and endangers livestock herds, the Agriculture Department freely gives away grain stockpiles to whoever qualifies. The program costs taxpayers anywhere from $100 million to $500 million a year. More adversely, it encourages ranchers to overgraze both private and public lands to qualify for the program. As in other federal welfare ranch programs, it is the wealthier ranchers that benefit most.[27]

How did federal grazing policy come to this? The federal policy of giving away lands and refusing to manage those retained was "successful." Between the Northwest Ordinance of 1785 and the Homestead Act of 1862, over 320 million acres of the 1.31 billion acres of public lands were given away to private interests. Another 325 million acres were given away from 1862 to 1920. During this latter period, the nation's cattle increased from 21 million to 45 million head, and sheep from 36 million to 50 million.

In the popular imagination, ranching takes place in the wide open grasslands of the American West. Although a ranch is anywhere livestock graze, much of the increase in the nation's herds following the Civil War did occur west of the Mississippi River. In 1866, enterprising Texas ranchers drove the first cattle north to the railhead at Abilene, Kansas, and eventually elsewhere. From those railheads the cattle were shipped east to feed an ever growing population. As hunters decimated buffalo herds across the Great Plains, ranchers drove their herds onto those public lands and claimed them. Beginning in 1874, barbed wire began to be used on the plains, thus making it infinitely easier for cattle barons to lock up the public land and its scarce water for themselves. By the late 1880s, 7.6 million cattle foraged across eleven western states.[28]

The land grabs inevitably fostered domination and abuse

by rich and powerful special interests. Complaints about the domination of public grasslands by livestock barons are not a recent phenomenon. In 1883, Congress issued a report which detailed the abuse of public lands by ranchers who fenced it off, monopolized the water, and forced out any competitors. However, until recently, the fiercest battles livestockers fought were among themselves. Throughout the late nineteenth century and into the twentieth century, cattle and sheep herders feuded incessantly over grazing lands; hundreds of men died.

The reason for these conflicts was the "first come, first exploit" or the "law of capture" land-use policy. Without property rights, anyone could graze their herds anywhere. Privatization did not alleviate these problems. The 1887 Desert Land Act exacerbated them by allowing ranchers and farmers to claim up to 640 acres of land if they irrigated it, thus encouraging entrepreneurs in arid regions to take over entire watersheds. Those who owned the water that snaked through dry regions, indirectly owned vast dry grasslands all around. Rival ranchers fought bitterly for scarce water resources.

To worsen matters, during the 1880s a series of droughts, overgrazing, and freezes devastated ranching across much of the West. The winters of 1886 and 1887 in particular ruined ranchers across the northern plains; some ranchers lost as much as 80 percent of their stock. Over 43 million acres of grazing lands were lost during the 1880s alone. Losses thereafter were insidious rather than dramatic. Between 1890 and 1930, over 184 million acres were converted from grass to crop lands.

The earliest effort to regulate public grazing lands was initiated by ranchers themselves. The National Cattleman's Convention in 1884 resolved to demand that Congress lease public lands to established ranchers to offset the influx of newcomers. Nothing came of the initiative. Newcomers kept squeezing in and the bloodshed continued.

It was not until 1897 that Washington first tried to regulate some public lands when that year's Forest Management Act authorized the government to manage access to forest reserves. Under that law, the Interior Secretary imposed the first significant grazing restrictions on public lands by ruling on June 30, 1897 that:

the pasturing of livestock on public lands in forest reserves will not be interfered with, so long as it appears
that injury is not done to the forest growth, and the rights
of others are not jeopardized. The pasturing of sheep is,
however, prohibited in all forest reserves except for those
in the States of Oregon and Washington, for the reason
that sheep grazing has been found injurious to the forest cover, and therefore of serious consequence in regions
where rainfall is limited.[29]

Thus were cattle interests able to prevail over sheep interests.
    The cattle victory, however, was fleeting. Three years later
the cattle industry's access to public lands would be regulated. In 1900, the General Land Office began issuing grazing permits in which AUMs were based on the number of
livestock that a region could carry without deterioration. Fees,
seasons, types, and numbers were designated. In 1905, President Roosevelt transferred forest reserves from the corrupt
Interior Department to the Agriculture Department. Agriculture Secretary James Wilson issued a policy statement that
emphasized conservation and that national interests would
shape the use of any lands under his jurisdiction:

> all land is to be devoted to its most productive use for
> the permanent good of the whole and not for the tempo-
> rary benefit of individuals or companies . . . where con-
> flicting interests must be reconciled, the question will always
> be decided from the standpoint of the greatest good for
> the greatest number of the long run.[30]

In 1911, the Supreme Court reinforced the federal government's power to regulate public lands when it ruled that
"any previous implied license to graze stock on public lands
did not confer any vested rights on the users, nor did it
deprive the United States of the power of recalling licenses."[31]
Privileges could be revoked without compensation. In 1910,
the Forest Service created the Office of Grazing Studies to
survey public grazing lands.
    Unfortunately, Wilson's ideals have not been systematically
implemented. When the Agriculture Department tried to
impose its permit and fee system on public grasslands, ranchers

shrilly protested. In the first of several "sagebrush rebellions" they demanded that the federal government transfer grasslands to the states, whose legislators were even more in the pocket of special interests than congressmen. Special interests soon succeeded in corrupting the Agriculture Department as thoroughly as they had the Interior Department; the fee system was poorly managed. Ranchers scored an important victory in 1916 when Washington passed the Stockraising Homestead Act, which allowed the government to sell more land to ranchers. Still, ranchers demanded more. On March 29, 1930, President Calvin Coolidge signed into law the Mizpah–Pumpkin Creek Act, which leased public lands to associations of private ranchers in Montana who would in turn manage them by collecting fees, making range improvements, and determining the amount of Animal Unit Month (AUM) fees. If that pilot study was successful, it would be implemented across all public lands. President Herbert Hoover hoped to transfer more than 200,000 acres of federal grazing lands to state control. Bureaucratic politics rather than conservation ideals blocked this transfer. The US Forest Service, which would have lost the land, protested against the initiative while the states themselves rejected the offer because they feared the administrative costs would exceed any benefits.

The government did not attempt to regulate grazing on public lands strictly until 1934 when Congress passed the Taylor Grazing Act, which asserted a management policy over 150 million acres of public rangelands. The Act created a Division of Grazing within the Interior Department and authorized it to license access collect fees, and improve rangeland. District managers were appointed to oversee the grazing on public lands. Advisory committees, usually packed with local ranchers, were set up to "assist" the district managers. Ranchers applied for permits to run livestock on public lands. The bill initiated the AUM system throughout the public rangelands.

The initial AUM fee was only a nickel a month, hardly enough even to cover expenses. The assessed fees were a tiny fraction of what it would have cost ranchers to graze their livestock on private lands.

Ranchers resented even these fees. Nevada Senator Pat

McCarren helped slash appropriations for the Grazing Service by two-thirds. Proponents of range management realized that a stronger agency was needed to fulfill the law. In 1946, the Division of Grazing was combined with the General Land Office to form the BLM. AUM's were raised to fifteen cents.

The West's ranchers howled in protest. Later in 1946 some 150 of the West's richest ranchers, mostly representing the American National Livestock Association and National Wool Growers Association, gathered in Salt Lake City to debate what to do about the newly created BLM and its policies. They quickly, boisterously, and unanimously agreed on demanding that Washington grant them ownership not only of all 142 million acres of BLM lands, but of all other public lands including the national forests and parks as well. Wyoming Senator Allan Robertson wrote up the proposals in a bill and submitted it to committee. Historian Bernard DeVoto led the conservationist charge against what he called "one of the biggest landgrabs in history." In a *Harpers* article, DeVoto pointed out the irony that "at the very moment when the West is blueprinting an economy which must be based on the sustained, permanent use of its natural resources, it is also conducting an assault on those resources with the simple objective of liquidating them."[32] Other powerful voices protested at the livestock barons' landgrab. The bill died in committee.

Although the ranching lobby has yet to own the public lands outright, it has overpowered nearly every reform proposal. Most bills die in committee, often when senators threaten to filibuster to death any that reach the floor. When pressure builds on the BLM or Forest Service to enact reforms, they simply announce that they will study the problem.

Few federal agencies have been as thoroughly captured by special interests as the Grazing Service, and its successor, the BLM. The BLM is largely staffed by the sons and daughters of Western ranchers who attended local land-grant colleges. Local ranchers control the local grazing boards which allocate permits. Even the fees end up being used to subsidize the ranchers who pay them. Most fees have been returned to rural counties and ranchers via the BLM, which subsidizes the building of wells, roads, fences, water tanks, windmills, and other ranching infrastructure. Much of the money goes to destroying natural grasslands by burning, spraying chemicals, and plowing those lands, then reseeding them with exotic grasses better suited for cattle. Not just ranchers ride roughshod over BLM lands.. The Fish and Wildlife Service's Animal Damage Control Service spends tens of millions of dollars to kill livestock predators like coyotes, mountain lions, bears, and eagles. Although the AUM is now about $1.86, the fees collected contribute only a fraction of the BLM's operating costs. So the BLM annually diverts hundreds of millions of taxpayer dollars to subsidize ranchers. While most ranchers may denounce welfare mothers, they fervently believe their taxpayer-financed entitlements are a sacred right rather than a privilege secured by their political power.

Special ranching interests have used their political clout to gain special privileges even in some of the nation's parks. Former Wyoming Senator Clifford Hansen received a permit to graze 569 cattle in Teton National Park. Here is how he got away with it. The original conception for Grand Teton National Park was to have included much of adjacent Jackson Hole Valley, but local residents resisted the park's expansion. When it was established in 1928, the park included only the Grand Teton peaks. In 1943, however, President Roosevelt overrode local interests and declared part of Jackson Hole a national monument. Then county commissioner Clifford Hansen and other local ranchers protested by illegally grazing cattle on those national monument lands. In 1950, when Hansen had become a US Senator, Congress expanded Grand Teton National Park to encompass Jackson Hole National Monument. To gain the votes of Hansen and other Western congressmen, supporters of the measure agreed to the extraordinary concession of allowing hunting and grazing in Grand Teton National Park. Hunters are temporarily designated "deputy park rangers," which allows them to carry firearms in the park and kill predators. The illegal grazing of Hansen and his cronies was not only tolerated but officially permitted. Such can be politics in a "free" country.

Ever since the Taylor Act was passed, conservationists and environmentalists have complained about the low AUMs and other government subsidies for the ranching industry, along with the way the federal bureaucracies often turned a blind eye to their own laws. Laws in the 1940s and 1950s required those federal agencies managing grazing lands, such as the Agriculture Department, Forest Service, BLM, and Soil Conservation Service, to inventory and classify the lands under their jurisdiction; conservation measures, however, were not strictly required. It was not until the passage in 1960 of the Multiple-Use, Sustained Yield Act that agencies were required to adopt sweeping conservation practices in administering rangelands, among other public lands.

A contribution to federal grazing policy was made by Velma Johnson, a rancher who dedicated her life to preserving wild horses, which competed with ranchers for forage and were slaughtered for dogmeat. Johnson's efforts led Congress to pass range wildlife-protection laws in 1959, 1971, and 1978. Despite these efforts, 80 percent of the public range remains dominated by livestock, leaving only 13 percent solely to wild horses and burros, and a mere 7 percent to wildlife.

In the mid-1970s, two environmental measures provoked a fierce cornucopian backlash. In 1974, the National Resources Defense Council won a suit which required the BLM to write 144 environmental-impact statements on grazing. The 1976 Federal Land Policy and Management Act (FLPMA) mandated the BLM along with other federal agencies to use conservation practices in managing the lands for multiple-use purposes. The FLPMA mandated that half of all grazing fees be used for range improvements.

These environmental victories were pyrrhic. Livestock barons who enjoyed easy access to public lands fought fiercely against these limited measures. The livestock industry united with loggers, miners, and farmers to stage the "sagebrush rebellion" which raged throughout the 1970s into the 1980s. The sagebrushers scored some notable victories. For example, ranching interests were able to water down the FLPMA's impact. Idaho Senator James McClure, chair of the Energy and Natural Resource Committee, attached a rider to the BLM's budget that limited ability to control overgrazing. According to the rider, the BLM could only reduce grazing levels by 10 percent a year in any area. The trouble was that vast realms of grasslands had degraded so thoroughly that they demanded a long moratorium on any use in order to revive. But McClure and other Western politicians were concerned with reelection and the viability of their rich financial contributors rather than the long-term viability of the public's lands.

The livestock industry was also instrumental in getting Congress to pass the 1978 Public Rangelands Improvement Act, which allowed those agencies managing rangelands to favor "exemplary" permittees by allowing them more autonomy in setting AUMs and managing their portions. A federal court, however, ruled that the law violated the 1976 Federal Land Policy and Management Act, and thus could not be enacted.

With Ronald Reagan's election in 1980, the sagebrushers were able to roll back some federal restrictions on their operations and to lower fees. Robert Burford, the BLM head under the Reagan Administration, fulfilled the cornucopian vision by purging the agency of personnel, regulations, and programs. Grazing fees were lowered, while fees to adopt wild horses were raised to favor dogfood producers over families. Interior Secretary James Watt was the most virulent sagebrush supporter inside the White House. His resignation in 1983 proved a sharp blow to the "rebellion." At the state level, the sagebrushers had a mixed success, with victories in New Mexico, Wyoming, Utah, and Arizona but losses everywhere else. All told, the sagebrushers fell short of their ultimate goal – the massive transfer of federal lands to state ownership that they demanded.

They did succeed, however, in increasing subsidies for many ranchers. In 1986, the BLM issued access permits to 20,000 ranchers who grazed 4 million head of livestock on 163 million acres in 16 Western states. The Forest Service issued permits to 10,387 ranchers for 102 million acres. While only about 6 percent of the nation's AUMs are taken from public lands, in 11 Western states the percentage is 17 percent. Altogether, "89 percent of the cattle AUMs came from private ranges and irrigated pastures, 6 percent from public ranges, and 5 percent from residues from cropland. For sheep, 63 percent came from private ranges and pastures, 11 percent from public ranges, and 26 percent from crop residues."[33]

As if the giveaway of public lands to a small group of

often rich ranchers were not bad enough, the practice often devastated those rangelands. How badly eroded are the nation's rangelands? The BLM and other federal agencies provide statistics to show that public rangelands are in better shape today than they were sixty years ago. By the mid-1930s, generations of unlimited access by ranchers to the nation's public grasslands had steadily destroyed them. The 1934 Taylor Grazing Act saved them. In 1936, the newly created Division of Grazing rated only 1.5 percent of the rangelands under its jurisdiction excellent or good and only 14.3 percent fair; the rest, 84.2 percent, were poor. A half-century of management helped revive an increasingly larger percentage of public rangelands. By 1989, the BLM rated 4 percent of its rangelands excellent, 30 percent good, 41 percent fair, and 25 percent poor. The government's two other agencies whose duties include conserving rangelands reported similar results. The Forest Service rated 3 percent of its 4 million acres of rangeland excellent, 36 percent good, 44 percent fair, and 16 percent poor. The Soil Conservation Service reported that 4 percent of its rangelands were excellent, 30 percent good, 45 percent fair, and 21 percent poor.[34] Less sanguine was the Society for Range Management Committee, which had created the Range Inventory Standardization Committee (RISC) in 1978 to establish objective national standards for range classification. A 1989 Society for Range Management report revealed that ranges on 60 percent of private lands were in fair or poor condition.[35]

What all these studies clearly revealed was that, overall, the government did a better job of managing public land than ranchers did their own land. The studies belied the cornucopian claim that privatization would improve rather than destroy those rangelands. Deregulation worsened rather than improved range conditions. With nearly free access to grasslands, ranchers overgraze. Meanwhile, there is less land upon which to run livestock. Grazing pressures on land are exacerbated by its diminishing amount. Between 1945 and 1982, rangeland fell from 723 million acres to 659 million acres, mostly from the land's conversion to urban and suburban uses.[36] As rangelands diminish from conversion and desertification, ranchers squeeze their livestock into smaller areas, thus ruining yet more rangeland. Whether they graze their livestock on public or private lands, most ranchers are concerned only with short-term calculations of profit rather than long-term economic and environmental viability.

How has this immense loss of grazing land affected productivity? Fortunately, there is less livestock pressure on the land today than previously. The number of cattle peaked at 132 million in 1975 and declined to around 105 million cattle by 1986. Sheep peaked forty years earlier in 1935 at around 56 million then declined to around 10 million by 1982. Draft animals like horses and mules also declined steadily over the past half-century as they were replaced by tractors. In the 1920s, there were over 20 million draft animals; by 1982, only 2 million remained.[37]

By the late 1980s, the cornucopian agenda began to confront increasing resistance from conservationists and environmentalists alike under the "Save Our Public Lands" banner. Critics of ranch subsidies became increasingly vocal and well-organized. Some opponents rallied against public grazing under the slogan "Cattle-free by '93." Conservation and most environmental groups would allow limited grazing on healthy grasslands but called for the raising of fees to near levels for private lands.

Advocates of the sustained use of public lands cheered Bill Clinton's victory in 1992, and particularly his choice of Bruce Babbit as Interior Secretary. Upon taking office in 1993, Babbit promised that his Department would promote a new "land ethic" based on conservation and preservation rather than the rapacious cornucopian values of previous administrations. In particular, Babbit promised to promote higher fees and more restricted access for grazing, along with restrictions on logging and mining on public lands. So far he has lost in all three of those wars.

In spring 1993, Babbit proposed increasing AUMs on public lands from $1.86 to $4. After months of debate, a Senate and House conference on the grazing bill finally reached a compromise on October 7, 1993. The bill that was returned to each House would have raised AUMs to $3.45, revoked licenses for those ranchers who overgrazed and abused the land, enhanced the federal government's power to safeguard public water resources, and abolished grazing advisory boards by which local ranchers control federal policy over local public lands. The bill was filibustered to death in the Senate by a coalition of Western senators. Wyoming Senator Alan Simpson tried to justify the filibusters by claiming that he was "defending a Western life style in this administration's war on the West."[38]

In 1994, AUMs were $1.86 for public lands and $10.20 for private lands. While AUMs on private lands had increased from about $7.50 in 1980, federal AUMs actually declined from $2.15. All but two Western states charge more than the federal AUM rate. New Mexico recently doubled its own fee to $3.41 a month with no decline in participants.

Advocates of subsidized grazing on public lands claim that it helps keep poor ranchers in business who would otherwise succumb to market forces. In reality, ranch welfare benefits the rich rather than the poor. The top 10 percent of the wealthiest ranchers who enjoy subsidized access to public lands control about half of those 260 million acres. The largest public land handout to a welfare rancher goes to Daniel Russell, who has permits to 5 million acres in Nevada and California, an area larger than Massachusetts. In contrast, only 12 percent of those who graze their cattle on public lands are poor. About 30,000 individuals or corporations currently hold grazing permits for public lands. If grazing permits were given only to the poor, much of the overgrazing that destroys the resource would disappear.[39]

That is unlikely ever to happen. The ranching industry's vast wealth translates into vast political power. Perhaps no special ranching interest has been more effective in taking taxpayer dollars than the mohair industry. Mohair comes from goats and was once used by the military for uniforms. Synthetic materials all but eliminated the demand for mohair by the military and civilians alike. Rather than accept this market reality, mohair producers banded together to lobby Washington for federal subsidies. Mohair was labeled a "strategic commodity" and this made its producers eligible for huge subsidies. By 1990, mohair producers received $3.60 in subsidies for every $1 of mohair they sold to consumers, up from 88 cents in 1987. In 1991, over 10,000 mohair producers received $50 million in subsidies, of which 1 percent of producers received over 50 percent of the payments.

Ironically, in 1990, 60 percent of this "strategic commodity" was exported to the Soviet Union.[40]

Clinton came into office determined to eliminate subsidies for special interests like mohair and mink. He soon succumbed to political reality. In February 17, 1993, President Clinton proposed not to eliminate this welfare payment, but simply to reduce mohair subsidies from a maximum of $150,000 to $50,000 per producer, which would save taxpayers $212 million over four years. The ranching industry joined ranks and killed the proposal. In July 1995, representatives from 28 states in which mink farmers divvy up a $1.9 million annual subsidy succeeded in killing a proposal to end that subsidy.[41]

Reformers advocate four basic reforms for public rangelands. First, they call for raising AUMs on public lands to match fee levels on private lands. Secondly, the number of animals allowed to graze should be restricted to a sustainable level. Thirdly, there should be a moratorium on grazing for those rangelands which have already deteriorated badly. Finally, access to public rangelands should be managed for multiple uses rather than the special interest of ranchers. Reformers also argue that the BLM itself is in desperate need of reform. Rather than cornucopians, environmentalists and conservationists should run the BLM. These proposals are all pipe-dreams given the power of the ranching industry, the entrenchment of their welfare programs, and a Republican Congress.

HUNTING AND FISHING

Despite popular beliefs, from the Jamestown settlement in 1607 to the frontier's official closing in 1890, only a small percentage of Americans depended on hunting, trapping, and fishing to supply most of their food and clothing. Farmers produced most of the nation's sustenance. This was mostly from necessity. Wherever people settled, they soon decimated the local fish and game. As the nation's population and settled regions increased, the wildlife diminished both directly from hunting and indirectly from the destruction of habitat through its conversion to farms, towns and cities, and its exposure to pollution. The introduction of exotic animals either helped kill off native species or replaced those which had already died out. Among other species, pheasants, sparrows, and starlings have displaced native songbirds; wild hogs and horses, native mammals; brown trout, native trout.

Entire species were decimated for financial gain. In 1600, as many as 60 million buffalo may have ranged from the Rocky Mountains to the Atlantic Ocean. By the late nineteenth century, only a few hundred remained. Elk covered the same area; although much more numerous than buffalo, they now live only in the northern Rocky Mountains and in pockets elsewhere across the West. Wolves once lived in all of the lower 48 states. Today, there are viable wolf populations only in Minnesota, and tiny packs in Montana, Wyoming, and Washington. At one time, jaguars ranged as far east as North Carolina but they have long since disappeared from the United States. Passenger pigeons used to flock in such great numbers that they blackened the sky; the last died in 1912 at the Cincinnati Zoo. When the first settlers arrived, countless beavers dams diverted streams from coast to coast. By the 1840s, trappers had nearly wiped out the species. Though now so numerous that many suburbanites consider them a nuisance, deer had been hunted out across much of the country by the early twentieth century. Overfishing, dams, and pollution have destroyed salmon runs on the East coast and virtually all of the West coast. All these species were natural resources destroyed by free markets.

Probably many more animals died from the loss of their homes than from bullets, traps, or nets. Forest lands diminished from about 1 billion acres in 1600 to the nadir of 465 million acres in 1920; strict conservation measures have increased America's forests to 700 million acres at present. Unfortunately, American's wetlands have continued to decline from about 215 million acres in 1600 to 101 million in 1991. Wetlands include both estuarine (coastal) regions and palustrine (inland) regions. About 95 percent of all wetlands are palustrine. While draining wetlands, humans destroy millions of animals. In just one decade from the mid-1970s to mid-1980s the duck population dropped from 44 million to 30 million birds as the total amount of wetlands steadily diminished.

The federal policy of privatizing rather than managing public lands was the most important reason for this massive habitat destruction. The various homestead acts opened all the public lands to towns, farms, ranches, logging camps, railroads, and mines. The Swamp Land Act of 1847, amended in 1850 and 1860, gave away public lands to those who drained and converted wetlands. Altogether the government granted over 60 million acres under the Swamp Land Act, although many of those lands were actually dry.

As in so many other areas, just as some public policies accelerated environmental destruction, others have promoted conservation and in some cases preservation. Throughout American history, if hunting was at all regulated, it was first the colonies and later the states which did so. In 1694, Massachusetts enacted the first closed deer-hunting season; by America's independence twelve of the thirteen colonies had closed hunting season for various species. The states continued these policies. By 1880, every state had its own fish and game bureau. Writing a state law proved easier than enforcing it. Wildlife steadily died off despite all these laws; the responsible agencies were usually underfunded, under-manned, and overly corrupt.

It was not until the late nineteenth century that the federal government tried to oversee fishing and hunting. Concerned with diminishing fish stocks, the Agriculture Department created the US Fisheries Commission in 1871. In 1874, Congress pased a law forbidding any further buffalo killing on federal lands. President Grant pocket-vetoed the law when he was advised that the decimation of the buffalo was the best means of subduing the Plains Indians. Thus died the first federal attempt to preserve a species. Responding to complaints by trappers and hunters about the depletion of game, the Agriculture Department created the Bureau of Biological Survey (later renamed the Fish and Wildlife Service) in 1885. Lacking sufficient funds, expertise, and power, these new agencies could do little more than note the problem. Legally their hands were tied. The Supreme Court reaffirmed in 1896 in *Geer* v. *Connecticut* that the states had jurisdiction over hunting.

Federal jurisdiction was confined to federal lands. In 1894, Congress passed the Yellowstone Protection Act forbidding any hunting in the park, and in 1895 extended that restriction to all national parks with the Park Protection Act. Then, in 1900, Congress passed the 1900 Lacey Act, which made it a federal crime to cross a state border with wildlife killed in violation of another state's law.

The conservation movement led these first national efforts to regulate hunting. Magazines such as *The American Sportsman* and *Field and Stream,* and associations like the New York Sportsmen's Club (1844), National Audubon Society (1886), and Boone and Crockett Club (1887) advocated strict limits on hunting and fishing. In 1902, most of the lobby groups banded together under the International Association of Fish and Wildlife Agencies. The efforts of these "sport" hunters to conserve species conflicted with those of the "market" hunters to enjoy unrestricted freedom to hunt and fish.

The most important figure in the early wildlife conservation movement was Theodore Roosevelt. At times, T. R. could be the most appalling of cornucopians. During an extended African safari from April 1909 to March 1910, he and his companions shipped back to the United States the remains of over 3,000 animals.[42] And like the Western rancher he once was, he considered predators such as wolves, cougars, and coyote as so much vermin to be wiped out. Yet he saw most "game" as a resource that should be conserved like forests, streams, and grasslands. And he exulted in the beauty of wild animals – even as he gunned them down.

Roosevelt had founded the Boone and Crockett Club and throughout his life eloquently called for wildlife conservation. As president, Roosevelt converted his beliefs into policy. Roosevelt started the National Wildlife Refuge in 1903 when he created the Penquin Island Refuge off the Florida coast. With congressional approval for this precedent, within a year Roosevelt had established the National Bison Range in Montana and the Grand Canyon National Game Preserve to protect mule deer in northern Arizona. His actions were confirmed by the 1906 Antiquities Act, which empowered the president to protect public lands holding natural or cultural treasures. By the time he left office in 1910, Roosevelt had created 435,000 acres of wildlife refuges across the nation.

A series of laws have expanded wildlife protection since Roosevelt left office. The 1911 Weeks–McLean Act was important not just because it placed migratory birds under federal protection but because it allowed the government to buy land. Proponents argued that Congress was empowered to do so under the Constitution's interstate commerce clause. Opponents disagreed and sued. Federal district courts declared the law unconstitutional. The Agriculture Department appealed to the Supreme Court. Fearing it would lose, the Agriculture Department came up with a sounder legal basis to assert power over migratory species. It implored the State Department to negotiate a migratory bird treaty with Canada, since the Constitution requires all states to comply with international treaties. The Migratory Bird Treaty Act of 1918 at once repealed the Weeks-McLean Act and ratified the migratory bird treaty with Canada. In 1920, the Supreme Court upheld the 1918 Act in *Missouri* v. *Holland.* In 1928, the Supreme Court further extended the federal government's powers to regulate wildlife on private and state as well as federal lands by citing the Constitution's eminent domain clause. These powers were explicitly extended with the 1929 Migratory Bird Conservation Act.

As important as creating wildlife refuges is managing them properly. Although these laws began to slow and sometimes reverse the decline of many species, the government was and remains highly selective about which wild animals it conserves. While the government limited the hunting of browsing animals like elk, deer, and moose on public lands, it eradicated predators such as coyote, cougars, and bears. The government's predator control program started in 1915. Since then taxpayer dollars have financed the slaughter of hundreds of thousands of "predators" by poison, bullets, traps, burning, and drowning. While private hunters could not kill in the national parks, federal employees could.

These policies led to a tragedy on the Kaibab Plateau north of the Grand Canyon. In the 1920s, lacking human and animal predators, the deer population in the preserve soared beyond the ecosystem's ability to sustain it. After devouring the available foliage, the deer then starved to death by the thousands until only a few remained. Fortunately, lessons were drawn from the tragedy which stimulated advances in understanding ecology and devising sound conservation-management practices. After studying the Kaibab Plateau

deer population explosion and crash, Aldo Leopold concluded that every ecosystem had its own carrying capacity
for its species, whose numbers were kept in balance by predators and prey. When humans wiped out one link in that life
chain they inevitably disrupted the entire ecosystem. The
Bureau of Biological Survey began incorporating these lessons into its policies. Although the government's predator
control program continues, it is not as rapacious as before.

Leopold's contributions to ecology became the basis for
a range of new environmental organizations that joined older
ones in lobbying the government to expand its wildlife protection. Among the most prominent of these were the Izaak
Walton League (1923), Defenders of Wildlife (1926, originally called the Anti-Steel Trap League), the National Wildlife Federation (1934), and Wildlife Management Institute
(1936). Unlike the earlier generation of hunting clubs, which
advocated protecting certain game species for hunting, these
environmental organizations understood the importance of
preserving entire ecosystems from all human destruction –
including hunting.

Although by the 1930s the federal government had solidly established its right to purchase land, paying for it was
another problem. Land purchases under the 1929 Migratory Bird Conservation Act depended on congressional appropriations. Unfortunately, the United States was just
entering the Great Depression when the bill was passed;
Congress was not in a spending mood. Franklin Roosevelt
tried to emulate his cousin as a conservationist. He convinced Congress to pass two powerful wildlife-conservation
laws in 1934. The Migratory Bird Stamp Act required hunters
to buy bird stamps in return for a hunting license. The
government used stamp-sale revenues to purchase land for
refuges. The Fish and Wildlife Coordination Act required
wildlife-impact studies for all development projects on federal land. Then, three years later in 1937, Roosevelt signed
into law the Federal Aid in Wildlife Restoration (Pittman-
Robertson) Act, which further expanded the pool of funds
for land purchases by imposing an 11 percent excise tax on
all firearms and ammunition sales. To better enforce the
growing range of wildlife laws, Roosevelt pushed through
Congress the Reorganization Act of 1939, that consolidated

the Fisheries Bureau in the Commerce Department and the Biological Survey Bureau in the Agriculture Department into the United States Fish and Wildlife Service in the Interior Department. The tax was extended to handguns and archery equipment in 1972. In 1984, the Dingell-Johnson Act extended the tax to boats.

Despite the duck-stamp revenues, the US Fish and Wildlife Service cannot freely spend the money nor administer its lands as it sees fit. The first duck stamps cost one dollar. In 1949, when the US Fish and Wildlife Service proposed doubling the price, hunting groups convinced a majority in Congress to grant approval only if 25 percent of refuges were opened to hunting. When the duck-stamp price was later raised to three dollars, Congress mandated that hunting be allowed in 40 percent of all national refuges. The 1962 Refuge Recreation Act further eroded wildlife protection by opening those refuges to recreations such as boating and camping.

As if these incursions into wildlife sanctuaries were not intrusive enough, the Reagan White House tried to open them to commercial development! Interior Department head James Watt called for allowing, in the wildlife refuges, "grazing, haying, farming, timber harvesting, trapping, oil and gas extraction, small hydroelectric generation, concessions, commercial hunting and fishing guides, guided interpretive tours, and commercial fishing."[43] Of course, if the Reagan White House were allowed to implement those things, wildlife refuges would disappear. That, of course, was the cornucopian intention. Watt was forced to resign in 1983, but not before the Interior Department had received "144 lease applications for 614,876 acres on forty-six refuges in twenty-four states."[44] Under conservationist and environmental pressure, his successor agreed to discontinue the leases.

The states actually collect any wildlife fees on behalf of Washington. The federal government then gives back money to those states which have passed laws ensuring the fees will only be used for wildlife refuges. When a wildlife refuge is designated on private land, Washington will pay 75 percent and the state 25 percent of its cost. The 1980 Fish and Wildlife Conservation (nongame) Act grants money to states to help them restore nongame species to depleted ecosystems.

These laws only protect wildlife in federal and state preserves – and weakly at that. The 1966 Endangered Species
Preservation Act attempted to extend federal protection to
any animal threatened with possible extinction anywhere in
the United States. Unfortunately, the law lacked enforcement teeth. Environmentalists succeeded in vastly strength-
ening wildlife protection with the passage in 1973 of the
Endangered Species Act. The Interior Secretary, through
the US Fish and Wildlife Service, is responsible for listing
endangered species and protecting those species listed. Although the Act was designed to protect single species threatened with extinction, it soon became obvious that, in order
to do so, entire ecosystems had to be preserved. The Fish
and Wildlife Service evaluates all proposals for developing
"critical habitats" and then issues a "biological opinion" on
the impact of that development on any endangered species
in the area Development which destroys critical habitat can
be halted.

Cornucopians challenged the law's constitutionality and
applicability. In 1978, the Supreme Court ruled that the
endangered species law was constitutional and upheld an
injunction against finishing the Tellico Dam on the Little
Tennessee River because it threatened the snail darter, a
perch species protected under the Endangered Species Act.
Special interests twisted the arms of enough legislators to
bypass the Supreme Court's decision. Congress passed the
Endangered Species Act Amendment of 1978, which created the Endangered Species Committee – the so-called "God
Squad" – which would determine in future cases which species
would live or die as a result of development. Then in 1979
Congress passed a bill exempting Tellico Dam from the
Endangered Species Act, thus allowing it to be completed.

While the succession of new wildlife refuges and regulations have expanded the US Fish and Wildlife Service's duties,
the agency lacks a clear policy mandate like those of the
Forest Service, BLM, and Park Service. Today, the US Fish
and Wildlife Service oversees 91.5 million acres of 508 refuges and 100 fish hatcheries. Seventy-five million of those
refuge acres are in Alaska. The biggest problem is that the
US Fish and Wildlife Service often must share jurisdiction
over a refuge with other federal agencies, and often with

private corporations. In most of those areas designated as a wildlife refuge, the animals must compete with humans to survive. Of the nation's wildlife refuges, about 50 are open to gas and oil development, 100 to livestock, 100 to crops, and 259 to hunting, while only 200 are protected from commercial use and a mere 50 are wilderness areas. The expenses of managing refuges outstripped user fees by $1 million in 1994.

Given these hobbles, how effective have these refuge laws and the US Fish and Wildlife Service been in reviving depleted species? The 1970 Endangered Species Act, 1974 Forest and Rangeland Renewable Resources Planning Act, and 1989 Resources Planning Act require agencies to survey the animal and plant services under their jurisdiction. Between 1970 and 1990, 727 species were listed as threatened or endangered, half of which were plants. Only sixteen species were taken off the list – seven because they became extinct and nine because they had recovered. The greatest success story has been the nation's symbol, the American bald eagle, nearly extinct in the 1960s because of unrestricted hunting and DDT poisoning. Strict federal laws and enforcement have brought the bald eagle's numbers back to 6,000 in the United States. An additional 3,000 species are being considered for the list. Unfortunately, the law and its enforcement came too late for an estimated 500 species which have become extinct in North America since 1600. While it is relatively easy to determine some of the species the law has saved from oblivion, it is difficult to determine how many more species would have become extinct without the law.

Although cornucopians claim the Endangered Species Act halts development, in reality, of 34,203 proposed projects between 1987 and 1991 that potentially harmed an endangered species, only 18 were actually canceled because of the Act![45] At best it is difficult and usually impossible to determine the economic costs of species extinction. However, the depletions of some species such as salmon have inflicted enormous economic as well as environmental damage on America.

The wolf is one of the well-known animals on the endangered-species list. By December 1995, 30 wolves had been brought to Yellowstone National Park and released. It is hoped that these wolves, which were captured in Canada, will eventually breed into a stable population of 150. What happened to Yellowstone's previous wolf population? From the 1870s to the 1920s, various government bounties paid an average $1 million a year for killing wolves alone, including those in national parks. The last Yellowstone wolf was killed in the 1930s. Lacking this key environmental link, Yellowstone has been ecologically imbalanced ever since; elk and deer populations have exploded to unhealthy levels. Wolves can bring nature back into balance. A similar wolf-reintroduction program is targeted on central Idaho's wilderness.

Ranchers and hunters alike are opposed to any reintroduction of wolves because they might kill livestock and game. Yet it is cornucopian ideology rather than economic reality which motivates those who protest against the wolf programs. Wolves were never completely wiped out in Minnesota and are now expanding their range and population; wolves there kill only one cow in 10,000. An environmental fund of $100,000 has paid out only $17,000 in compensation to 20 ranchers since 1987. Ranchers receive this in addition to federal compensation for the full market cost of any livestock slain by wolves. Biologists believe that at most wolves would kill about 20 cattle and 110 sheep a year near Yellowstone. Those financial losses are more than offset by the estimated $19 million of additional tourism that wolves would bring to Yellowstone. Yellowstone visitors support the wolf-reintroduction program by a margin of six to one.[46]

Although they claim the issue is livestock losses, cornucopians are more concerned about the impact of wolves across the entire West. Wherever wolves appear, federal endangered-species laws protect them. Wolves have already spread into the northern Rockies from Canada. Yellowstone packs will eventually wander to the central Rockies and beyond from Yellowstone, a development environmentalists and most conservationists would heartily applaud.

"Wetlands" was an alien concept to most Americans until George Bush Pledged his commitment to "no net loss" of it during the 1988 presidential campaign. Bush himself may have been rather hazy about the concept even as he declared his support for it. It was Campaign advisor William Reilly who had urged Bush to make the declaration to entice an increasingly environmentally-aware public and as part of his "kinder, gentler" persona which would assuage the ravishes of the Reagan years. Bush later appointed Reilly to head the EPA. Although Reilly would remain at his post throughout Bush's term, the president would prove less committed to preserving wetlands.

Wetlands are not just sanctuaries for fish and fowl. Those long familiar with the concept know that wetlands are essential for absorbing floodwaters, refilling water tables, filtering pollutants, and providing refuges for complex wildlife ecosystems. Despite their vital importance for preserving environmental health, wetlands did not receive federal designation and protection until the 1972 Clean Water Act. Henceforth, anyone wishing to drain wetlands had first to obtain permission from the Army Corps of Engineers, an ironic assignment considering the Corps' own history of wetland destruction. A 1975 Court of Appeals decision gave teeth to wetlands protection when it ruled that the Clean Water Act applied not only to rivers but to all wet areas whether or not they drained into rivers. The jurisdiction for protecting wetlands is shared by at least four government bureaucracies – EPA, Agriculture Department, Interior Department, and Army Corps of Engineers. Turf battles among these bureaucracies abound. Not only does each have its own method of designating wetlands, but a range of powerful special-interest groups such as farmers, miners, loggers, ranchers, and other land developers exert enormous pressure on each to turn a blind eye to infringements of their respective legal missions.

Wetlands protection potentially affects farming most severely. Farmers traditionally drained away wetlands so they could plant crops. Under the 1985 "Swampbuster Law," farmers who destroyed wetlands could lose such government handouts as loans, disaster payments, subsidies, and price supports. The farm lobby fought back with millions of dollars in contributions and advertising. In 1989, farm, mining, and housing interests joined to form the National Wetlands Coalition, which then enlisted in its cause Vice President Quayle's White House Council on Competitiveness. In 1990, they succeeded in pressuring a majority in Congress to rescind Swampbuster. In 1991, Quayle's Competitiveness Council released the "Federal Manual for Identifying and Delineating Jurisdictional Wetlands," which could open about half of all existing wetlands for development.[47] The new criteria designated wetlands as those lands with water tables within eight inches of the surface during the growing season, fifteen days of consecutive flooding, or twenty-one days of saturation. These standards were far weaker than those environmentalists and most biologists advocated, and excluded altogether such vital wetland ecosystems as vernal pools, prairie potholes, and bottomland hardwood forests. The rule changes would also have forced the fourteen states with much stricter guidelines to retreat to the federal level. So much for the new federalism. Fortunately, environmentalists pressured the White House into shelving the recommendations.

Wetlands protection suffered yet another blow the following year in 1992 when a Court of Appeals decision released a developer who had been fined $55,000 by the EPA for failing to obtain a permit from the Army Corps of Engineers before filling a wetland. The judge reversed the 1975 precedent that to be protected wetlands did not have to be connected to a watershed; the pool was isolated, the judge ruled, therefore it did not come under the Clean Water Act. That same year, just before the election, President Bush tried to exempt Alaska from wetlands protection.

Thus, although theoretically protected by several national laws, wetlands continue to die at a rate of 200,000 to 300,000 acres annually. In 1991, less than half (103.3 million acres) of the wetlands in the lower 48 states remained from those that existed when the Pilgrims arrived (221 million acres).[48] The Clinton Administration has done nothing to reverse this destruction.

The first Europeans to sail to North America's shores were not explorers or settlers, but fishermen. Long before Columbus set sail, fishermen were casting their nets off the rich New Foundland banks, and perhaps elsewhere down the East coast. Fishermen have dropped nets and lines along America's streams and coasts ever since. No natural resource policy is more governed by the "law of the commons" than commercial fishing. Until 1976, America's ocean borders ended 3 miles offshore. American and foreign fishermen enjoyed completely unregulated access beyond those limits. And the "free market" to exploit those fisheries has nearly destroyed them.

The 1976 Magnusson Fishery Conservation and Management Act attempted to end overfishing by foreigners within waters claimed by the United States and thus boost America's fishing industry. The Act extended sea waters claimed by the United States from 3 to 200 miles offshore. Under the Act, 8 regional councils were set up to regulate offshore fishing in this "exclusive economic zone" (EEZ). The government pays Council members $300 a day for the 30 to 35 days they annually spend drawing up that year's plan for "regulating" their region. Each council's plan is then reviewed by the National Marine Fisheries Service and the National Oceanic and Atmospheric Administration. They then forward the plans to the Commerce Department, which ultimately approves or rejects them. In addition to these measures, the government boosted America's fishing fleet by extending low-interest loans and tax cuts to those who wanted to buy fishing boats. Between 1977 and 1980, New England's fishing fleet increased nearly 50 percent to 1,300 boats. Huge $250,000 fishing boats replaced the smaller boats.

Although the Magnusson Act prevented overfishing by foreigners, it allowed overfishing by Americans. Unfortunately the councils were exempt from conflict-of-interest laws. The regional councils were dominated by fishing interests who promoted short-term cornucopian rather than long-term conservation interests. In 1992, 84 percent of the Council members were drawn from the commercial or recreational fishing industries.[49]

Although each of the eight regional fisheries has experienced steady drops in fish species, none has been more exploited than that "managed" by the New England Fishery Management Council. In 1977, it adopted quotas only to drop them five years later in response to lobbying by fishermen. Fish stocks steadily declined. In 1991, the Conservation Law Foundation sued the Commerce Department to stop overfishing in the region. Although the Commerce Department continued to approve the Council's plans, it did suggest that it impose stronger measures. By 1994, overfishing off New England's coast had cost the region 14,000 jobs and $350 million in annual income.[50] On October 24,

1994, the New England Fishery Management Council recommended shutting down the entire Georges Bank off Cape Cod to fishermen. The 50 percent cut in fishing it had imposed in May 1994 had failed to slow that fishing ground's destruction. To save the industry, the government must save the fish. Even the fishermen now understand that. But the short-term price they and the nation will pay in unemployment and other socioeconomic ills throughout the region will be stiff until those fishing grounds recover – if they ever do.

LEGACY

The war over the nation's resources is fiercely fought in all sectors, particularly farming and ranching. Perhaps only the mining industry has greater political wallop than the farming and ranching industries. However, farmers and ranchers not only represent less than 1.3 percent of America's population, they are minorities in every rural area and congressional district. Even in the most "agricultural" congressional district, farmers and ranchers represent only 25 percent of the population; overall, they compose about 9 percent of rural populations.[51]

Two interlocked iron triangles largely determine agribusiness policy. Farmers and ranchers are represented not just by a majority of senators and representatives, but by a plethora of powerful national interest groups, both the Democratic and Republican parties, and the Agriculture Department and Bureau of Land Management. Given its political clout, agribusiness has long been a "sacred cow" whose tens of billions of dollars in direct and indirect annual subsidies are politically untouchable because they were bought with tens of millions of dollars in campaign contributions and other favors.

Agribusiness power seems greater than ever. Traditionally, Southern and Plains farmers formed a backbone of Democratic Party support in those regions. However, ever since Ronald Reagan's election in 1980, increasing numbers of farmers have switched their support to the Republican Party. With both the Democratic and Republican parties vying for the farm vote, farm subsidies will be unassailable for some time. Ranchers assert just as tight a control over policies that enrich them. It is ranchers who control the local advisory committees that set grazing-district policy. BLM-appointed district managers become mere figureheads. Range exploitation rather than management is inevitable with this system. Despite their tiny numbers, ranchers enjoy enormous political and cultural clout throughout the West.

With this enormous political power, farmers and ranchers have been able to amass and protect a range of direct and indirect taxpayer subsidies, including parity prices; export subsidies; payments to take land out of production; rural infrastructure development programs; below-market prices for public water, grazing land, and loans; monopolies, protection from competitive imports, foreign aid, food-stamp and nutrition programs; technology and science from government laboratories, and technical aid from government experts.

Washington's industrial policies toward farming and ranching have been successful in many ways. The average income for farmers and ranchers is now 20 percent higher than that for all other Americans' homes. The most important reason for the higher income of agribusiness families is that nearly 85 percent of it comes from jobs off the ranch or farm. Farming and ranching now supplements rather than supports most of its recipients. The prosperity of American agribusiness is becoming increasingly dependent on access to global markets. From 1962 to 1971, the United States exported 49.5 percent of its wheat, 13.0 percent of its corn, and 31.1 percent of its soybeans; from 1971 to 1983, exports had risen to 58.4 percent of wheat, 27.0 percent of corn, and 39.4 percent of soybeans.[52]

There are significant problems with Washington's industrial policies toward agribusiness. Because much of America's crops and livestocks are protected from foreign competition, consumers pay more than they would if there were free markets. This indirect subsidy is boosted by the higher taxes Americans pay for the range of other benefits to farmers and ranchers. And, not surprisingly, these federal farm-welfare programs favor rich rather than poor farmers. In 1989:

627,000 commercial farms each grossing over $40,000 per year received payments totalling $9.2 billion for an average of just over $14,000 per farm (the 39,000 farms each grossing over $500,000 per year had payments averaging approximately $32,000 per farm); whereas the 1,544,000 farms each grossing less than $40,000 per year received payments totalling $1.7 billion for an average of some $1,100 per farm.[53]

Farm policy is trapped in various political-economic vicious circles. Washington subsidizes certain crops whose overproduction causes low prices. Farmers naturally prefer to plant crops which are subsidized, thus adding to the very overproduction the government handouts are supposed to alleviate. Federal subsidies to farmers to take land out of production encourage them to cultivate the remainder more intensively, which results in greater erosion and chemical pollution. These price-support and soil-bank policies contribute both to greater overproduction and to soil depletion – the very problems they were intended to diminish – while exacerbating yet another problem, environmental destruction.

Likewise, ranch policy encourages the destruction of public and private grazing lands. Ranchers are allowed access to public lands at prices one-fifth of what they would pay in a free market. With this near giveaway of public grazing land, ranchers tend to crowd as many cattle on it as possible. If they destroy those lands, the loss is America's not theirs.

How can these government-generated problems be alleviated? Perhaps the conservative politicians who join with their liberal counterparts to vote for the bills and massive appropriations for their farm and ranch constituents could begin to act on their "small government" rhetoric. What would happen if the government withdrew all its direct and indirect subsidies to farmers and ranchers? At the supermarket, consumers would enjoy lower prices and greater choices. Taxpayers would pocket more savings. Without welfare, some farmers would have to take up another trade; most would specialize in niche crops which might well boost their income. Soil erosion, salination, and chemical use would slightly decline, thus slowing environmental degradation. Higher tobacco prices would discourage some from smoking, thus lowering health costs. Overall, the economy would grow faster, more efficiently, and more equitably.

And what about a third area of natural resource policy – the fate of wildlife? The licenses that hunters and fresh-water fishermen buy to pursue their interests help pay for maintaining and expanding federal and state wildlife habi-tats. While hunters and fishers alike have a vested interest in conserving wildlife, without governmental regulation of their industries, there would be no fish and game left. As with any other natural resource, if people are allowed to exploit wildlife freely, they will eventually destroy it. The "tragedy of the common" led first the colonies, then later the states, and finally the federal government to regulate hunting and fishing. Today all fifty states regulate hunting and fishing, and maintain their own wildlife sanctuaries, while the US Fish and Wildlife Service oversees 476 national wild-life refuges comprising 91.5 million acres. Less successful have been federal efforts to protect wetlands and saltwater fish stocks – both of those natural resources continue to diminish at alarming rates. The "tragedy of the commons" has been lessened but not eliminated.

2 Forests, Parks, and Wilderness

America's national park system has been called the best idea the country ever had. Apparently many think so. People are literally loving America's national parks to death. The number of visitors is expected nearly to double from 275 million in 1992 to 500 million in 2010. Overcrowding brings big city problems to the national parks, including traffic jams, crime, crumbling infrastructure, tacky strip malls, and air, noise, and water pollution. Rangers increasingly find themselves acting as law enforcement officers rather than as ecologists. Wilderness areas and national forests have their own respective sets of problems. While the easy access to the national parks partly accounts for their popularity, overcrowded trails and campsites are damaging even roadless wilderness areas. Meanwhile, critics have labeled the Forest Service the "Tree Farm Service" for allowing huge logging corporations to clear-cut vast and often ancient forests and replant them with rows of identical trees.

How did this happen? After all, the government created national forests, parks, and wildernesses to allow people to enjoy rather than destroy those natural resources for all time. Essentially, the conflicting demands for all three resources have far outstripped the supplies.

When the first European settlers arrived in what is now the lower forty-eight North American states, forests covered over 1 billion acres of that future country. By 1850, Americans had cleared and converted over 114 million acres of forests to farms, towns, and cities, mostly east of the Mississippi River. As the population soared from 23.2 million in 1850 to 105.7 million in 1920, and spread across the country, the demand for wood increased steadily. By 1920, America's forestlands had diminished to 600 million acres, 400 million less than existed when the first Thanksgiving was celebrated.[1]

The designation of natural parks and forest reserves in

the late nineteenth century slowed rather than reversed the destruction of America's natural wonders. Although "conservation practices" were mandated in the first natural resource acts, they were rarely acted upon. The National Park, National Forest, and other new natural resource agencies were underfunded, understaffed, underutilized, and, often, overly corrupt.

The turning point in policy did not occur until the 1920s when the nation's forests reached their nadir in acreage and viability. Since then, a series of influential environmental writings and lobbying efforts, shifts in national consciousness, and new laws, have led to the better implementation of conservation and preservation policies. The 1964 Wilderness Protection Act created a new designation for some of America's remaining natural treasures. But, like national forests and many parks, even wilderness areas are open to mining, grazing, and some other private interests. This chapter will explore the evolution and effectiveness of the policies which have created and managed America's national parks, wildernesses, and forests.

THE EVOLUTION OF POLICY

Forests were the first natural resource regulated by government policy. As early as 1626, Plymouth Colony faced a growing timber shortage as farmers clear-cut and burned the surrounding forest. The government passed ordinances which regulated the cutting and sale of timber. William Penn's forest policy of 1681 was even more far-sighted. Penn required one of every four forest acres to remain virgin. A decade later, in 1691, Massachusetts designated the first "forest reservations." The object was not to preserve "forests for forests' sake" but to save particularly large groves of pines, which would eventually be downed for ship masts. These and similar policies elsewhere slowed rather than stopped deforestation in those colonies and later states. America's swelling population spilled over into a frontier that they steadily pushed westward, slashing and burning forests as they went.

Throughout the mid-nineteenth century, several influential

voices championed the concept of national parks. As early as 1832, the painter George Catlin, who had traveled to the Rocky Mountains to record the revels of Indians and mountain men, declared that the government should protect the sublime stretches of nature he had witnessed in a "magnificent park." He justified his idea as "a beautiful and thrilling specimen for America to preserve and hold up to the view of her refined citizens and the world, in future ages! A nation's Park, containing man and beast, in all the wildness and freshness of their nature's beauty!"[2] Few listened and none acted on Catlin's vision.

A generation later, other more influential voices seized upon the same idea. In 1851, newspaper publisher Horace Greeley called on Americans "to spare, preserve and cherish some portion of your primitive forests."[3] In 1858, Henry David Thoreau asked rhetorically in an *Atlantic Monthly* essay "why should we not . . . have our national preserves . . . not for idle sport or food, but for inspiration and our own true recreation."[4] Elsewhere he justified national parks "for modesty and reverence's sake, or if only to suggest that earth has higher uses than we put it to."[5] George Perkins Marsh tried to root these sentiments in science. In his 1864 book *Man and Nature: or, The Earth as Modified by Human Action,* Marsh analyzed the fall of past civilizations and found that most shared one thing – the civilization died when its demands on natural resources exceeded the land's ability to provide those demands. Deforestation in particular led to desertification and the collapse of civilization. Marsh was the first significant scientific voice in the United States raised in favor of conservation.

Several governmental attempts to preserve scenic wonders occurred during this time independently of the pleas of people like Catlin, Greeley, Thoreau, and Marsh. In 1832, Washington designated Hot Springs, Arkansas, as America's first "national reservation." The intention was to preserve the Hot Springs for its assumed health properties rather than for its natural wonders. It did not become a national park until 1921.

On June 30, 1864, Congress took time off from fighting the Civil War to grant Yosemite Valley to California "for public use, resort, and recreation." This act was an extraordinary shift from the traditional policy of giving away public lands for human exploitation. The landscape architect Federick Law Olmstead was instrumental in saving Yosemite. During a visit to California in 1863, Olmstead visited and became entranced by Yosemite, and lobbied Sacramento for its protection. Swayed by Olmstead's eloquent arguments and fame, California then asked Washington to cede the valley.

Another state initiative occurred on April 10, 1871, when Nebraska newspaper editor J. Sterling Morton and future governor Robert W. Furia succeeded in getting the legislature to designate that date Arbor Day as an integral part of a comprehensive campaign to make that largely treeless plains state "mentally and morally the best agricultural state in the Union." Nebraskans planted over a million trees that first year alone. A nation-wide consensus was building in favor of conservation practices.

The turning point in the national debate over public land use was over Yellowstone. In 1869 and 1870, the government sponsored exploration expeditions through the Yellowstone region. One of the participants in the 1870 expedition, Nathaniel P. Langford, was so inspired by Yellowstone's beauty and wonders that upon his return back East he publicized his idea of converting the region into a national park. *Scribners' Monthly* published two of Langford's articles and its accompanying illustrations. Inspired by hearing one of Langford's lectures, Ferdinand Hayden, the director of the Geological and Geographical Survey of the Territories, put Yellowstone on the list of regions he would visit during an expedition in 1871. Accompanying Hayden's party were the painter Thomas Moran and photographer William Henry Jackson. The published reports, photographs, and paintings inspired by the 1871 expedition generated yet more popular support for the national park idea.

Ironically, it took a huge corporation interested in reaping profits to bring the idea to fruition. The conglomerate Jay Cooke and Company was financing the building of the Northern Pacific Railroad across the continent. Its leaders conceived of sending a spur down to Yellowstone that would convey tourists and generate additional income. Jay Cooke and Company got Montana's representative, William Clagett, to sponsor a bill in Congress. On December 18, 1871, a bill was introduced in Congress to convert the Yellowstone region into a national park.

The strategy for passing the bill involved dismissing the region as useless for any other purpose. Its proponents reassured their colleagues that designating the region a national park would cause "no harm to the material interests of the people."[6] The strategy worked – Congress approved the bill and President Ulysses S. Grant signed it into law on March 1, 1872. The law stipulated that Yellowstone would forever be a "public park or pleasuring ground" whose "timber, mineral deposits, natural curiosities, or wonders" would be left in their "natural condition."[7] Hunting in Yellowstone, however, was not prohibited until 1883.

Corporate interests soon challenged the sanctity of the new national park. Although Cooke and Company could not financially float their own scheme, throughout the mid-1880s, the Cinnabar and Clark's Fork Railroad Company lobbied Congress for a right of way across Yellowstone, eliciting barrages of eloquent arguments from cornucopians and environmentalists alike. Illinois Representative Lewis E. Payson argued that Yellowstone's worth should be "measured by the millions of dollars" that could be extracted by businessmen who "shall be permitted to have access to the markets of the world." Payson went on to assert an argument that has been repeated by countless cornucopians ever since: "I cannot understand the sentiment which favors the retention of a few buffaloes to the development of mining interests amounting to millions of dollars." A railroad spokesman echoed Payson's arguments, "Is it true that the rights and privileges of citizenship, the vast accumulation of property, and the demands of commerce . . . are to yield to . . . a few sportsmen bent only on the protection of a few buffalo?"[8]

The environmentalists were just as powerful in resisting Yellowstone's desecration. New York Representative Samuel Cox bluntly pointed out that the right-of-way measure was "inspired by corporate greed and natural selfishness against national pride and beauty." New Jersey Representative William McAdoo asserted that Yellowstone's purpose was to preserve "in the great West the inspiring sights and mysteries of nature that elevate mankind and bring it into closer communion with omniscience" and thus "should be preserved on this, if for no other ground." He then elaborated Yellowstone's virtues: "The glory of this territory is its sublime solitude. Civilization is so universal that man can only see nature in her majesty and primal glory, as it were, in these virgin regions."

In a stunning reversal of the relative power of conflicting American values, the environmentalist arguments defeated those of the cornucopians – Congress rejected the right-of-way measure by 107 votes to 65. The success in creating and defending Yellowstone inspired similar efforts elsewhere.

Consevationists and environmentalists alike warned against the rapid destruction of the nation's forests. Of the 384 million acres of forests clear-cut from the nation's founding to 1920, 270 million were lost after 1850. America's population doubled during those seventy years, and with it the demand for trees as lumber to build homes, fuel to cook meals and heat homes, and pulp to satisfy the intellectual needs of an increasingly literate people. Lumber prices rose eight-fold during that period. Higher prices, of course, encouraged yet more clear-cutting.[9] Both for crossties and fuel, railroads devoured much of the forests. Railroads were built directly into the forests to take wood to market. Inventions like the chainsaw and electric sawmills transformed the logging industry. Although, by the 1920s, coal and increasingly oil had replaced wood as America's most important fuel, and logging yields diminished, the damage had been done.

In 1871, Congress first appropriated money to enforce existing timber laws. The $5,000 appropriation had merely symbolic importance. Six years later, Agriculture Secretary Stephen Watts asked Franklin Hough to investigate the private use of public forests. Hough's "Report Upon Forestry" bluntly revealed that logging firms were looting America's forests, and argued that the United States should adopt European techniques to manage its natural resources scientifically. Hough expanded upon these ideas in his 1882 book *The Elements of Forestry*. Meanwhile, in 1875, Bernhard Fernow helped found the American Forestry Association, which was dedicated to promoting conservation. Fernow was born in Prussia and trained there as a forester. He only immigrated to the United States in 1872 after falling in love with and marrying an American woman.

Pressure began to mount for the federal management of public lands. But the timber interests succeeded in defeating even mild federal attempts to slow the devastation of the nation's forests. In 1876, Congress debated a bill which recognized the vital relationship between forests and watersheds and called "for the preservation of the forests of the national domain adjacent to the sources of navigable rivers and other streams of the United States." Logging interests defeated the bill.

Conservationists warned that unless forests were managed on a sustained basis the nation would eventually face a "timber famine." As early as 1877, Interior Secretary Carl Schurz warned that unless conservation measures were immediately imposed, the United States would not only begin suffering shortages of lumber, firewood, and paper pulp within a generation, but as clear-cutting devastated watersheds, shipping, farming, and cities would suffer from increasingly severe water shortages. Schurz argued that if the nation clear-cuts

at the present rate, the supply of timber in the United States will, in less than twenty years, fall considerably short of our home necessities. How disastrously the destruction of the forests of a country affects the regularity of the water supply in its rivers necessary for navigation, increases the frequency of freshets and inundations, dries up springs, and transforms fertile agricultural districts into barren wastes, is a matter of universal experience the world over.[10]

Schurz introduced the concept of forest-management techniques during his tenure as Interior Secretary between 1877 and 1881. The key to forest conservation, according to Shurz, was for the federal government to begin enforcing its own laws which prohibited unauthorized logging on public lands, and that it should value forests according to their impact on other economic sectors. Penalties for violations should be severe enough to deter the practice.[11] To fulfill these goals, Schurz dispatched rangers into the nation's forests to arrest the most rapacious loggers. The timber barons pressured their representatives and senators to cut congressional appropriations for the Interior Department. Schurz had to recall his rangers.

Over the next fifteen years, over 200 forestry bills were submitted to Congress. Nearly all were defeated. In 1886, Congress did create the Division of Forestry within the Interior Department, and named Fernow its first head. Fernow had a title but no real powers or duties. Yet, largely because of his persistent efforts, on March 3, 1891, Congress passed the Forest Reserve Act, which gave the president the authority to set aside public lands as forest reserves "to preserve the lands therein from destruction." Over the next decade, Presidents Benjamin Harrison, Grover Cleveland, and William McKinley protected 40.6 million acres in forty-one reserves.

The war between cornucopians and conservationists over the nation's forests was waged at the state level as well. One of the biggest battles was fought over the fate of upper New York state where scores of logging companies were clear-cutting the Adirondacks. This destruction did not just make a future "lumber famine" more likely. By destroying the watershed, the loggers threatened the Hudson River valley with worsening cycles of flood and low water which would disrupt navigation, along with the soiling of drinking water.

In the mid-nineteenth century, a growing chorus of voices pointed out these dangers and demanded relief for the Adirondacks. As early as 1857 the rich businessman and sportsman Samuel H. Hammond had called for protection of a 100-mile-diameter circle of the Adirondack region of upper New York state. In 1859, the Northwoods Walton Club took up the cry. In 1864, the *New York Times* threw its weight behind the proposal. The publication in 1869 of William H. H. Murray's *Adventures in the Wilderness: or, Camplife in the Adirondacks* generated yet more popular support.

Despite these appeals, it was not until 1872 that Albany actually created the New York State Park Commission to investigate proposals to protect the Adirondacks and other natural resources. The Commission rejected the environmentalist argument of wilderness for its own sake but did embrace the conservationist position that preserving the Hudson River watershed was essential to the state's economic vitality. The 1873 report argued that "without a steady, constant supply of water from these streams of the wilderness, our canals would run dry, and a great portion of the grain and other produce of the western part of the State would be unable to find cheap transportation to the markets of the Hudson River valley."[12] However, Albany rejected the Commission's recommendations.

Proponents of an Adirondack reserve continued their efforts and expanded their allies. In 1873, the new national magazine *Forest and Stream*, took up the cause on the utilitarian grounds that businessmen and the mass public alike should "look at the preservation of the Adirondacks as a question of self-interest."[13] In 1876, the Appalachian Mountain Club was formed to help lobby for reserves in the Adirondacks and elsewhere.

Until the 1880s, the threat of watershed destruction on navigable waterways was largely theoretical. However, during that decade, water levels for navigation and city drinking water did drop noticeably. Along with virtually all the city's newspapers, the New York City Chamber of Commerce weighed into the battle, arguing that if the Erie–Hudson canal dried up, corporations and farmers would be at the mercy of extortionist prices charged by the railroad monopoly.

In 1886, proponents of preservation introduced a bill in the New York State Assembly. After considerable debate, the Assembly passed a bill which would "preserve forever" 715,000 acres "as wild forest lands." The governor signed it into law on May 15, 1886. Almost immediately, conservationists argued that even this bill was not tough enough in enforcement or extensive enough in area. In 1892, the Assembly passed another law which designated Adirondack State Park as a "ground open for the free use of all the people for their health and pleasure, and as forest land necessary for the preservation of the headwaters of the chief rivers of the state, and as a future supply of timber."[14] Even then, the Adirondacks' fate remained insecure. The law's environmental provisions on preservation and conservation provisions on sustained yield of timber conflicted. This discrepancy was cleared up during New York's 1896 constitutional convention. Article 7, Section 7, of the proposed constitution emphasized Adirondack State Park's environmentalist value. The constitution was approved overwhelmingly by the voters.

The debate over the Adirondacks' fate, and subsequent victory by conservationists and environmentalists, inspired similar efforts elsewhere, particularly at the national level.

An expanding range of conservation and environmental groups such as the American Forestry Association (1875), Appalachian Mountain Club (1876), Boone and Crockett Club (1887), and Sierra Club (1892) at once pushed government for more favorable policies and were strengthened by subsequent policies to seek yet more protection. Charismatic leaders like John Muir in California and John Burroughs in New York inspired environmentalists while Theodore Roosevelt was the most outspoken conservationist.

But during the 1890s and into the early twentieth century, no voice on the specific issue of scientific forest conservation was more influential than Gifford Pinchot. He had studied at the French forestry school in Nancy and then applied those management techniques to the North Carolina Biltmore estate of multimillionaire George Vanderbilt. Like Shurz and Fernow, Pinchot understood the reality that the failure to conserve would lead to a chain reaction of ruined economic sectors dependent on those resources.[15]

In 1895, Pinchot collaborated with John Muir on a forestry symposium in *Century* magazine. At the time, Muir uncomfortably agreed with Pinchot that the forests should be conserved on a sustained-yield basis rather than preserved untouched. This coalition would not last. In 1896, Washington appropriated money for a nation-wide forestry audit and appointed Pinchot its leader. Pinchot in turn got Muir to join the commission. As the Forestry Commission met that autumn to write its report, it split between Pinchot who advocated sustained logging and Muir who just as vociferously called for preservation. During the debate, Forestry Division head Fernow argued that "the main service, the principal object of the forest has nothing to do with beauty or pleasure. It is not, except incidentally, an object of esthetics, but an object of economics."[16]

The environmentalists won out in the short term when on February 22, 1897, President Grover Cleveland set aside an additional 21 million acres of forest reserves with no talk of future logging. Pinchot, joined by logging, grazing, and mining interests, fought back in Congress. Bills were introduced calling for the sustained yield from America's public lands. Muir's eloquent appeal for forest preservation in an *Atlantic Monthly* article could not overcome the business interests lobbying Congress. On June 4, 1897, Congress passed the Forest Management (Organic) Act, which stated that: "No national forest shall be established, except to improve and protect the forest within the boundaries, or for the purpose of securing favorable conditions of waterflows, and to furnish a continuous supply of timber for the use and necessities of citizens of the United States."

Pinchot's efforts were soon rewarded with his ultimate ambition. In 1898, after twelve years at the helm of the Division of Forestry, Fernow resigned to join the faculty of Cornell University where he created the nation's first university forestry program. Pinchot took Fernow's place as Chief Forester. There he deepened his friendship with Theodore Roosevelt who was then serving as vice-president, and who, after McKinley's assassination in 1901, became president.

Pinchot was not Roosevelt's only conservation advisor. The scientist William John McGee extended conservation advice to several administrations, including Roosevelt's. McGee blasted the public land giveaway policies which allowed the exploitation of public lands by the few for the few. He rhetorically demanded, by

> what right has any citizen of a free country, whatever his foresight and shrewdness, to seize on sources of life for his behalf that are the common heritage of all; what right has the legislature or court to help in the seizure; and striking still more deeply, what right has any generation to wholly consume, much less to waste, those sources of life without which the children or children's children must starve or freeze.[17]

When it came to forests, Roosevelt was clearly a conservationist first and environmentalist second:

> [P]rimarily the object is not to preserve forests because they are beautiful – though that is good in itself – not to preserve them because they are refuges for the wild creatures of the wilderness – though that too is good in itself – but the primary purpose of forest policy . . . is the making of prosperous homes, is part of the traditional homemaking policy of our nation.[18]

In 1901, he asserted that the "fundamental idea of forestry is the perpetuation of forests by use. Forest protection is not an end in itself; it is a means to increase and sustain the resources of our country and the industries which depend on them."[19]

During his years as president, Teddy Roosevelt added 148 million acres to the forest reserves, and asserted protection over an additional 80 million acres in public lands rich in coal and 4 million in lands rich in oil. Taking Pinchot's advice, Roosevelt transferred the Bureau of Forestry from the Interior Department to the Agriculture Department, and renamed it the Forest Service in 1905. The transfer at once removed the Forest Service from corrupt interests in the Interior Department and emphasized the idea that trees were a crop to be managed like any other. Pinchot went on to organize the Society of American Foresters (SAF) to promote tree farm-management techniques.

Roosevelt could also be an environmentalist. In 1903, he single-handedly created yet another designation to protect America's national wonders when he ordered protection for three-acre Pelican Island off Florida's coast, thus making it the nation's first wildlife refuge. He helped assert national park status for Mesa Verde and Bandolier. Frustrated with congressional impediments to further national parks, Roosevelt worked with Iowa Congressman Lacey to write a bill which would allow the president to protect more lands. In 1906, Congress passed the Lacey or Antiquities Act, which empowered the president to withdraw public lands with cultural, scientific, or historic value. Roosevelt took full advantage of the law, protecting as national monuments Devil's Tower, Petrified Forest, Montezuma Castle, El Morro, Chaco Canyon, Lassen Peak, Tonto, Gila Cliff Dwelling, Muir Woods, Jewel Cave, Natural Bridges, Lewis and Clark Cavern, Tumacori Mission, and, in 1908 as one of his last acts, the jewel in the crown, Grand Canyon. In 1906, Roosevelt got Congress to approve Yosemite's reversion from state to federal control as a national park.

Roosevelt attempted to globalize his conservation efforts. In February 1909, he convened and presided over the North American Conservation Conference. The conference's most important action was to call for a world conference the following year in the Netherlands. Roosevelt sent out invitations to 58 governments. Roosevelt left office before the world conference could take place, and was succeeded by his vice-president, William Howard Taft.

President Taft was an old-fashioned cornucopian who believed the earth's resources were endless and that business should be allowed unrestricted access to those riches. Upon entering the White House he pushed policies to weaken the wealth of conservation policies and protection Roosevelt had enacted. He refused to attend the conservation conference Roosevelt had organized. His Interior Secretary, Richard Ballinger, reversed the Forest Service's conservation policy and instead allowed loggers virtually unlimited access to clear-cut the nation's forests. When Chief Forester Pinchot protested, he was fired.

Despite Taft's cornucopian policies, some conservation measures passed during his tenure. The most important was the Weeks Act of 1911, which authorized the government to purchase forest lands to protect watersheds. Under this law, Washington has since bought 24 million acres, which became part of fifty national forests, largely in the eastern United States. New environmental organizations emerged to struggle alongside older ones. The National Audubon Society (1905), National Recreation and Park Association (1908), American Camping Association (1910), Boy Scouts of America (1910), Girl Scouts of America (1912), and National Parks and Conservation Association (1919) raised national consciousness and pressured government for greater environmental protection in various ways.

From 1886 to 1916, the War Department had managed the national parks. In 1916, Congress passed and President Woodrow Wilson signed the National Park Service Act, which brought together the country's then thirty-six national parks under one administration. The Park Service's first director, Stephen Mather, was an excellent choice. Mather was a Sierra Club leader and naturalist, and completely dedicated to fulfilling the national park ideal. The legacy of his 1917 to 1928 tenure was a National Park Service dedicated to preserving rather than exploiting those lands in its care. Attendance at the nation's parks rose from 200,000 in 1910 to 1 million by 1921. The more people enjoyed the national parks, the more support and pressure increased for expanding the system. In 1933, Congress transferred control over all national monuments, battlefields, and cemeteries to the National Park Service.

Twelve years of Republican rule from 1921 to 1933 were not a total reversion to cornucopianism.[20] Although presidents Warren Harding and Calvin Coolidge did try to cut back government conservation programs, they did not succeed in destroying any institutions or programs. The Teapot Dome scandal exploded in 1923 amidst Harding's term. Revelations of the illegal attempts by Interior Secretary Fall to sell off the nation's naval petroleum reserves cautioned Harding and later Coolidge.

Although philosophically Herbert Hoover was also a cornucopian, he did promote conservation policies by regulating Alaskan salmon fishing, curbing water pollution, building the St Lawrence Seaway and other inland navigation projects, and authorizing what would become Hoover Dam on the Colorado River, and other dams to promote flood control, irrigation, and hydroelectric power. Hoover advocated "Organized Cooperation" in which individuals, groups, and the federal and state governments would voluntarily work together to promote goals that benefited all. Great Smokey Mountain National Park was created in 1931.

Although Hoover proclaimed himself a conservationist, at times his cornucopian instincts proved overwhelming. In 1930, he proposed and Congress approved a federal–state study of land-use policy. The subsequent 1931 report called for the federal government to manage national land-use policies such as the forests, parks, wildlife refuges, and so on, while the states managed all other public lands. Although Hoover fought fiercely for the study's conversion into law, conservationists and environmentalists protested at the vast giveaway of public lands that it would entail. The proposal failed to pass Congress.

By 1920, humans had destroyed 400 million acres of the 1 billion magnificent acres of the nation's forests that had existed only three centuries earlier. Of the remainder, the federal government owned some 150 million acres and state and private owners held the rest. Since then, for several important reasons, the nation's forests have steadily expanded.

Conservation played only a secondary role. Perhaps the most important reason was the declining demand for timber. For crossties and fuel, railroads consumed one-quarter of the nation's timber between 1850 and 1900. The railroad's conversion to coal for fuel, and chemical wood preservatives for crossties, sharply cut its timber demand. Meanwhile, most cities passed ordinances requiring buildings to be built of brick rather than wood to allay fire hazards. Not only brick, but cement, steel, and iron largely replaced wood in construction. By the 1920s, most homes and businesses were heated by coal rather than wood. Thus, by 1920, the demand for timber was one-half its peak level of around 1870. Meanwhile, as demand dropped, prices rose as more accessible forests were devastated. Technological advances rather than conservation practices accounted for these changes.

The most important conservation policies behind the expansion of the nation's forests were fire suppression, acquisition, and replanting. Chief Forester William Greeley had championed fire suppression during his 1920s tenure. The 1924 Clark/McNary Act funded federal and state cooperation in firefighting. During the 1920s and 1930s, the Forest Service purchased and replanted over 27 million acres of lands which had been destroyed by clear-cutting and abandoned. Most of these lands were included within twenty-six new national forests in the eastern United States. Other agencies got involved in forest conservation. For example, the Civilian Conservation Corps replanted over 1 million acres of clear-cut lands. In 1939, the Agriculture Department's Bureau of Biological Survey was transferred to the Interior Department and renamed the US Fish and Wildlife Service. To finance the purchase and maintenance of wildlife refuges, Congress taxed hunting equipment.

Bureaucratic politics led inadvertently to some progressive policies. For example, the Forest Service had continually rejected as "sentimentalist" the environmentalist emphasis on nature's psychological and spiritual values. Yet during the 1920s, the Forest Service adopted the rhetoric of aesthetics and recreation when the National Park Service threatened to take its scenic lands. In 1924, the Forest Service established its first wilderness area. More than anyone else, Forest Service employee Aldo Leopold was responsible for this policy of his own agency.

Aldo Leopold was to environmentalism, in the interwar era, what Muir was to it at the century's turn. However, unlike Muir, Leopold grounded his environmentalism in hard science rather than lofty sentiment. As both prophet and activist, Leopold helped forge for environmentalism philosophical arguments and political victories.

Like all thinkers', Leopold's perspectives evolved through decades of study, career and life experiences, and reflection. A passion for ornithology and forestry carried him to a career in the Forest Service. Sent to the territories of New Mexico and Arizona, Leopold first accepted the bureau's perspective that predators should be hunted to extinction and the lands exploited solely for human use. In 1913, an attack of Bright's Disease incapacitated Leopold for a year. Like Muir, the brush with debilitation catalyzed Leopold's thinking. After his health revived, he organized game protection associations and promoted the idea that animals have their own right to exist and should not be hunted to extinction. The Forest Service rejected his activism and forced him out in 1918. However, the Forest Service's competition with the newly created National Park Service caused it to accept some of Leopold's views. The Forest Service allowed Leopold to rejoin in 1919.

Over the next decade, Leopold developed his ideas for wilderness preservation and forest management. Leopold echoed Frederick Jackson's arguments that wilderness was essential for shaping American civilization and, for that reason alone, should be preserved. He argued that rather than struggle to transform wilderness, Americans can define themselves by seeking spirituality in its midst. Leopold's efforts paid off. In 1929, the Forest Service adopted a policy of preserving the forests and recreating others through massive tree plantings. In the 1930s, Leopold taught ecology at the University of Wisconsin.

In his study of ethics, Leopold concluded that virtually all previous moral systems had focused on relations among humans. Leopold went one vital step forward. As a system of right and wrong, Leopold's "land ethic" included not only human relations with each other, but humanity's interrelationship with nature:

> All ethics so far evolved rest upon a single premise: that the individual is a member of a community of interdependent parts. . . . The land ethic simply enlarges the boundaries of the community to include soils, waters, plants, and animals, or collectively, the land.

Man thus had a moral imperative to seek to live in harmony within nature rather than systematically destroying it for short-term material gains. A heart attack killed Leopold on April 21, 1948, while he was fighting a forest fire.

Yet another brilliant thinker emerged during the interwar era to advance sharply environmental thought and policy. Perhaps no national environmental leader since John Muir has experienced and exulted in wilderness as much as Bob Marshall. Although he was born into a wealthy family in New York City in 1901, Marshall early on was shaped by environmental ethics and wilderness experience. His lawyer father had successfully led the 1915 fight at the New York state convention to retain the wilderness clause for Adirondack Park. The family spent summers at their home on Lake Saranac in the Adirondack's heart. Marshall received a master's degree in forestry from Harvard and eventually a Ph.D. in plant physiology. He then embarked on his "missionary work" for environmentalism. He developed his ideas in field work as an official with the US Forest Service and Office of Indian Affairs and numerous extended backpacking trips through wilderness regions.

Whereas Leopold had grounded his environmental ethics in hard science, Marshall made psychology the basis of his. He saw wilderness as an essential escape valve for modernity's stresses and constraints. It was certainly essential for Marshall; as a high school student he wrote, "I love the woods and solitude. . . . I should hate to spend the greater part of my lifetime in a stuffy office or crowded city."[21] Cornucopians argued that keeping the nation's resources locked up into wilderness benefited only the elite few who could afford to backpack there. Marshall replied that only a relatively few enjoyed the nation's art museums, libraries, and universities, yet no one advocated converting those institutions into "bowling alleys, circuses, or hot dog stands just because more people would use them."[22] Much later, when asked how many wilderness areas America needed, he replied, "How many Brahms symphonies do we need?"[23] Marshall summed it all up when he exclaimed, "Wilderness furnishes perhaps the best opportunities for . . . pure esthetic rapture."[24]

Marshall was no armchair environmentalist. He spent years alone exploring different wilderness areas, including thirteen months above the Arctic Circle. He returned from these expeditions to publish his perspectives in various scientific and environmental journals. All of these writings expounded the view that wilderness must be preserved. In 1933, Marshall submitted his "Plan for American Forestry" to the Forest Service. His call for setting aside large tracts of forest beyond the chainsaw's bite was noted and filed away. He did not give up. In a 1934 memorandum to Interior Secretary Harold Ickes, Marshall urged that currently undeveloped public lands should remain roadless to preserve a "certain precious value of the timeless, the mysterious, and the primordial in a world overrun by spilt-second schedules, physical certainty, and man-made superficiality . . . life's most splendid moments come in the opportunity to enjoy undefiled nature."[25]

On January 21, 1935, Marshall and a coterie of supporters announced the creation of the Wilderness Society, whose purpose was to protect "wilderness and stimulat[e] . . . an appreciation of its multiform emotional, intellectual, and scientific values."[26] Ever since, the Wilderness Society has been among the most effective environmental groups shaping natural resource policy. Early on, the Wilderness Society and the eloquence and persuasiveness of its leaders paid off. On October 25, 1937, the Supervisor of Indian Affairs, John Collier, approved a Marshall-drafted plan to designate sixteen wilderness areas on Indian reservations. In 1939, Forest Supervisor Ferdinand Silcox imposed wilderness protection on 14 million acres of the national forests. Wrung out by decades of strenuous wilderness exploration and advocation, Marshall died of a heart attack in November 1939.

The postwar economic and baby boom increased the demand for wood, mostly for new homes, and recreation. Between 1950 and 1959, the amount of timber cut on federal lands increased from 3.5 billion to 8.3 billion board feet annually. Fortunately, prosperity also increased the demands of Americans for natural recreation areas. In 1950, there were 26 million visitor days at the nation's parks and forests; by 1960 the number had leaped to 81.5 million.[27]

While increasing numbers of Americans embraced environmentalism, the nation's policies remained a mix of cornucopian and conservationist values. For example, in 1950, Congress passed a bill joining Jackson Hole National Monument with Grand Teton National Park. The bill was not an unqualified victory for environmentalists; it allowed grazing and hunting in the national park. The Eisenhower Administration embraced cornucopianism. Anticipating the "give away" behavior of the future Reagan White House, Eisenhower's Interior Secretary, Douglas McKay, tried to eliminate eleven Fish and Wildlife refuges and donate the Desert Game Range in Nevada to the Nevada Fish and Game Department. Congress blocked his efforts.

There were some environmental victories. Environmentalists blocked a proposed dam that would have flooded Echo Canyon in Dinosaur National Monument. The establishment in 1959 of the Minute Man Historical Park created an important precedent. National parks and monuments were previously culled from public lands. Minute Man Historical Park was the first to be created through purchases of private lands. Similar purchases for a range of other parks on former private lands followed. By the late 1950s, conservationist and environmentalist forces were strong enough to convince Congress to pass the Multiple Use and Sustained Yield Act of 1960, which required all government bureaucracies to fulfill those ideas in managing the public lands under their sway.

In the mid-1950s, fresh from their Echo Canyon victory, environmentalists targeted the passage of a wilderness-protection act as their next national campaign. Wilderness Society head Howard Zahniser issued a plan for wilderness protection which included 160 separate areas in public lands. The Wilderness Society proposal was soon championed by a range of other environmental organizations such as the Sierra Club, Izaak Walton League, American Forestry Association, and National Parks and Conservation Association, among others. Together they continually lobbied all levels of government to preserve the nation's natural treasures.

When Congress reconvened in 1957, Senator Hubert Humphrey and Representative John Saylor introduced wilderness-protection bill based on Zahniser's plan in their respective congressional Houses. The battle for wilderness protection raged from then until a bill's final passage seven years later in 1964. During that time, the bill was altered or resubmitted 66 times and the 9 hearings over the proposals accumulated 6,000 pages of testimony.[28] All along, it faced the concerted opposition of miners, loggers, grazers, drillers, many recreation advocates, and their national, state, and local political representatives. Ironically, the cornucopian ranks were joined by the National Park and Forest Services, which feared the bill would mean encroachments on their bureaucratic turf.

The arguments for wilderness protection were profound. Noting that the proposed bill would protect only 50 million acres or 2 percent of the nation's lands, Sierra Club president David Brower reminded the public that "the wilderness we now have is all . . . men will ever have."[29] Describing wilderness as "an intangible and spiritual resource," novelist Wallace Stegner argued for

> the wilderness as something that has helped form our character and that has certainly shaped our history as a people. . . . Something will have gone out of us as a people if we ever let the remaining wilderness be destroyed. . . . For an American, insofar as he is new and different at all, is a civilized man who has renewed himself in the wild . . . it does not matter in the slightest that only a few people every year will go into it. . . . That is precisely its value. . . . [T]hey can simply contemplate the idea, take pleasure in the fact that such a timeless and uncontrolled part of earth is still there."[30]

The Senate passed the bill on April 10, 1963, by 73 to 12 votes, and the House on July 30, 1964, by 373 votes to 1. President Johnson signed the Wilderness Protection Act into law on September 3, 1964. The final bill was a pale version of Zahniser's original proposal. The bill designated 9.1 million acres in 54 areas of public lands, a fraction of the 50 million acres in 160 areas first advocated. Wilderness is a misnomer for those lands so designated: mining claims could be filed until January 1, 1984, and mining continued for all claims approved prior to that date; grazing, hunting, and fishing would be allowed indefinitely; and the president was empowered to approve dams, roads, and power plants in wilderness if he deemed it in the national interest. Thus, private interests such as ranchers and miners have as much right to exploit those lands as backpackers have to hike it. When the right to file mining claims in wilderness areas finally expired in 1984, 10,000 permits were in private hands. Those with permits can fence off their stake, build roads to it, blast and steam shovel the earth, and use cyanide and other chemicals to leech the debris for its minerals.

Additional wilderness areas could be created only with congressional approval. All roadless public lands 5,000 acres or larger in national forests, national parks, or wildlife refuges would be reviewed for inclusion in an existing wilderness, or public lands of 100,000 acres or more for a separate designation. Three government bureaucracies – the Forest Service, Park Service, and Fish and Wildlife Service – would administer the National Wilderness Protection System created by the Act. The BLM was left out because it was then thought that its largely grazing and desert lands were unsuitable for wilderness designation. Since then, wilderness areas have been created on public lands administered by the BLM.

That same year, Congress passed another environmental bill that was almost as important as the Wilderness Protection Act. Most of the nation's parks, monuments, and forests had been designated before World War II. Since then, Congress had been extremely stingy in funding the existing systems, let alone enlarging them. The Land and Water Conservation Fund was designed to make protection of America's natural heritage independent of congressional whims and special interests. Financed from such sources as park entrance fees, sales of federal property, taxes on motorboat fuel, and oil leases on the continental shelf, the fund is used to buy federal park and recreation lands, or matched with funds from state and local government so that they can buy lands for the same purpose.

Then, on October 2, 1968, President Johnson signed two laws that represented major conservation steps. The National Wild and Scenic Rivers System Act protects designated rivers from development up to a half mile on either side. To date, Congress has designated 10,574 miles of 212 river segments as wild and scenic. Likewise, the National Trails System Act protects trails so designated – 23,650 miles to date.

Despite these victories, some environmentalists were deeply disappointed over the compromises their organizations had made in winning approval for the Wilderness Act. These dissidents founded organizations such as the Environmental Defense Fund (1967), Friends of the Earth (1968), and Natural Resource Defense Council (1970), which were less willing to compromise on vital issues. They lobbied hard and eloquently to get Congress to approve Zahniser's proposal that at least 2 percent of the lower 48 states be designated as wilderness. The poet Gary Snyder called wilderness his constituency and spoke powerfully for its defense. A real democracy, according to Snyder, would represent and defend the rights of all living creatures, not just those of humans.[31] The consequences of destroying wilderness, according to A. J. Rush, was the equivalent of farmers eating their seed corn: "When man obliterates wilderness, he repudiates the evolutionary force that put him on this planet. In a deeply terrifying sense, man is on his own."[32] As Rod Nash put it, "Wilderness should no longer be seen as a threat to civilization, but rather as a valuable part of a rich and full civilization – an asset and not an adversary."[33] Nash finds seven values in wilderness – scientific, spiritual, aesthetic, heritage, psychological, cultural, and intrinsic; he asserts that any one of those values should be reason enough to conserve wilderness.

One of the first victories of the reinforced environmental coalition was over Mineral King Valley in the Sequoia National Forest. In 1965, the Forest Service tried to cede Mineral King to the Disney Corporation to build a ski resort there. The Sierra Club sued Disney and the Forest Service. The defense argued that the Sierra Club could not sue because it had no property in the disputed region. In the 1972 case of *Sierra Club* v. *Morton*, the Supreme Court ruled that the Sierra Club did in fact have standing. Disney abandoned its effort to incorporate Mineral King Valley. In 1978, Congress added Mineral King to Sequoia National Park. While the Sierra Club's efforts had saved a magnificent valley from development, they had gained much more. The Supreme Court's ruling that an interested group could enjoy standing even if they had no direct financial stake in an issue helped make lawsuits the ultimate weapon of environmentalists in the natural-resource war.

Continued lobbying and lawsuits by environmental groups led to more victories. In 1969, the Sierra Club and National Resources Defense Council sued the Forest Service to stop its clear-cutting in watersheds of the Monongahela National Forest. The West Virginia District Court ruled in the environmentalists' favor and ordered the Forest Service to end clear-cutting on those lands.

In the mid-1970s, the coalition of conservationists and environmentalists succeeded in pushing through Congress three natural-resource management laws. The 1974 Resources Planning Act established comprehensive planning for each national forest. The 1976 National Forest Management Act imposed stricter standards on the Forest Service for clear-cutting, species diversity, and multiple use. But even more decisive was the Federal Land Policy and Management Act (FLPMA) of 1976, that not only imposed new and elaborate multiple-use regulations upon the federal agencies but also required them to protect the nation's historic and cultural legacy. And, perhaps most importantly, henceforth all policies were to be open to public review and comment. The Act also required the BLM to conduct wilderness studies for those lands under its jurisdiction. Finally FLPMA proclaims unambiguously that "Congress declares that it is the policy that the public lands be retained in federal ownership."

Those three laws were a reaction against decades of policies by the various natural-resource bureaucracies which largely gave away public land riches to special interests. But even with new, comprehensive conservation laws on the books, it was difficult to get the bureaucracies to stop catering to the special industrial interests.

Meanwhile, the Forest Service's wilderness studies of its lands – called the Roadless Area Review and Evaluation (RARE) program – was becoming increasingly controversial.

RARE's initial review was completed in 1972. It found that 1,449 areas totaling 56 million acres met the basic requirements for possible wilderness, but only recommended that about 12 million of those acres be designated as wilderness. Environmentalists protested that too few acres would be protected. The Carter White House got the Forest Service to begin a second review in 1978. Completed the following year, RARE II expanded the list to 2,919 areas consisting of 62 million acres. Of these lands, the Forest Service recommended that 15 million actually be named wilderness, 10.8 million be studied further, and the rest opened for multiple use. Once again, environmentalists protested that RARE II designated too few lands as wilderness. Huey Johnson, California's Resources Secretary, sued the Forest Service for not complying with federal law in its RARE studies. The court ruled in his favor, as did an appeals court. The Forest Service was required to conduct yet another review. Unfortunately for wilderness advocates, RARE III was conducted during the Reagan White House years. Assistant Agriculture Secretary John Crowell was in charge of RARE III, which advocated the immediate opening for development of all lands not designated as wilderness under RARE II, and yet another review of those lands that the previous study had designated as possible wilderness.

When the BLM finally got around to reviewing its realm for possible wilderness designation in 1979, it helped spark the "sagebrush rebellion" among ranchers and miners with operations there. Those special interests demanded that the federal government transfer BLM lands to state and private ownership. Nearly two decades later, the deadlock over the fate of BLM lands remains.

The greatest recent victory by conservationists and environmentalists was during the 1970s over Alaska. Today, those in search of true American wilderness can only head for Alaska. Half of Alaska is treeless. Only 20 million of 376 million total acres are fit for cultivation or grazing. Throughout much of Alaska, temperatures hover around minus 20 for months. Even in southern Alaska, winter days last a few hours; some days there is no sun in the north.

These harsh extremes have attracted environmentalists, while its natural resources have been a magnet for developers.

Fur trappers and commercial fishermen were the most important early developers, and have been exploiting the region since the Russians' first arrival in the eighteenth century. In the generation following America's purchase of Alaska from Russia in 1867, a trickle of wealthy tourists made the pilgrimage to the far north and returned with tales of its sublime beauty. As early as 1879, John Muir and writer Sheldon Jackson visited Alaska and then publicized its virtues. In 1890, the railroad millionaire Edward Harriman packed a score of scientists aboard his ship and explored the Alaskan coast and hinterlands. Other scientific expeditions followed. In 1898, prospectors discovered gold in Alaska and the rush was on. Within a few years, Alaska became a household image. National Geographic published stories and photographs. For millions of readers, Jack London explored Alaska's harsh, unforgiving nature through novels like *Call of the Wild* and *White Fang*. Robert Service's colorful poems captured Alaska's frontier characters and mores. Protection followed publicity. In 1917, President Wilson signed a bill establishing Mount McKinley National Park. In 1925, Congress designated Glacier Bay as a national monument.

Despite these initiatives, relatively few people visited Alaska; fewer stayed. After the gold rush played out, Alaska was home to less than 10,000 permanent non-native residents. While national interest in Alaska died during the Great Depression of the 1930s, Bob Marshall explored regions of Alaska never before seen by a white man. Marshall's reports of the late 1930s urged the government to protect more of the state, including entire mountain ranges and ecosystems. His reports were unheeded.

During World War II and the Cold War, Washington valued Alaska primarily for its natural resources and strategic location. Military bases across Alaska were linked in 1948 by the Alaska Military Highway extending to the lower forty-eight states. During the 1950s, several prominent American leaders and writers spotlighted Alaska. Supreme Court Justice William O. Douglas made several well-publicized annual treks there. Sally Carrigher's *Icebound Summer* (1951), Robert Marshall's *Alaska Wilderness* (1956), Lois Crisler's *Arctic Wild* (1958), and Frank Dufresne's *My Way Was North* (1960) inspired millions of readers.

Alaska intrigued not just environmentalists; developers coveted the seemingly endless treasure trove of natural resources. The land's vastness seemed to elicit extreme proposals from developers. In 1958, the Atomic Energy Commission proposed dredging a harbor near Point Hope by exploding nuclear bombs. Mercifully, the plan was rejected. In 1959, the Corps of Engineers proposed Rampart Dam across the Yukon River, which would have created a reservoir larger than Lake Erie. Territorial Governor Ernest Gruening seized on the proposal as the means of economically developing his realm. Ecologists protested that drowning an area the size of Lake Erie would be an uprecedented environmental crime with little economic payback. The scheme died more from lack of funding and political support than from the ironclad environmental rationale.

Instead, in 1959 Congress not only granted Alaska statehood, but promised that it could take 103 million acres of public lands anywhere it chose across the territory. Unlike elsewhere in the United States, the Americans never fought with the natives of Alaska or forced them to sign treaties ceding their land. So when Alaska became a state, the Indians asserted claims to immense realms of land. The new state and native Alaskans deadlocked over which lands each was entitled to. Meanwhile, vast oil fields were discovered at Prudhoe Bay in the Arctic Circle. Only a pipeline from Prudhoe Bay to the south Alaskan coast could get that oil to market. But the pipeline could not be built until the state and Indian land claims were settled.

This standoff began to crack on December 18, 1971, when President Nixon signed the Alaska Native Claims Settlement Act, which awarded the state's Indians $1 billion and 44 million acres of federal lands. The Act also set a deadline of eight years for a comprehensive land-use plan for Alaska which would divide its lands between federal, state, local, Indian, and private interests. In 1972, the petroleum lobby succeeded in overwhelming environmentalist protests and getting Congress to pass a law allowing a pipeline to be built across public lands. The pipeline was soon begun and was completed in 1977.

Although they had decisively lost the pipeline battle, throughout the 1970s the Alaskan Coalition of 52 organizations, including environmental heavyweights like the Sierra Club, Wilderness Society, National Audubon Society, Friends of the Earth, and National Parks and Conservation Association, fiercely lobbied for a sweeping wilderness-protection bill for Alaska. A new generation of environmental writers extolled Alaska's virtues and advocated various degrees of protection. Joining the bookshelves were John Milton's *Nameless Valleys, Shining Mountains* (1970), Sierra Club's *Wilderness: Edge of Knowledge* (1970), Booton Herndon's *The Great Land* (1971), Dale Brown's *Wild Alaska* (1972), Sam Keith's *One Man's Wilderness: An Alaska Odyssey* (1973), Paul Johnson's *Alaska* (1974), Paul Lewis's *Beautiful Alaska* (1977), Boyd Johnson's *Alaska, Wilderness Frontier* (1978), capped by John McPhee's bestseller *Coming into the Country* (1977). The publicity paid off. In 1961, only 57 backpackers reached Mount McKinley National Park; in 1977, 32,000 hiked its back-country.[34]

More importantly, political forces in Congress rallied around the Alaskan Coalition proposal. On January 4, 1977, Representative Morris Udall submitted to Congress a bill designating wilderness protection for 115 million Alaskan acres. A coalition of oil, timber, and mining interests and Western congressmen vociferously opposed the bill. Alaskan Governor Jay Hammond protested at locking up such an immense stretch of land; he counterproposed setting aside only 25 million acres to be jointly administered by state and federal officials and open to hunting and fishing. The Carter White House worked with Udall to produce a compromise bill protecting 92 million acres. The bill reached the House floor on May 17, 1978. Although the House overwhelmingly approved it two days later, a Senate filibuster by Alaskan Mike Gravel stalled the bill.

The White House sidestepped the gridlock. On November 16, 1978, Interior Secretary Cecil Andrus withdrew 110 million acres of federal land in Alaska from mining designation. On December 1, President Carter granted national monument status to 56 million acres, and ordered Andrus to set aside 40 million acres of wildlife refuges, and Agriculture Secretary Bob Bergland to designate 11 million acres of national forest free from mining claims. Carter's decisive actions encompassed virtually all lands originally targeted for protection.

In 1979, Udall introduced yet another bill protecting 127.5 million acres of Alaskan lands, of which 67.5 million would remain wilderness. Once again, the developers rallied their forces against the bill. On May 4, the bill passed the House by 268 votes to 157, but a Senate filibuster derailed it. Over a year later on August 19, 1980, a stripped-down Senate version passed by 64 votes. The Senate–House conference gridlocked over reconciling the two very different Alaskan bills. Environmentalists threatened to withdraw and pass an even tougher bill the following year, but Ronald Reagan's victory on November 4, 1980, cast a cornucopian pall over the congressional conference. Conservationists and mainstream environmentalists joined in backing the compromise bill. House proponents approved the Senate version on November 12.

On December 2, 1980, President Carter signed into law the Alaska National Interests Lands Conservation Act, thus setting aside 104.3 million acres of public lands, or 28 percent of the state, for various forms of protection. The Act doubled the national park and wilderness acreage. Of the 56 million acres designated wilderness, Indians and homesteaders were allowed special subsistence privileges such as hunting, fishing, snowmobiling, motorboating, and floatboating. The 1.5 million acres of the Arctic National Wildlife Refuge was opened to oil exploitation. The Act also transferred lands from federal to state ownership. All together, the federal government retained title to 33 percent of unprotected public land and 28 percent of protected, the state gained access to 27 percent and native Alaskans to 12 percent, while only 1 percent of the total state was privately owned.

While conservationists applauded the bill as a sensible compromise, cornucopians were no more happy with it than were environmentalists. What was the point of locking up all that wilderness, the cornucopians demanded. Edward Abbey made perhaps the best environmentalist reply:

Man could be a lover and defender of the wilderness without ever in his lifetime leaving the boundaries of asphalt, powerlines, and right-angled surfaces ... I may never in my life get to Alaska ... but I am grateful that it is there.

We need the possibility of escape as surely as we need hope.[35]

Environmentalist hopes for preserving yet more wilderness withered during the dozen years of cornucopian presidents Reagan and Bush, who declared war on not only environmentalist, but conservationist concerns. John Crowell, Reagan's Agriculture Secretary, expanded logging in the nation's forests, particularly its old-growth "decadent" forests, and even called for canceling old contracts and issuing logging corporations new ones with even more generous terms. Interior Secretary James Watt opened the national parks to snowmobiling and tried opening wilderness areas to oil and gas exploration. Watt succeeded in giving away 63 million acres of Forest Service and BLM land in the lower 48 states to petroleum corporations, along with 100 million acres of Alaskan lands, and 1 billion acres of outer continental shelf (OCS) lands. In 1982, the Reagan White House created the cabinet-level Property Review Board, which would evaluate all federal lands and sell at least $17 billion worth to private interests within five years. Although George Bush declared himself an "environmental president," he was a cornucopian at heart and in policy. Style was the only difference between the cornucopian policies of Reagan and Bush – the latter promoted a less destructive image. However, in reality, the federal government's cornucopian policies of giving away the nation's natural resources either free or at below-market prices remained unchanged.

Environmentalists and conservationists alike tried to stem the cornucopian onslaught, with limited success. Nowhere has the battle over the nation's forests raged more fiercely than in the Pacific Northwest. At stake are some of the world's most complex and beneficial ecosystems. No tropical or temperate forest in the world absorbs more carbon dioxide than that of the Pacific Northwest. Clear-cutting the region's forests not only worsened the greenhouse effect, but threatened the water supply of Pacific Northwest cities, destroyed salmon fisheries, and depressed the tourist trade. Clear-cutting results in a permanent net economic loss for the entire region.[36]

The Reagan and Bush administration unofficially ordered the Forest Service to break the laws governing its operations and open the Pacific Northwest, along with other national forests, to unrestricted clear-cutting. Although environmental groups could have sued the Forest Service for breaking a variety of laws, they eventually used the Endangered Species Act to halt clear-cutting. The spotted owl lives throughout the western regions of Washington, Oregon, and northern California. The destruction of the Northwest forests would have been far more devastating had it not been for the spotted owl, which was designated "threatened" under the Endangered Species Act. A 1989 court order forced the Forest Service to set aside for the spotted owl millions of acres which otherwise would have fallen to chainsaws.

The Forest Service had long feared just such a ruling. In 1984, as required by law, the Forest Service included in its "Regional Guide for the Pacific Northwest" an initial management plan for preserving a viable spotted owl population. Then, over the next four years, the Forest Service revised its plan in response to criticism by the logging industry and the White House. In 1987, the BLM joined ranks with the Forest Service and bluntly announced its refusal to submit a plan for spotted owl protection on lands it administered. Logging on BLM lands would proceed unhindered by any conservation, let alone environmental, concerns.

In 1987, a coalition of environmental groups petitioned the US Fish and Wildlife Service to designate the spotted owl endangered or threatened. In December 1987, the US Fish and Wildlife Service announced that its investigation revealed that the spotted owl deserved neither designation. A GAO analysis of the US Fish and Wildlife Service study revealed that it had been shaped by cornucopian politics rather than science. A coalition of environmental groups then sued the US Fish and Wildlife Service. On November 17, 1988, the US District Court in Seattle ruled against the US Fish and Wildlife Service and ordered them to restudy the issue by May 1, 1989. Not surprisingly, the US Fish and Wildlife Service report, issued just weeks before the deadline, concluded that the spotted owl was indeed a threatened species. On June 26, 1990, the EPA officially listed the spotted owl as an endangered species. Environmental groups then sued logging firms which continued to clear-cut in the spotted owl's domain. In May 1991, Judge William

Dwyer ordered a logging ban in those areas.

Since the first court order in 1989 to protect the owl, the regional timber harvest had been halved. The logging industry howled in protest. The Bush White House ordered the US Fish and Wildlife Service to conduct a study on the restriction's impact on jobs. The subsequent report issued in January 1992 claimed that continued protection of the spotted owl habitat would halve the number of logging jobs from 66,395 to 32,436 by 1995 in all three northwest states.[37]

Environmental groups protested that political motivations had deeply flawed the study. They pointed out that although logging industry executives blamed regulations for job losses in their industry, the real reasons were their investment in labor-saving technologies and exports of raw logs. During the 1980s, over 200 mills closed in the Pacific Northwest. Between 1977 and 1987, Oregon lost 12,000 logging and milling jobs or 15 percent of the total, while the amount of logs actually cut increased by 10 percent.[38]

While the industry shed all those jobs, the amount of trees harvested nearly doubled. Exports alone increased from 2.6 billion board-feet in 1980 to 3.7 billion in 1989. Thus, the major reason for these shutdowns was that 25 percent of all Northwest logs are exported without refining, and most of those go to Japan. Japanese and other foreign corporations pay as much as $750 for 1,000 board-feet of Douglas firs, or twice their domestic value, then ship them to their own refineries. Wealth, thus, flows to Japan that otherwise would be created among sawmills, pulp mills, furniture producers, and so on in the United States. One way to maintain well-paying jobs in the region would be to impose export tariffs or to ban outright the export of logs. Logging industry profits would drop if they could no longer sell ancient trees to Japanese corporations for twice the domestic price. But the number of logging industry jobs and regional wealth would increase significantly.

Given how hard-pressed environmentalists were in battling the cornucopian agenda in the Pacific Northwest, and a range of other natural resource policies, it was with tremendous relief and hope that they greeted Bill Clinton's electoral victory in November 1992. Disappointment soon followed. Despite naming avid environmentalists such as Al Gore as

Vice President and Bruce Babbit as Interior Secretary, Clinton himself is a conservationist. On one environmental issue after another – forests, grazing, mining, farm subsidies – he compromised and sometimes caved in to those special interests in order to gain crucial votes on other issues. Given the power of special interests in shaping congressional votes, Clinton really had little choice but to compromise.

Clinton did make a strong effort to resolve the logging standoff in the Pacific Northwest along with the Forest Service's giveaway of the nation's timber. In April 1993, Clinton convened a "Forest Summit" in Portland in which he listened carefully to arguments from cornucopians and environmentalists. He promised to issue a policy within six months. The White House announced on April 29, 1993, that it would end low-price logging in 62 of the 156 national forests by 1998.[39] On June 30, 1993, Clinton approved a $1.3 billion plan to reduce logging on public lands, retrain loggers, and aid logging communities. Logging in national forests would be restricted to 1.2 billion board-feet a year, down from the current 3 billion level, and far below the peak of 5 billion board-feet annually taken from the nation's forest during the Reagan years. Most of the money would be transferred to this program from other ones.

On October 7, 1993, President Clinton forged an agreement with twelve environmental groups to allow annual logging of an additional 83 million board-feet in forests where the spotted owl lives, and 1.2 billion board-feet from the entire Northwest. The figure is only one-fourth the amount that loggers cut during the Reagan years. The compromise dissatisfied all parties to the conflict, with environmentalists lamenting the continued clear-cutting, particularly in old-growth forests, and loggers angry they cannot cut more.

In addition to these measures, Clinton attempted to reduce the demand for timber through conservation. The average American uses 700 pounds of paper annually for such uses as toilet paper, books, newspapers, paper towels, plates, and napkins, packaging, and so on. Even a small reduction in the average waste would translate into millions of forest acres. During the April 1993 Earth Day celebrations, President Clinton announced that after a half-year of studying the problem he would issue orders to all federal

agencies to recycle between 10 and 20 percent of their paper
to reduce waste and stimulate the nation's recycling industry. The government annually buys 300,000 tons of paper
or about 1 to 2 percent of the total national consumption
of 22 million tons of paper worth about $20 billion.[40]

Environmentalists, of course, cheered Clinton's remarks.
They favored as high a percentage of recycled paper as
possible, along with a prohibition on any paper bleached
with chlorine or chlorine-based chemicals, which spew a variety
of toxins including dioxins. Alan Hershkowitz, the solid-waste
specialist for the Natural Resources Defense Council, re-
marked that if the White House chose a 20 percent standard, "it will do more for recycling in 6 months than the
environmental community was able to accomplish in 20
years."[41] Allied with the environmentalists were municipalities
and local governments, which have either filled or will soon
fill local dumps and face ever higher dumping costs; they
favored the 20 percent recycling standard but rejected the
chemical processing ban as imposing costs too high for the
paper industry, and thus being a political non-starter.

Many powerful interest groups oppose recycling. Logging
and paper-making corporations, of course, resist any effort
to reduce the demand for virgin timber. They called for
federal standards at most no higher than 10 percent and
wanted to include papermill scraps as part of the recycling
definition. Standing firmly on cornucopian assumptions, most
Republicans either favored minimal standards or opposed
any recycling measures.

The issue split Democrats. Most declared in favor of the
high standard. However, the party's leaders, House Speaker
Tom Foley and Senate Majority Leader George Mitchell, both
come from states with large logging operations. Not surprisingly, they pressed Clinton for the 10 percent standard.
In October 1993, President Clinton gave the recycling industry a major boost when he decreed that henceforth at
least 20 percent of paper procured by the federal government
would be recycled. He mentioned nothing about banning
paper recycled with a chlorine-based process. Compromise
with powerful special industrial interests, as usual, diluted
the environmentalist agenda.

These environmental gains were undercut on July 27, 1995,

when Clinton signed a popular budget bill with a rider attached that allowed logging firms to clear-cut in fire- or disease-ravished areas. The president signed the bill despite receiving 50,000 calls, letters, and names on petitions urging him to veto it. The environmentalist fears were realized as logging corporations clear-cut previously little touched regions. The result has been a disaster for the nation's forests, especially its old-growth stands.

LEGACY

As in other environmental issues, the fate of the nation's forests, national parks, and wildernesses pits groups of different ideals, motivations, and goals against each other. The policy results in continual compromise for all three of those designated areas.

Several vital issues concern the nation's forests. The most important issue swirling around those regions which have already been destroyed and replanted into tree farms is sustainability. Are trees from those national, state, and private farms being replenished at a rate where the resource remains constant over time?

Certainly the nation's forests are in better shape today than they were earlier this century. In 1987, about 728 million acres or one-third of the United States was forest, a figure well above the nadir of 600 million acres in the 1920s but still well below the 1 billion acres of forest that covered the United States four centuries ago. But the fate of the nation's forests lies largely in private rather than public hands, and the government does not regulate logging in the former. Jacqueline Switzer writes that:

> about one-third, approximately 730 million acres of the U.S. land area is forested, two-thirds of which (about 480 million acres) is considered timberland, capable of growing crops of trees. The federal government owns about 20 percent of those lands, with 7 percent owned by state and local governments, 1 percent by Indian tribes, 58 percent by private nonindustrial owners, and 14 percent by the forest industry.[42]

In 1991, the national forests provided 7.3 billion board-feet of timber, about 12 percent of the 58 billion board-feet consumed in the United States. In other words, the sustainability of America's forests is beyond Washington's present control. Overall, America's commercial trees are slightly increasing in total acreage. Critics, however, distinguish between forests and tree farms.

A related issue is the fate of the nation's remaining "old-growth" forests, or those which have evolved uncut for at least 500 years, and often several millennia. Logging corporations value the lumber they can rip from an old-growth forest's huge trees. Environmentalists mourn the loss of ancient and complex ecosystems. Most remaining old-growth forest is located on federal lands. The Forest Service has allowed the virtually unlimited clear-cutting of old-growth forests. Over the past four centuries, Americans have destroyed about 95 percent of the nation's original forests in the lower 48 states. Throughout the 1980s, the logging industry destroyed around 70,000 acres of old-growth forests every year. Most of these forests have been replaced by tree farms, monocultures of one or two tree species planted largely in neat rows.

Whether old-growth or not, how valuable are the nation's forests? Traditionally, forests were valued only for their stumpage. Even today, the cost-benefit models that economists use in evaluating resource exploitation remain crude and inaccurate. It is easy to compute the market value of the board-feet of lumber a tract of forest can yield to clear-cutters. Economists have yet to create a formula sophisticated enough to incorporate all the tangible costs of clear-cutting. Yet, even by the most tangible economic estimates, the benefits of preserving the nation's forests far outweigh the benefits of destroying them. In 1990, the nation's forests generated $122 billion in tourism, hunting, fishing, and other recreation while the Forest Service received a mere $13 billion in logging receipts.[43]

Much more difficult to calculate are the intangible benefits of the national forests. Environmentalists consider them priceless. Forests absorb enormous amounts of pollutants that would otherwise damage our bodies and worsen the greenhouse effect; they moderate climates and promote moisture; they cleanse, store, and keep waters flowing, and moderate flooding and drought; they support vast, intricate webs of plant and animal life, many of which can benefit humanity with foods and medicines; they create soils and prevent their erosion; they create oxygen through photosynthesis; they provide, for many people, deep aesthetic and spiritual needs; and they have an intrinsic value which would persist even if no humans existed to appreciate what forests can do for them.

For new-growth forests, the controversy is not so much over whether but how they are cut. Nothing devastates a forest worse than clear-cutting, although even limited logging damages an ecosystem. According to Eliot Norse, logging operations "reduce biological diversity in three ways: by destroying, fragmenting, and simplifying ecosystems."[44] Every phase of logging, including road building, cutting, and fire suppression, destroys forests. Logging anywhere can lead to soil erosion and compaction; the worse these effects are the less likely it is that a forest will ever regenerate. The most destructive logging operations are along watersheds. Without tree cover, streams silt up, fish die, temperatures rise higher in summer and fall further in winter; precipitation diminishes. By definition, destroying a forest to create a tree farm means the loss of a complex ecosystem. Yet, ironically, monoculture tree farms themselves can become vulnerable to nature. Because they lack genetic diversity, tree farms are susceptible to disease and pests.

Chainsaws are not a forest's only enemy. Airborne pollutants can ravish a forest. Acid deposition includes acid rain, snow, fog, and dry deposition of acidic particulates. The burning of fossil fuels and melting of metal ores create acid deposition. The chemical reaction can damage or kill trees, soils, streams, and lakes, along with the lungs of humans and other animal species. Animals and plants damaged by acid deposition are more likely to succumb to diseases and pests. Most of the eastern forests and much of the western forests have experienced varying degrees of acid deposition damage. For example, the rainfall on Mount Mitchell in western North Carolina is as acidic as vinegar; the accumulation of acidity in those soils is slowly and steadily poisoning the forests.

So what role has the Forest Service played in either enchancing or destroying the national forests? Critics have attacked the Forest Service ever since it was established in 1873 when it was known as the Division of Forestry. The Forest Service is blasted by cornucopians for not allowing loggers to clear-cut more forests, and by environmentalists for allowing too much destruction. Is the Forest Service "tree-oriented" or "forest-oriented"? Environmentalists derisively call the Forest Service the "US Tree Farm Service," which gives away the nation's forests to logging corporations at the taxpayers' expense. Cornucopians counter that a "tree farm service" is exactly what the Forest Service should be. In contrast to these critics, conservationists generally believe that existing Forest Service policies are largely based on that resource's sustained yield.

In the eyes of environmentalists, the Forest Service is as bad a villan as the BLM, and just as much the captive of a special-interest group to the detriment of the nation's interests. Critics argue that because the Forest Service is attached to the Agriculture Department rather than the Environmental Protection Agency, its mission is "tree farming" rather than "forest management." They point out countless examples of the Forest Service promoting massive giveaways of public resources, converting complex forest ecosystems into tree farms or even semi-deserts, and decimating old-growth forests.

Are these charges true? The Forest Service is a massive bureaucracy with 35,000 employees. Many of those employees are in the road-building division whose web of logging roads cutting through the national forests is eight times larger than the federal highway system, and in total mileage could go all the way to the moon and half-way back. Although most Forest Service employees seem to support tree farming rather than forest management, about 2,000 are members of the Association of Forest Service Employees for Environmentalist Ethics.

Unlike most federal agencies, the Forest Service pockets most of the fees it collects to cover its operating expenses; the rest is redistributed to local governments and school districts. In 1990, the Forest Service collected $629 million of which it returned $327 million to local governments.[45]

Thus the incentive for the Forest Service is to sell off as much of its assets as possible, a task reinforced not only by the logging industry but by all those local governments and school boards that depend on the fees and which would otherwise have to raise taxes.

Despite contrary Forest Service claims, mismanagement is rife. During the 1980s alone, mismanagement cost taxpayers $5.6 billion in lost revenues. Of the nation's 122 national forests, the US Forest Service estimates that 65 lost money on timber sales in 1990. Studies by the Wilderness Society and Cascade Holistic Economic Consultants estimate that actually somewhere between 98 and 108 of the national forests lost money. The Forest Service claims that its operations yielded $629,727,247 in 1990. The Cascade Consultants looked at the Forest Service's books and calculated that it had actually lost $118,895,390. What the Forest Service failed to include in their calculations were much of the costs of surveying, personnel salaries, road building, management, and payments to counties of 25 percent of revenues, all of which are essentially subsidies to the logging corporations.[46]

One of the most outrageous examples of special interests pillaging America's natural resources occurs in the Tongass Forest of Alaska where two corporations, one Japanese and the other American, were given monopoly rights for fifty years to clear-cut under the 1947 Tongass Timber Supply Act. The vast profits these two corporations annually reap are supplemented by Forest Service-supplied roads and other benefits. The 1990 Tongass Timber Reform Act was supposed to halt the destruction of that forest with its tremendous loss to American taxpayers – the US Forest Service lost as much as 95 cents on every dollar it spent in the Tongass Forest. Yet even under the new law, the two logging corporations are still paying a mere $3 for 500-year-old sitka spruces.[47]

Likewise, the US Forest Service grossly overestimates the success of replanting its tree farms – while the official percentage was a 99 percent success rate, a congressional report in June 1992 revealed that in many forests it may be as low as 50 percent.[48] Ironically, while the Forest Service's success rate in replanting lands under its jurisdiction was mixed at best, a federal program of encouraging private landowners to replant trees has been more successful. The government gave landowners incentives to preserve or re-create forests through the 1943 change in the Internal Revenue Code, which imposed capital gains treatment of income from timber harvests, while the Soil Bank after 1958 has subsidized the conversion of farmland to forest. The Federal Forestry Incentives Program of 1973 offered additional subsidies for forest conservation. In 1986, Congress created the Conservation Reserve Program, which further subsidized the conversion of eroded farmlands to trees. That same year, the Federal Tax Reform Act eliminated the special capital gains treatment for timber harvesters. Tree planting by all owners increased from about 500,000 acres in 1950 to around 3 million by 1987.[49]

Forest Service fire suppression has been an increasingly effective means of conserving the nation's forests. Fires annually devastated large swathes across the country. During the 1930s, about 30 million acres of forests burned annually. After 1945, better fire-control tactics and technologies steadily diminished the amount of forest lost annually to fire. By the 1950s, the annual average number of acres burned had dropped to 5 million, and by the 1970s to 3 million, one-tenth the average a mere four decades earlier.

Yet, fire suppression is not an unmitigated benefit for the nation. To varying degrees, fire is a vital natural regulatory force for every forest. Some trees, like Douglas firs, germinate better after a fire exposes the soil to more sunlight. Fire creates ash which enhances soil, and burns erratic patches of forest that become meadows with even richer ecosystems of plants and wildlife. When fires disappear or dwindle, an ecosystem may develop in unexpected ways. By suppressing limited fires in the short term, the Forest Service allows debris to build up on the forest floor that may eventually spark into uncontrollable conflagrations that devastate entire regions.

The Forest Service's priorities clearly favor the logging industry to the detriment of other interests. Within the 1992 federal budget, $1.17 billion was allocated to manage the national forests. Of that amount, $583.4 million went to the timber industry, $342.1 million went to promote recreation, $92.9 million to wildlife protection, $71.2 million to watershed protection, $43.2 million to promote the grazing industry, and $38.0 million to promote the mining industry.[50]

The 1976 Forest Management Act attempted to curb some of these abuses and disincentives by requiring the Forest Service to engage in comprehensive, scientific forest planning and limited clear-cutting. The Forest Service designates three uses for forests – preservation, which forbids any cutting; intensive, which allows clear-cutting; and non-intensive, which allows selective cutting. Yet, designation decisions have often been shaped by political rather than professional criteria, particular during the Reagan years.

The Forest Service Employees for Environmental Ethics is struggling hard to reform their agency. Increasing numbers of Forest Service employees support "new forestry" techniques "to sustain biological diversity, ecosystem services, recreation, scenic beauty, and timber production."[51] New forestry would completely protect old-growth forests and watersheds, allow selective and irregular cuts elsewhere, and ban clear-cutting.

Technological advances are aiding progressive Forest Service employees in reducing the demand for wood. Wood preservatives allow telephone poles, crossties, and house siding to last much longer before they rot. Concrete substitutes for products like telephone poles and crossties further reduce timber demand. Lumber mills have adopted waste-reduction methods such as thinner saws, which reduce dust, computer-guided cutting, and smaller logs. Steel is replacing wood for building trusses. Genetically improved seedlings have increased the yield and uniformity of America's tree farms. Although wood stoves became popular during the energy crisis of the 1970s and early 1980s, wood now supplies only a minute amount of the nation's energy and the household demand for logs remains limited.

Enormous criticism has been heaped upon the Forest Service. Yet the Service has achieved the sustained yield of America's forests, which are now nearly double their size a century ago when there were no logging regulations. The Forest Service is starting some pilot programs involving "new forestry" techniques of selective and less frequent cutting, protection of riparian (riverside) zones, and selective burns so that the forest's vitality is preserved. Whether or not new forestry becomes standard management policy for the national forests remains to be seen.

Meanwhile, the nation's parks and wildernesses are endangered not so much by mismanagement as by overuse. While the amount of national parks and other natural areas has increased steadily since Yellowstone's creation in 1872, the demand for nature has outstripped and sullied the existing supply. In 1910, there were 250,000 recorded visits to the nation's parks; in 1990 there were 300 million; by the year 2010 over 500 million people may descend on the system of 51 national parks comprising 80 million acres.

Americans are literally loving their national parks and wilderness areas to death as tourists and backpackers overwhelm the carrying capacities of those protected lands. Smog, at times, blankets most national parks; trails are turned to mud soup by backpackers and pack animals. In increasing numbers of national parks, visitor impact is limited through lottery systems and reservations often made months in advance.

The National Park mandate is clear: "conserve the scenery and the natural and historic objects and the wildlife therein . . . provide for the enjoyment of the same in such a manner and by such means as will leave them unimpaired for the enjoyment of future generations." The achievement of these ideals varies considerably from one national park to the next. But every national park is plagued by a lack of money to fulfill its mission. National Park employees are overworked, underpaid, lack promotion opportunities, and, not surprisingly, have low morale.

Congress is mostly to blame for not appropriating enough money for the National Park Service. But, like the Forest Service, the National Park Service worsens matters by selling out its resources to special interests. For example, in 1991, the 560 concession businesses earned $500 million in sales but returned only $12.5 million to the National Park Service.[52] About 6 million national park acres are open to several thousand mining claims. Although no new claims have been allowed since the 1976 Mining in the Parks Act, those with existing mining rights can still operate unhindered.

Today Americans enjoy the legacy of 591 wilderness areas comprising 95 million acres. Yet this is less than half of the 200 million acres that still qualify as wilderness in the lower

48 states. And the existing national wildernesses have their own set of problems. As with the national parks, the demand for wilderness is exceeding the supply. Far more important than the increased number of backpackers who venture into those limited areas is the fact that many of the "forever wild" areas are assailed by mining, logging, and grazing. And America's wilderness system is far from complete. Only 81 of the 233 distinct ecosystems recognized by the Forest Service are represented in the National Wilderness Preservation System.[53] Today, less than 1 percent of America's total land area and 2.5 percent of federal lands are designated wilderness. Given the Republican-controlled Congress, the short-term outlook for stopping the existing mining and grazing of the national wildernesses, let alone designating more, is bleak.

3 Mines, Drills, and Energy

Traditionally, a nation's security rested on possessing a military strong enough to deter or defeat invaders, and self-sufficiency in food and mineral resources. Strategic minerals were those smelted and hammered into weapons or coin. Those strategic minerals of the pre-industrial age included tin, copper, gold, silver, and iron ore. Nature's uneven distribution of minerals has shaped the course of history. Over the millennia, nations that lacked natural resources often conquered other peoples to get them. In the pre-industrial era, the most successful conquerors were the European states which subjugated the entire western hemisphere and knit the world's far corners within an increasingly dense trade network in search of minerals and other sources of wealth. But this first great wave of global imperialism died with the American Revolution of the late eighteenth century and the Latin American revolutions of the early nineteenth century.

Industrialization expanded the range of strategic minerals, in particular creating a demand for those that produced energy, such as coal, oil, natural gas, and eventually uranium. More than ever, industrializing nations were dependent on foreign mineral sources. During the late nineteenth century, the world's industrial powers, which now included the United States and Japan, embarked on an imperial drive which encompassed virtually all of Africa and Asia. These powers strove to create autonomous empires in which to extract minerals and other natural resources and sell industrial goods. This second global imperial age collapsed after 1945 as the peoples of one colony after another sought and received independence.

As the world became increasingly interdependent, national security depended less on self-sufficiency in natural resources. For many reasons, most governments now understand that it is much cheaper to buy than to capture minerals from foreign sources. National competitiveness depends on many factors, not the least of which is the ability to buy minerals and other raw materials from the cheapest sources. Nations that cling to extracting raw materials rather than refining them into sophisticated, popular products drop further behind in global competitiveness rankings. As such, a nation with minerals that are abundant but expensive to extract may be burdened rather than strengthened in an increasingly dynamic global economy.

Unlike most countries, the United States was blessed with self-sufficiency in minerals for most of its history. That did not stop Americans from searching for more. As America's population expanded, the pressure to take adjacent lands across the continent expanded as well. Within less than a century after winning independence, the United States had grown from its thirteen original states huddled along the Atlantic Ocean into a dynamic industrial power stretching three thousand miles across the continent to the Pacific Ocean. Then in 1899, after defeating Spain in war, the United States acquired a small overseas empire in the Philippines, Puerto Rico, and elsewhere.

Until well into the twentieth century, federal policies toward minerals did not vary much from one policy to the next. Given the abundance of minerals within the ever expanding United States, mineral policy consisted mostly of giving away lands to prospectors whether they were a man with a shovel, pan, and donkey, or Standard Oil. These policies changed little over the decades, even when the United States became a net importer of a particular mineral, including oil in 1949. America had been so mineral rich for so long that it was hard for most people to believe that it could ever be otherwise.

The policy watershed was 1973 when OPEC succeeded in quadrupling oil prices, thus inaugurating a decade of low economic growth and high inflation. The American public finally realized a truth that experts had been telling for decades – minerals are unevenly distributed around the world; the United States was increasingly dependent on a range of minerals from distant, politically unstable, and unfriendly regions. The result was a change in both perceptions and policies for energy-producing minerals, less so for other minerals. Conservation, efficiency, new sources, and alternatives became the guidelines for mineral policy.

And yet, in the mid-1990s, the continuities in mineral

policies seem to outweigh the changes. A global oil glut beginning in the mid-1980s still persists, bringing gasoline and most other energy prices down to their lowest real levels ever. Iraq's invasion of Kuwait in 1991, and the subsequent removal from global markets of oil exports from both countries, caused barely a blip in global oil prices. Meanwhile, new extractive technologies and freer markets have stimulated a new rush for gold and other minerals across the United States.

These events have reestablished the traditional American cornucopian belief that mineral resources are endless and government policy should simply encourage their extraction without regard for conservation, efficiency, or alternatives. How long cornucopianism will shape the nation's mineral perceptions and policies remains to be seen.

THE 1872 LAW AND THE MINING INDUSTRY

In 1872, President Ulysses Grant signed two laws whose completely different policies symbolized the schizophrenia that would increasingly characterize American attitudes toward its natural resources. One law created Yellowstone National Park. The other was the General Mining Law, which allowed anyone who strikes ore on public land to enjoy mineral rights or a patent to it for either $2.50 an acre for placer (surface) or $5 an acre for lode (underground) mining. Miners pay no royalties on the wealth they extract from the land. Although the law was billed as targeting small-time miners, it has mostly subsidized the profits of huge mining corporations.

Whether the claimant is a lone prospector or huge corporation, filing remains easy. A prospector need only extract a trace amount of the mineral to "prove" the area's mining viability. Entitled to at least twenty surrounding acres, he then piles rocks at his claim's far corners, and posts a written notice warning others that the land is now his. Finally he files his claim at the nearest courthouse and with the BLM. That's all there is to it!

The claimant then owns mineral rights to that land in perpetuity, unless he decides to sell his stake. There is no limit to the number of claims anyone can own. Once staked, the owner can treat it like private property, even if it is on public land. He need only spend $100 a year on developing his stake, which could involve no more than building a fence, shack, or road. Many "miners" claim a chunk of public land with no intention of ever wielding a pick to the hard earth. Instead, they build a second home or hunting camp on the land. Or they clear-cut the land and sell the logs at a handsome profit.

Mining itself is very environmentally destructive. Miners freely pollute. Huge piles of toxic tailings accumulate, leeching poisons into streams and aquifers; massive amounts of cyanide are poured through tons of crushed rock to separate it from ounces of glittering minerals. If any cleanup occurs, the cost is borne by taxpayers. Regardless of what activities occur on staked public land, the owner pays no royalties or fees on any wealth subsequently extracted. And all this is legal – at the taxpayer's loss.

Today, there are over 1.5 million mining claims of at least 20 acres each scattered across the nation's public lands. Nearly all public lands, including even some national parks, are open to mining. Although over 70 million acres of public lands are designated wilderness, new claims could be and were staked anywhere in those regions until 1984 and can be exploited by those claimants forever thereafter.

Why does the government give away trillions of dollars of public metal wealth to private interests? As in any other natural resource policy, the answers are rooted deep in American history and culture. From the first English colonies in North America until 1872, government policy was based on the idea that by definition the nation's minerals on public lands belonged to its citizens. The enterprising were allowed to exploit them, but only by paying royalties for the privilege. In 1785, the Continental Congress passed America's first law governing mining – it required prospectors to hand over one-third of their take to the US Treasury.

Of course, it was easy for mining companies and individuals alike to cheat on their royalties. The government had only a rudimentary inspection and accounting system. The government's flimsy regulations were shredded during the 1849 gold rush in California. Miners largely ignored and sometimes murdered those few inspectors who tried to collect royalties. This vast looting of public wealth by private interests was repeated in gold and silver strikes across the West and eventually in Alaska. Rather than enforce the 1785 law, Congress chose in 1872 simply to legalize the massive expropriation of America's mineral riches by mining corporations.

In every mineral strike, grizzled prospectors soon panned all the available ore glittering in streams; the rest was locked up deep within the surrounding rock and mountains. Capital and technology revolutionized mining. Extracting minerals from hardrock is a highly capital- and technology-intensive industry. Picks and shovels gave way to water cannon and mountain-boring drills; burros to railroads. Lone prospectors were shoved aside by increasingly huge corporations that monopolized the exploitation of the local minerals. For example, by 1940, three corporations – Kennecott, Phelps Dodge, and Anaconda – mined 80 percent of America's copper.

Until the 1970s, two obstacles inhibited gold mining in the United States. One was price – an ounce of gold was fixed at $32. The other was technology. All the easily available gold had been extracted – miners today must mine an average of four tons of rocks to extract one ounce of gold; in some mines an ounce of gold is fragmented among 27 tons.

The gold-mining industry got a rocket boost when President Nixon abandoned a fixed price for gold in 1971. The price of gold rose from $32 an ounce to a height of $800 an ounce by the late 1970s. The higher prices gave mining entrepreneurs an incentive to invest in the technology necessary to literally move mountains and extract the ore.

By the 1980s, miners had perfected a new technology to do so, a technology that potentially was more environmentally devastating than any which preceded it. Contemporary miners use cyanide to leach out ore specks so tiny they cannot be seen. The means of moving and crushing the ore has been revolutionized as well. Today, there are $6 million shovels to dig the earth and $1 million trucks to move it. Cyanide-leaching, earth-moving, and rock-crushing technologies increased America's gold production 1,000 percent during the 1980s. They also made half of all miners redundant; they were fired.

In 1993 alone, mining corporations crushed and leached 10.6 million ounces of gold in the United States, three times more than was extracted during the height of the California gold rush in 1853. Of all gold produced in 1993, 43 percent was dug from public lands. That same year, miners filed 612 patent claims to over 24,000 acres of public lands.[1] And those corporations extracted all that gold, silver, copper, and uranium without paying a penny in royalties. Hardrock mining executives claim that the uncertainties of prospecting justify the government subsidy. But certainly, those who mine other minerals could make the same claim. Somehow the royalties that private companies must pay for extracting other mineral resources have not inhibited their operations. The oil, surface coal, and natural gas industries must pay royalties of 12.5 percent, the underground coal industry 8 percent, sulfur and phosphate industries 5 percent, and sodium and potash industries 2 percent. Ironically, all other countries charge mining royalties. Many of the foreign corporations given patents to American public lands are Canadian; Canada requires that mining corporations pay royalties of 12 percent.

The 1872 mining law has essentially allowed a handful of families and corporations to "rape and run" away with public wealth worth trillions of dollars. The mining industry is concentrated in few corporate hands, many of which are foreign. In 1993, 283 mining corporations accounted for 92 percent of all production. Much of the mineral wealth extracted from America's public lands ends up in foreign hands. In 1993, 23 of the 40 largest producing mining corporations were the subsidiaries of foreign conglomerates. For example, in May 1994, the Canadian Barrick Resources Corporation paid $9,765 for a patent to 1,949 acres of public lands with an estimated 30 million ounces of gold worth $8–10 billion. Barrick had filed for the patent in 1992, but the Clinton White House tried to delay granting it. Barrick sued. The US District Court in Nevada agreed that under the 1872 law the administration's delay was illegal and they had to grant the patent. To illustrate the 1872 law's absurdity, Interior Secretary Bruce Babbit called a news conference and had a huge facsimile of a $10 billion check as a backdrop. After signing the patent, Babbit described it as "a historic giveaway," but added that Barrick Resources Corporation, like other mining conglomerates, was "ripping off the American people fair and square."[2]

Perhaps even more devastating to American interests is the fact that no law requires miners to clean up the environmental horrors they cause. Mining creates huge mountains of tailings filled with heavy metals and cyanide. The 1872 law's ultimate monument is 500,000 abandoned mines, 50 billion tons of toxic waste, and 10,000 miles of dead streams. Altogether, the taxpayers must hand over $72 billion to clean up this toxic mess. The legacy of the Canadian corporation Galactic Resources is typical; it extracted 280,000 ounces of gold worth $3.2 billion and left behind a poisoned landscape that will cost taxpayers $100 million to clean up.[3]

In 1994, President Grant's conflicting 1872 laws collided three miles from Yellowstone National Park's northern boundary. Crown Butte Mines, a subsidiary of the Canadian conglomerate Noranda Inc., filed a $225 claim to 45 acres of federal lands worth an estimated $500 million in gold, silver, and copper. As if this handout of a half-billion dollars of public wealth were not bad enough, the project will pose enormous risks to Yellowstone's fragile environment. Crown Butte Mines will extract and process 1,800 tons of ore daily for ten to fifteen years until it has squeezed out the last recoverable ounce of mineral wealth. To help process those riches, Noranda will hollow out a mountain and then fill a 10-story deep, 77-acre lake with the resulting cyanide and heavy-metal wastes. That pool must last intact for eternity. The chances of an environmental catastrophe are great. The site is 10,000 feet above sea level, is frost-covered for eleven months a year, and is not far from an earthquake fault.

As if such giveaways of national wealth were not egregious enough, the Western States Public Lands Coalition lobbies government for the right to mine anywhere, including national parks, wilderness, and wildlife refuges. Perhaps no special industrial interest has as much political and financial clout and employs as few workers as the mining industry. Although Western senators and representatives are the most obstinate in opposing mining reforms, only a tiny percentage of their constituents are actually miners. Across the entire West in 1994, there were only 40,000 hardrock miners –

0.1 percent of the population or fewer than one Westerner in 1,000! In contrast, the recreation industry employs about 10 percent of the region's workforce. The ski industry in Colorado alone employs 60,000, which is more than the total number of hardrock miners in the entire country.[4]

Although those in Congress claim they are concerned about job losses, there is no evidence that the imposition of royalties, higher filing fees, or environmental regulations would cost jobs – in fact, they would probably create them because of the requirement that mining corporations clean up their messes. The reality is that those congressional opponents of reforms receive huge political donations from the mining industry and fear its power.

Ironically, the mining industry gets popular support for its government subsidies from any of those who sentimentalize about the myths of "rugged individualism" – often the same people who claim they want minimal government and decry "welfare" subsidies for, say, inner-city single mothers. As Wyoming Senator Alan Simpson put it: "This is not about money. We are defending our Western heritage."[5] Alas, the ironies in that statement seem to have escaped the good senator.

Most Americans and a majority in the House of Representatives have long supported mining reforms. But the mining industry can usually buy enough senators to filibuster any reform bills to death. The latest success of the mining industry in destroying proposed reforms occurred in 1993. That year the House of Representatives by a large majority passed a bill which would have imposed 4 percent royalties on the values of minerals extracted, raised filing fees, and set environmental standards for cleanup. The bill's initial version had an 8 percent royalty, but the Mineral Resources Alliance succeeded in forcing representatives to lower it as far as 4 percent; they had opposed any increase at all. The Senate version written by the Energy and Natural Resources Committee, chaired by Louisiana Senator Bennett Johnson, had only a 3.5 percent royalty. Yet, even that was too much for the mining lobby. Those senators in the pocket of the mining industry cried that the bill would, in the words of Wyoming Senator Malcolm Wallop, "be the death knell of American mining."[6] The House and Senate bills then went to a conference. On September 29, 1994, those proponents of a tougher bill rejected any more concessions to the mining industry, thus killing a potential bill that session. The decision represented a massive defeat for the Clinton White House, conservationists, and environmentalists. The best Congress could do in 1994 was to impose a one-year moratorium on the granting of new mining patents.

ENERGY POLICY: AN OVERVIEW

The United States lacks a comprehensive, far-sighted energy policy.[7] The reason is simple. The popular perception of a looming energy crisis was recent and fleeting. The hodgepodge of energy laws largely written by the industries themselves goes back a century and more. Until recently, the United States always seemed to have an endless supply of energy sources – wood, water, coal, oil, uranium. When one supply seemed to dwindle, others emerged to take its place. Each industry accumulated enormous political power in Washington and the state capitals, and milked those governments for direct and indirect subsidies. Federal policy largely consisted of giving away those energy sources on public lands to private businesses. Since renewable and clean sources such as solar, wind, and geothermal energy threaten the politically entrenched fossil-fuel industries, not surprisingly, they have been shunted aside and neglected.

Thus, as in so many other natural resources, energy policy is shaped by special interests rather than national interests. In addition to the obvious industrial interests like coal, oil, nuclear, natural gas, and alternative energies, there are bureaucracies. Over the decades, a plethora of agencies and the Energy Department have emerged to squabble over policy and laws.

Despite President Nixon's declaration in November 1973 that the nation faced an energy crisis, and the agreement by presidents Ford and Carter, the federal government has yet to devise and implement a systematic energy policy. Ever more laws, agencies, and regulations have spilled from Washington in the two decades since, but many were contradictory and short-lived. Ever since Nixon declared an energy crisis, politicians, scientists, bureaucrats, and academics have debated just what it meant and at times whether it even existed. As a former congressional representative put it:

> It is much easier for politicians ... to visualize building gargantuan machines to provide new energy supplies than it is to visualize how to influence millions of individuals and businessmen to adopt conservation practices. ... It is also politically more rewarding to finance big production units with their influx of megabucks and jobs than it is to achieve conservation.[8]

The energy industry supplies four broad economic sectors – transportation, households, manufacturing, and businesses. Each of these sectors demands abundant and cheap energy sources. With only 5 percent of the world's population, Americans account for 26 percent of its energy consumption. Americans remain indifferent to the reality of finite sources of oil, natural gas, uranium, and coal. Likewise, they deny their increasing dependence on foreign and often unstable energy sources despite a quadrupling of oil prices in 1973, a further doubling in 1979, and the 1991 war against Iraq for Kuwaiti oil fields.

Meanwhile, global demand for oil is outstripping supplies. The crunch in electricity and oil energy sources may come as early as the late 1990s. In 1990, Americans imported nearly half of all their oil needs. Overall, however, the United States depended on crude oil for only 15.5 percent of its energy needs, surpassed by coal for 22.6 percent and dry natural gas for 18.1 percent. Nuclear power accounted for a small 6.2 percent of total energy consumption, while hydroelectric power contributed 2.9 percent, liquid natural gas 2.2 percent, and other sources including wind, solar, geothermal, and wood a minuscule 0.2 percent.[9] America's electricity consumption soared nearly 100 percent between 1970 and 1990, and has expanded at a rate of around 2.5 percent throughout the 1990s. At this rate by the year 2015, the United States will need an additional 270,000 megawatts – the equivalent of 270 large coal or nuclear power plants.[10] The construction of new electricity plants may not keep up with the demands later in the decade.

All too many Americans consider the terms natural "resources" and "reserves" synonymous. In fact, there are considerable differences between the two. A reserve includes that which can be exploited; a resource includes both what can and cannot be exploited. For example, no matter how sophisticated the oil-drilling technology or how high the price of oil, there will always be some oil that can never be recovered. Oil reserves are only those that can be exploited; oil resources include the total amount. A natural resource remains fairly constant, its total diminished by the amount of it people exploit or by new discoveries. In contrast, the amount of estimated reserves of a resource may vary widely as technology, extraction costs, and demands change over time. Twenty years ago, the standard estimates of the earth's oil reserves were enough to last about thirty years. Today, the reserves are still enough for about thirty years despite the enormous exploitation of the earth's oil resources over the past two decades. Technological advances and the discovery of new oil fields have expanded the world's estimated oil reserves. But inevitably, they will run dry.

The federal government underwrites America's energy industries in three broad ways. In energy research and development (R&D), the federal government contributes a small but often decisive 13 percent, while private businesses conduct 72 percent, and universities and think tanks 16 percent. However, in alternative energy R&D, Washington contributes nearly as much money (47 percent) as private business (49 percent), while universities and think tanks bear the remaining costs. Without federal funds, private industry would neglect research and development of many vital and alternative energy fields – the start-up costs and development times are just too expensive.

Yet another important energy-policy tool is the federal government's rules for exploitation of public lands. Washington owns one in every three acres in the United States, and those public lands contain about 40 percent of America's coal reserves and 80 percent of its shale oil reserves. Some of the 1.1 billion acres encompassing all of the seabed as far off as 200 miles from America's shores also have enormous reserves of oil and natural gas. The 1920 Mineral Leasing Act empowers the Interior Department to lease access to energy sources on public lands under its jurisdiction.

Finally, the United States spends tens of billions of dollars annually on maintaining troops capable of defeating an aggressor in the oil-rich Persian Gulf and elsewhere. The price tag for the American-led coalition which expelled Iraq from Kuwait in 1991 was about $53 billion. Fortunately, Washington got its allies to pay for nearly all of these costs. Many analysts have pointed out the irony that among America's allies, the United States depends the least on the Persian Gulf for its oil imports (7 percent) and yet devotes the most military, financial, and diplomatic resources to its defense. Nation-wide conservation measures could eliminate the need for any Persian Gulf oil.

The Clinton Administration recognized this and ordered the Energy Department to lead the shift to more fuel-efficient and alternative energies. The Energy Department attempted to create a market and scale economies for natural-gas-powered vehicles by converting the federal vehicle fleet from gasoline to natural gas. President Clinton signed an executive order in April 1993 by which the government would buy 34,000 electric vehicles over the next three years. Resources were shifted from research and development of fossil fuels and nuclear power to clean energies like wind, solar, and water. Of the Energy Department's $3 billion budget, $1.3 billion went to coal and nuclear energy and only $212 million to renewable clean energies. It redoubled efforts to clean up the nuclear waste-dumps scattered across the United States in military bases, power plants, and laboratories. Finally, the Clinton Administration vowed to work closely with the pollution-control industry. Currently, America's pollution-control industry has only $6 billion of a $50 billion global market. President Clinton argued that investing in all of these areas would accelerate America's economic growth and prosperity beyond what would have occurred.[11] The Republicans oppose all of these policies, and have used varying means to smother them. What effect these policies have on reducing America's vulnerability to foreign oil remains to be seen.

COAL POLICY

For all recorded history until the mid-nineteenth century, most humans relied on wood as their primary energy source, and dried dung as a secondary source. Coal is a relatively recent addition to the energy pie.[12] The quality of coal varies considerably from the lowest of thirteen grades, lignite B, with a heat content of only 6,000 British thermal units (Btus) per pound and 30 percent or less fixed carbons, through the highest, meta-anthracite, with 14,000 Btus per pound and 90 percent fixed carbons. The best coals are middle-grade bituminous coals with 50 to 70 percent fixed carbons.

The United States is estimated to have 2.8 trillion tons of coal resources, of which 439 billion tons are recoverable reserves. Virtually all of these reserves are scattered across three regions – Appalachia with 112 billion tons, the Midwest with 105 billion tons, and the West with 222 billion tons. The United States consumes about 90 percent of its coal production and exports the remaining 10 percent. Of the coal consumed at home, about 87 percent is used for generating electricity, 4 percent for creating steel, and 9 percent for creating other products. Coal mining once consisted of burrowing deep into the earth after a coal seam. Today, most coal is produced by strip mining the earth's surface and shoveling it out.

Of all America's natural resource policies, coal is the only one that has been shaped by labor interests. However, until the turn of the twentieth century, as in other natural resources, Washington's traditional policy toward coal consisted of encouraging corporations to extract as much of it as possible from public and private lands alike. By 1900, coal accounted for 90 percent of all American energy. The nation's economic dependence on coal gave coal-miners increasing power. Coal policy in the early twentieth century was largely shaped by the United Mine Workers (UMW) and other unions, which fought for higher wages, safer conditions, and shorter work weeks. In 1900, fearing a continued coal strike would jeopardize President William McKinley's chance for reelection, Republican Party head Mark Hanna pressured coal-mine owners to compromise with UMW demands. In 1902, President Theodore Roosevelt intervened in a UMW strike by establishing an arbitration commission overseen by the federal government. From then on, the White House would intervene whenever a strike proved economically crippling and the positions irreconcilable.

Roosevelt was concerned about more than the labor conditions in the mines. As a fervent conservationist, he was troubled by the giveaway of America's natural resources, including coal, to huge corporations with no regard for future needs and sustained yields. In November 1906, he tried to sidestep the law and the mining interests' power in Congress by withdrawing 66 million acres of coal-rich lands from development. He justified his action in conservation terms, arguing that the public's wealth must be conserved for future generations rather than consumed by contemporary special interests. The mining lobby blasted Roosevelt's action as illegal but he got away with it.

Meanwhile, the war between coal-mine owners and workers continued. Unions and strikes in any industry lacked legal protection until President Franklin Roosevelt got Congress to pass his National Industrial Recovery Act (NIRA) in 1933. Union membership soared in all industries, including coal. Although the Supreme Court struck down the NIRA in 1935, within months of the decision Congress passed the National Labor Relations Act, which firmly and irrevocably legalized unions and strikes. Most craft unions were affiliated with the American Federation of Labor (AFL). In 1935, a group of unions split with the AFL to form the Congress of Industrial Organizations (CIO), which was based on industrial unions. In 1936, the UMW rewarded Roosevelt by switching its support from the Republican to the Democratic Party. Both the AFL and CIO followed suit.

During World War II, the coal workers experienced their own victories and defeats. Safety has been a persistent demand of mine unions. Since 1902, 90,000 people have died in coal mines alone; since 1930, 1.5 million have been grievously injured. It was not until 1941 that Congress passed the first law regulating mine safety, and subsequently strengthened it in 1947, 1952, and 1969. Roosevelt's sympathy for unions was challenged in 1943 when a coal strike threatened to cripple America's war production effort. Roosevelt ordered the army to seize and operate the mines. Within months, Roosevelt agreed to a slight wage increase for the miners and allowed them to return to work.

In 1946 and 1947, the UMW again threatened America's economy by shutting down most coal mines. President Truman emulated his predecessor by ordering that the mines be seized and run by the government, then negotiating a compromise with the miners. Meanwhile, in 1946 a Republican-controlled Congress passed over Truman's veto, the Taft-Hartley Act, which required an 80-day cooling-off period of mediation before a union could strike. This Act weakened the UMW's power considerably as it was invoked three times over the next three years. Although the AFL and CIO combined in 1955, neither they nor the UMW have been able to reverse a steady decline in union power ever since.

More important to the UMW decline was petroleum's rise as the most important energy source for the American economy, and the development of strip mining for the coal indutry. Of the two, strip mining weakened the UMW's power the most. In 1950, deep mines accounted for two-thirds of coal production; today, strip mining supplies 60 percent of all coal. Strip mining combines giant shovels twenty-two stories high, which tear away the earth's surface to the coal seam below. The shovels then can strip away 90 percent of a coal seam, compared with only 50 percent for a deep mine. One-hundred-ton capacity trucks then haul away the coal to trains with 100 cars carrying 100 tons each. A half-dozen engines then drag the 10,000 tons of coal directly to an electricity plant.

Strip mining is more profitable, safer, and less labor-intensive than deep mining; its workers enjoy higher pay and benefits and have far less reason to organize, let alone strike. Strip-mined coal has diluted the UMW power in the older deep mines. The more coal dumped on the markets, the cheaper the prices.

The only drawback is that strip mining is even more destructive to the environment than deep mining. Strip mining converts once-rich grasslands or forests into barren wastelands leaching toxic minerals into watersheds. Although state governments were aware of this environmental and economic devastation, they were reluctant to regulate the pollution for fear that it would increase the cost of their coal compared with that from other states. Only national strip-mining regulations could slow the environmental and economic destruction, and those did not emerge until recently.

Increasing amounts of this strip mining occurred on public lands. In 1950, about 50,000 acres of public lands were leased to coal corporations. Then, between 1950 and 1980, the government leased an additional 800,000 acres. The percentage of coal mined from public lands rose from 1 percent to 10 percent during that period, or a total of 17 billion tons of coal. During those three decades, individual coal-mining leases of public lands dropped from 27 percent to 5 percent, while corporate leases soared from 26 percent to 78 percent.[13]

The more coal flooded onto markets, the lower the price that could be charged for it, and the lower the total royalties private corporations paid for coal extracted from public lands. President Richard Nixon imposed a moratorium on coal leases because the price and, thus, royalties had dropped so much. As a conservationist and fiscal conservative, Nixon argued that public wealth should not be given away at such low prices. In 1971, after discovering that only 10 percent of the 773,000 acres of public lands leased to coal companies were actually being mined, Interior Secretary Rogers Morton forbade the issuance of any new coal leases. In 1973, Morton issued a policy which regulated the rate at which lands could be leased for coal, based on overall production.

Meanwhile, since the 1960s, the COALition Against Strip Mining had been lobbying Washington for laws forcing coal-mine corporations to restore the land as closely as possible. The National Coal Association (NCA) of coal corporations succeeded in killing any mining legislation that came before Congress until the mid-1970s when environmental forces tipped the political balance. Then, in 1974 and 1975, President Gerald Ford vetoed strip-mining laws, claiming that they would cost 40,000 jobs and cut coal production by 187 million tons.

President Carter was much more sympathetic to environmental concerns. In 1977, he signed the Surface Mining Control and Reclamation Act (SMCRA), which set strict national standards for stripping and reclaiming land which the states are responsible for fulfilling. A mining tax would raise money for the government's cleanup of "orphan sites." The Act also created the Office of Surface Mining Reclamation and Enforcement (OSM) within the Interior Department to police the industry. Virginia and West Virginia challenged SMCRA's constitutionality, arguing that the clause allowing federal takeovers of orphan sites violated the due process of law. The Supreme Court upheld SMCRA. Most states grudgingly went along with it. Of the 27 states with some coal production, 24 have created their own mine-regulatory agencies as required and 3 with negligible industries simply allow the OSM direct controls.

After asserting strip-mine regulations in 1977, Carter boosted coal production in 1978 by pushing through the Land Use Act, which prevented utilities from building new oil-fired and gas-fired plants, and required them to convert existing ones to other fuels by 1990. To supply the increased demand, Carter also opened public lands for lease containing an estimated 771 million tons of coal. In all, Carter followed a balanced approach to coal which encouraged both greater production and stricter environmental regulations.

His successor, Ronald Reagan, supported a cornucopian policy for coal which emphasized production, dismantled environmental regulations, and removed any advantages coal had received as a fuel for electricity. In 1981, the White House convinced Congress to abolish the requirement that all utilities convert from oil- and gas-powered electricity to other fuels. Meanwhile, Interior Secretary James Watt attempted to lease public lands which contained an estimated 2.2 billion tons of coal. Holdings were sold at well below market rates.

As in other industries, the Reagan Administration disdained any environmental constraints on coal production. If they could not change the law, they could at least inhibit legal enforcement. Interior Secretary Watt gutted his Office of Surface Mining, Reclamation and Enforcement; the number of full-time inspectors was halved; field offices were reduced from thirty-seven to twenty; three out of five regional offices were closed; 91 percent of coal regulations enacted during the Carter years were revised or dropped; it failed to collect over $150 million in fines against various mining companies. The Bush Administration continued these policies of preventing the Office of Surface Mining, Reclamation, and Enforcement from fulfilling its legal duty to regulate the industry. The Director, Bush appointee Harry Snyder, ordered his inspectors to end investigations of abuses, inspections, prosecutions, and penalties of the 1977 law that regulates strip mining. In Kentucky alone, 90,000 of the 100,000 acres of strip-mined lands remain devastated. Meanwhile, Interior Secretary Manuel Lujan proposed that a million acres of additional public lands be opened to strip mining. Environmentalists retaliated through the courts. Between 1981 and 1985, various courts issued over 1,700 cease and desist orders to violators of federal coal-mining regulations.[14]

Meanwhile the battle lines shifted as the coal-mining industry gradually shifted further west. As recently as 1970, coal mines east of the Mississippi River produced more than half the nation's supply; today, they produce less than 20 percent. This shift occurred as the most accessible eastern seams played out while western public lands were opened to coal mining. New strip-mining regulations after 1977 compounded costs for eastern producers in the mountainous Appalachian terrain; coal seams in western and midwestern lands were much more accessible and more easily reclaimed. Eastern coal firms tended to be smaller and less able to comply with the new regulations; western miners tended to be huge corporations with deep financial pockets. Because of these corporate and geological differences, the western producers actually welcomed the regulation because they knew it would damage the competitiveness of their eastern rivals.

As other resources dwindle, coal will become an increasingly important energy source. Fortunately, the United States rests atop vast coal fields – one-quarter of the world's known reserves and enough to supply America's energy for 250 years. Technological advances have made coal ever easier to extract: "The development of gargantuan, electric-driven shovels weighing 27 million pounds with 32 story booms allowed mining to proceed rapidly, sometimes twenty-four hours daily, on big seams."[15] Because it has become cheaper than petroleum, utilities prefer using it; coal powers about 60 percent of all electricity. The United States annually exports over 100 million tons of coal. In all, coal is a $20 billion American industry.

Coal's downside is the catastrophic economic and environmental effects of strip mining it, and the filth produced when it is burned. Perhaps no more succinct account of the disaster wrought by strip mining has been written than that of a 1954 Kentucky legislature report:

> unregulated strip mining of coal causes soil erosion, stream pollution, and the accumulation of stagnant water and the seepage of contaminated water, increases the likelihood of floods, destroys the value of land for agriculture purposes, counteracts efforts for the conservation of soil, water, and other natural resources . . ., creates fire hazards dangerous to life and property, so as to constitute an imminent and inordinate peril to the welfare of the Commonwealth.[16]

Coal is one of the worst sources of smog, acid rain, and the greenhouse effect. The 1970 and 1990 Clean Air Acts require utilities to further curtail the sulfur dioxide emissions. Unfortunately, the pollution spewed by burning coal is not restricted in the United States and most other advanced industrial countries. Like their Western counterparts until recently, most Third World countries value industrialization over environmentalism. Their factories and electricity plants run on cheap, sulfur-heavy coal. Thus, the reduced pollution caused by environmental regulations in the industrial democracies are undercut by Third World countries creating global-warming emissions and acid rain which know no national boundaries.

PETROLEUM POLICY

Federal oil policy has been torn between the long-term national-security outlook of foreign-policy experts and the short-term-profit outlook of producers. America remains dependent on oil and increasingly dependent on foreign oil sources as its most important energy source. This dependence on foreign oil will steadily increase as America's own reserves gradually diminish.

Oil is a relatively new addition to America's energy pie –

in 1900, it accounted for only 2 percent of the nation's energy.[17] In the early twentieth century, petroleum corporations expanded their sources and ability to extract oil. This, combined with the soaring demand for automobiles, stimulated the petroleum age. Not only automobiles, but ships, trains, and electricity plants switched from coal to oil. As a result, oil use in the United States expanded steadily for the next seven decades until it peaked at 49 percent of all energy in 1978.

Unfortunately, America's demand for oil eventually exceeded its domestic supply. The United States became a net oil importer for the first time in 1949. America's oil production peaked at 3.5 billion barrels in 1970 and has decreased every year since, except for slight upward surges in 1978 and 1984. In contrast, America's dependence on foreign oil has varied considerably. Although domestic oil production has sagged since 1970, conservation and efficiency reduced demand even more. Thus, America's dependence on imported oil peaked at 46.5 percent of total consumption in 1977 and decreased to 27.2 percent by 1985.

In 1990, American oil reserves were estimated to be 26 billion barrels (one barrel equals 42 gallons) of 139 billion barrels of resources. Altogether the United States has only 5 percent of the world's oil reserves and 8 percent of its resources, and that percentage is diminishing. Sixty percent of the world's reserves are in the explosive Persian Gulf region, and a further 12 percent in the former Soviet republics.

No one could have foreseen the revolutionary changes that oil has wrought since 1859 when Colonel Drake drilled the world's first oil well in Titusville, Pennsylvania. Drake's initiative was capitalized on by other more enterprising, ruthless, and lucky men, most notably John D. Rockefeller. In 1862, Rockefeller formed his Standard Oil Company; by 1900, Standard Oil controlled 87 percent of the nation's crude oil supplies, 82 percent of its refinery capacity, and 85 percent of its kerosene, gasoline, and fuel oil. Standard Oil's near monopoly over the oil industry was extended through 37 subsidiaries across the United States and overseas. Rockfeller used the monopoly to keep oil prices high and gouge consumers. When a competitor arose, Rockefeller succeeded in either buying him out or bankrupting him through price wars.

As oil demand for businesses and households rose, so too did complaints about Standard Oil's monopoly. State governments began suing Standard Oil for its price gouging practices under the provisions of the 1890 Sherman Anti-trust Act. In 1906, President Theodore Roosevelt decided to champion the crusade against Standard Oil as part of his general policies toward promoting both greater competition and conservation. He ordered the Commerce Department's newly created Bureau of Corporations to investigate Rockefeller's empire. The Bureau of Corporations found evidence that Standard Oil was guilty of price gouging, railroad rebates, and noncompetitive distribution, and sued in the Federal District Court at St Louis. Standard Oil lost and appealed to the Supreme Court. In 1911, the Supreme Court ruled in *Standard Oil* v. *the United States* that Rockefeller's empire was indeed guilty as charged, and ordered Standard Oil's breakup.

Ironically, Standard Oil's domination of the industry had been eroding for a decade before the Supreme Court ruling. Oil strikes in Oklahoma, Texas, and Louisiana shifted the nation's production center and flooded markets, thus easing Rockefeller's stranglehold over the industry. By 1910, Standard Oil's market share had dropped to 60 percent, and new corporations such as Gulf, Texaco, Sunoco, Union, and Phillips emerged to compete fiercely. With or without Standard Oil's monopoly, the petroleum industry continued to promote their interests by corrupting public officials and policies.

As in other natural resource industries, federal government policies helped develop and enrich the oil industry. Under the 1872 Mining Act, huge oil corporations and wildcatters alike could freely drain public lands. The Geological Survey revealed the most likely places to strike oil. The oil industry could not buy every prominent politician, bureaucrat, or institution. The Geological Survey tried to curb some of the wasteful practices spurred by the "rule of capture," which allowed the producer who first tapped into the oil to keep it. "Rule of capture" stimulated a frenzied competition for draining oil fields dry that often left oil pools above ground which evaporated rather than made it to market. In addition, the Interior Department stepped into some of the Oklahoma oil fields to ensure that Indian tribes there were not cheated by oil companies. But in all, federal regulation of the oil industry was minimal. It was left to the state governments to regulate the oil tycoons in their midst. States began to impose royalty taxes on oil production and laws that regulated prices.

Roosevelt sought not only to bust the trusts but also to conserve petroleum production so that its use could be stretched out as far into the future as possible. The Navy had recently converted from coal to oil. Claiming a national security prerogative, Roosevelt withdrew 3 million acres in the Elk Hill, California, and Teapot Dome, Wyoming, oil fields from private exploitation; he designated them naval petroleum preserves, that would be allocated to the Navy only if other sources had withered. Unfortunately, the government had to buy back some of those reserves that it had already given away to private corporations.

When World War I broke out in Europe, President Woodrow Wilson set up the Petroleum Advisory Committee composed of corporate leaders to allocate oil use and prices. Britain's fleet was dependent on American sources for 85 percent of its needs. The Committee ensured that Britain's needs were met. In 1915, Wilson created within the Bureau of Mines the Petroleum Division to catalog that resource. When the United States entered World War I in 1917, Wilson converted the Committee to the National Petroleum War Service Committee. When public interests complained that Wilson was granting vast, uncontrolled powers to the oil industry, Wilson created the US Fuel Administration to watch the Committee. But the Fuel Administration was simply another bureaucratic level that allowed the industry to manage its own affairs. When the Fair Trade Commission (FTC) complained about oil anti-trust practices, the Fuel Administration resisted. The two bureaucracies compromised; the FTC would investigate and perhaps act against Standard Oil if it left the other corporate giants alone. Although Wilson disbanded the Petroleum Committee in 1919, the participants continued their collusion through the American Petroleum Institute (API).

Increasing numbers of Americans resented freely giving away billions of dollars of public wealth to the oil giants.

This rising political pressure finally resulted in the 1920 Mineral Leasing Act, that required petroleum developers to pay 12.5 percent royalties on the oil they extracted. To pass that law, the sponsors had to compromise away the federal government's share of those royalties – 90 percent of royalties are returned to the state or reclamation fund, and only 2 percent goes to the US Treasury.[18]

President Warren Harding was a classic cornucopian, and appointed men of a like mind to his cabinet. He named New Mexico Senator Albert Fall as his Interior Secretary. Fall was determined to destroy the 1920 Mineral Act – and make a fortune in the process. The Act had empowered the Interior Secretary to lease public lands to private corporations for energy exploitation. First, he succeeded in transferring control over the Elk Hills and Teapot Dome naval petroleum reserves from the Navy Department to his Interior Department. Then, in return for a $200,000 bribe, he quietly leased some of those lands to Harry Sinclair, the owner of the Sinclair Oil Company. Each lease was estimated to contain $100 million worth of petroleum. Rumors of the bribe spread after Fall dove into an orgy of conspicuous consumption. An investigation led by Montana Senator Thomas Walsh exposed the scandal in October 1923. Fall was convicted and imprisoned on bribery charges. The contracts, however, could not be cancelled until after a long and expensive legal repeal process.

The Teapot Dome scandal was not an isolated corruption case. The investigation revealed how the petroleum industry "bought" leases to pump oil from public land by giving huge bribes to government officials. Washington responded by creating the Federal Oil Conservation Board to regulate the industry in 1925. The oil industry complained that the regulations hurt their profits and production. In 1926, the Interior Department responded with depletion allowances that permitted the industry to write off its diminishing fields at 27 1/2 percent of gross production. These tax advantages combined with new discoveries and drilling techniques to create an oil glut which worsened with the Great Depression of the 1930s.

Franklin Roosevelt's policies were largely based on conservation rather than cornucopian values. He tried to regulate

oil prices and production through the National Recovery
Administration (NRA) he set up in 1933. The NRA allowed
the API to create and run a national oil industry cartel.
The cartel was strengthened by the Interstate Compact to
Conserve Oil and Gas, which created state quotas for oil
production, and the Hot Oil Act of 1934, which outlawed
oil sold outside the state quotas. The White House had essentially set up the domestic equivalent of the Organization
of Petroleum Exporting Countries (OPEC).

Interior Secretary Harold Ickes strongly shared Roosevelt's
belief that the nation's public resources should be managed
in the public's best interests rather than given away to private interests. Acting on this belief, he not only tried to
regulate the private exploitation of public lands, but asserted
a federal claim over yet more land. In 1937, Ickes claimed
the nation's "tidelands" from state and private interests for
the United States. The issue was not resolved until long after
Ickes left office.

In June 1941, as the United States moved closer to entering World War II, Roosevelt named Ickes the Petroleum
Coordinator for National Defense, with powers to set aside
the Sherman Anti-trust Act and Federal Trade Act. Ickes's
most important accomplishment was to build a vast network
of pipelines across the country to transport oil, and more
refineries to produce 100-octane fuel for America's air force.

Following World War II, President Harry Truman dismantled the regulatory regime and sold off the pipeline network to private interests. In addition, Truman created separate
oil and gas divisions in the Department of Mines, and the
National Petroleum Advisory Council (NPC) composed of
100 leading corporate executives to advise the government
on oil policy. In other words, the federal government allowed
the oil-industry cartel to continue under a different name.

Truman's most controversial act was to announce in 1945
that henceforth the federal government owned the entire
continental shelf out to twelve miles. The coastal states protested and continued to lease lands to oil firms and reap
revenues. The states and the oil industry managed twice to
get bills passed in Congress denouncing the federal conti-
nental-shelf claim. Truman vetoed both bills. The controversy continued until Dwight Eisenhower became president.

In 1953, Eisenhower signed two laws resolving the issue. The Submerged Lands Act, which gave the states all continental shelf up to three miles from shore on the Atlantic and Pacific, and 10.5 miles (three leagues, reflecting the region's historic administration under Spanish rule) on the Gulf Coast. The Outer Continental Shelf Act gave the federal government jurisdiction over the ocean bottom beyond the state's limits out to twelve miles. Although the 1920 Mining Lease Act applied to these offshore lands, the royalty rate was increased to 16.66 percent. Instead of sharing such revenues with the states, the federal government scooped all revenues from these offshore lands into its own coffers. In 1958, the Eisenhower White House negotiated international treaties by which coastal countries could claim the continental shelf as far as 200 miles from shore. Then, in 1976, Washington claimed an exclusive economic zone (EEZ) out to 200 miles from the nation's coastline, regardless of where the continental shelf ended.

The United States would increasingly value these offshore claims. In 1949, the United States could no longer supply all its oil needs and began importing more oil than it exported. Fearing that domestic production would be hurt by cheap imports, the oil industry succeeded in getting Congress to pass laws imposing import restrictions that maintained high prices. In 1959, Eisenhower succumbed to oil-industry pressure and imposed formal quotas administered by the Interior Department that prevented foreign oil from exceeding 12.5 percent of domestic production. Throughout their lifetime, the quotas cost American consumers $4 billion to $7 billion annually and hurt the competitiveness of American industries compared with overseas rivals who enjoyed cheaper-priced oil. More importantly, the result was a "drain America first" policy that has weakened American national security over the long term by making it increasingly dependent on foreign oil sources.

The federal government also acquiesced to foreign oil interests. Starting in 1950, the United States has tried to enlist the support of oil-rich Muslim states through the "golden gimmick" of allowing American oil firms to deduct the taxes paid to foreign producers. Washington did this to assuage Muslim resentment over America's support for Israel

since sponsoring its creation in 1947. Ever since, the policy
has cost the United States hundreds of billions of dollars in
lost tax revenues.

Although many questioned the wisdom of these policies,
the oil bloc in Congress, built around senators from Texas,
Louisiana, and Oklahoma, proved invincible. The oil industry lined the pockets of senators and representatives beyond
the oil belt to ensure the passage of favorable laws and the
defeat of regulatory measures.

America's economy expanded for a quarter-century after
World War II, bringing most people an unprecedented standard of living. Although the number of automobiles on
American roads doubled between 1952 and 1972, real oil
prices (adjusted for inflation) remained relatively stable until
the late 1960s. By that time, expanded government spending on Vietnam and welfare sparked increasingly severe inflation. As demand drained America's oil fields, production
costs and thus prices increased.

Since the oil industry was adamantly opposed to lifting
the oil-import quota, the only other way to bring down oil
prices was to increase production. In 1968, oil was discovered in Alaska. The oil firms announced plans to build a
trans-Alaska pipeline from Prudhoe Bay on Alaska's north
slope where the oil fields were located to the ice-free port
of Valdez on Alaska's south coast, from which it could be
transported by ship elsewhere. Environmentalists sued, arguing that the pipeline violated the 1969 National Environmental Policy Act (NEPA). Congress intervened by passing
a law asserting that the pipeline was in compliance with NEPA.
Those who hoped Alaskan Oil would help fight inflation
would be disappointed – it took eight years and $7.7 billion
just to build the Alaskan pipeline. Production costs for Alaskan
oil were high. Producers passed the costs on to consumers.

On August 15, 1971, President Richard Nixon addressed
the nation's worsening economic problems by announcing
his Economic Stabilization Program, which, among other
measures, froze wages and prices for 90 days, including those
of gasoline and heating oil. The decree only briefly checked
inflation. After the three months concluded, prices continued
to rise. In April 1973, Nixon lifted the mandatory oil-import
quota for four months. Although oil imports surged, prices

remained high. The president also formed a Special Committee on Energy within his administration to address related problems. To dilute costs, the Committee emphasized increasing supplies rather than promoting conservation and alternative energies.

Compounding the problem of rising oil prices was America's increasing vulnerability to supply disruptions. After 1949, when America's demand for oil first exceeded its supply, the United States became increasingly dependent on foreign sources. This growing vulnerability to foreign supply or price disruptions would not become apparent for another two decades because international oil production, shipping, and refining were largely controlled by the "seven sisters" oil corporations, of which five were American. By 1973, the United States daily imported one million barrels of oil, an amount which accounted for 30 percent of the demand.

In 1960, an international producers' cartel, called the Organization of Petroleum Exporting Countries (OPEC), was formed among the Arab states of Saudi Arabia, Libya, Kuwait, United Arab Emirates, Iraq, Algeria, and Qatar, along with Iran, Nigeria, Indonesia, Gabon, Venezuela, and Ecuador. Among OPEC's members, only Venezuela and Ecuador are not Muslim. By the early 1970s, OPEC accounted for nearly two-thirds of global oil exports, of which about 70 percent came from the Middle East. The American and global economies were thus vulnerable to the ability of an international cartel, which was predominantly Arab, Muslim, and concentrated in the Middle East, to turn off the oil spigot or demand higher prices.

OPEC remained ineffective until 1969 when Libya demanded a greater share of oil production profits from the foreign oil producers operating there. Other OPEC members issued similar demands. The international oil corporations had no choice but to concede. Over the next four years, OPEC gradually increased its share of oil production profits and ownership, and pushed oil prices higher.

Then, in late 1973, the age of cheap and seemingly endless petroleum came to an abrupt end with OPEC's quadrupling of prices from $2.75 to $11.65 a barrel. On October 6, 1973, Egypt and Syria launched surprise attacks on Israel. Aided by American intelligence reports and $2 billion in military assistance, the Israeli army succeeded in defeating both Egypt and Syria. Unable to win on the military battleground, the Muslim states used their most powerful weapon – oil. On October 17, OPEC voted to reduce oil production by 5 percent every month until Israel surrendered to Arab demands. The following day, Saudi Arabia cut its own oil production by 10 percent and severed all shipments to the United States. With control over two-thirds of the world's oil exports, OPEC had succeeded in quadrupling global oil prices. Prices would continue to rise steadily until they doubled again in 1979 to reach about $34 a barrel. The result was a decade of largely double-digit inflation, slow growth, and the global debt crisis.

The Nixon White House responded in several ways. On November 7, 1973, President Nixon made a televised speech articulating the energy crisis afflicting the nation and world, and announced Project Independence, which was designed to supplant oil imports by 1980 through the development of domestic energy sources. To achieve this goal, Nixon formed the Federal Energy Office within the White House headed by an "Energy Czar". In January 1974, the president announced to Congress that he favored a windfall-profits tax on the oil industry to help finance a range of other proposals to counter the energy crisis. He also got Congress to pass the Energy Provision Allocation Act, which empowered the president to allocate all energy so that industries received priority. In May 1974, he created the Federal Energy Administration (FEA) with the duty to forge a comprehensive energy policy. These actions had no discernible effect on prices or supply. The Watergate scandal forced Nixon to resign in August 1974.

President Gerald Ford was just as candid as Nixon about the severity of the energy crisis. In his speech before Congress in January 1975, Ford admitted that, "We face a future of shortages and dependency which the nation cannot tolerate and the American people cannot accept." He then called on Congress to pass his bill which included a range of new federal initiatives to manage varying aspects of the energy crisis. Congress passed the Energy Policy and Conservation Act of 1975, which empowered the president to ration gas, imposed a windfall-profits tax on oil to encourage conservation and increase revenues, demanded increased miles-per-gallon (mpg) for new cars, and required the government to create a 1 billion-barrel Strategic Petroleum Reserve. The petroleum reserve was not just for the United States. Under treaty, the United States was committed to share that reserve with its allies through a newly created International Energy Agency if worldwide petroleum supplies ever dropped 7 percent. That same year, Congress also enacted the Corporate Average Fuel Economy (CAFE), which targeted average miles-per-gallon standards for each automobile producers' fleet.

Accurate information about energy reserves was obviously essential to formulating energy policy. The Ford White House created the Project Independence Evaluation System (PIES) to provide the FEA with essential information. Congressional energy committees dominated by Democrats resented the creation of this alternative information system, particularly when PIES' numbers and subsequent FEA policies began to conflict with their own. The conflict between these alternative information sources would continue for years.

In 1977, shortly after taking office, President Carter declared that the energy crisis was the "moral equivalent of war." He called for the implementation of a range of measures to wage that war, some of which would be enacted by executive fiat and others through legislation. Unless sweeping measures were taken, according to the president, the future was bleak, "the nation's economic security and the American way of life will be gravely endangered."[19]

Within a month of his speech, Carter submitted his National Energy Plan (NEP) to Congress; the NEP had over 200 separate proposals. Among other things, the NEP called for the increased substitution of coal for petroleum, mandatory fuel efficiency standards for applicances, the decontrol of petroleum and natural gas prices, tax hikes on "gas-guzzler" vehicles, tax cuts for households and businesses investing in insulation and other conservation measures, and increased R&D spending for energy development. NEP's centerpiece was the creation of a Department of Energy (DOE) to devise, coordinate, and implement comprehensive policies.

Although Carter did succeed in converting the FEA into the Energy Department, implementing his comprehensive energy policy proved elusive. Energy's primacy as an issue during the 1970s complicated rather than eased the system's ability to deal with it. Carter's plan ran into the phalanx of new "committees and subcommittees claiming jurisdiction over energy policy which dramatically expanded the number of members, congressional staff, and lobbyists participating in the issue."[20] During the 92nd Congress of 1970–72, only two committees and subcommittees addressed energy issues; in the 97th Congress of 1978–80, the number had risen to eighteen![21]

Carter's ambitious plan stumbled in Congress, the victim of "excessive haste in formulation and complexity in design, from incompetent political management and feeble public appeal, from bad timing and incohesive congressional support for its major objectives."[22] After months of political horsetrading, in October 1978, Congress finally passed a version of Carter's National Energy Act that included 113 provisions. Carter got much of what he wanted, but the new programs complicated rather than eased the energy crisis. Existing powers to regulate energy were concentrated in the new Department of Energy, along with energy conservation incentives, subsidies for standard and alternative energies, and fuel-consumption regulation. The newly created Federal Energy Commission (FERC) replaced the Federal Power Commission which had been created in 1920 to regulate the electric and natural gas industries. In addition, Congress passed the 1978 Solar Voltaic Energy Research, Development, and Demonstration Act that sought to achieve a commercially viable photovoltaic cell by 1988. PIES remained as controversial under Carter as it had been under Ford. The "solution" was to change PIES' name to the Midterm Energy Forecasting System.

In 1979, Carter asked Congress to appropriate $88 billion over the next decade for his synthetic fuel (synfuels) program, which he hoped would eventually daily produce 2 million barrels of oil. The following year, Congress passed and the president signed the Energy Security Act creating, among other things, the semipublic Synthetic Fuels Corporation, which would facilitate the creation of a viable synfuels industry. A petroleum synfuel can be created by coal liquefication; a natural gas synfuel by coal gasification.

Unfortunately, synfuels must burn energy to make energy. Synfuel costs were enormous. Carter also pushed for a massive oil-shale conversion process that eventually wasted over $3 billion without producing anything marketable.

While these massive energy-intensive and expensive alternative energy programs were spectacular failures, Carter did make some positive contributions to easing the energy crisis by promoting conservation, efficiency, and diversification of sources and types of renewable energy. Over the long term, his policies did reduce energy demand substantially over what they would have otherwise been. But in the short run, these efforts did nothing to prevent oil prices from doubling to $34 a barrel by 1980.

In stark contrast to his three predecessors, after entering the White House in 1981, Ronald Reagan and his administration denied that there was any energy crisis at all. The problem, according to Reaganites, was not supply but production. And the only thing inhibiting production was regulation. If the red tape were cut and public lands opened, oil and mining companies would dig out all the energy demanded by the American public. According to this ideology, the DOE inhibited rather than promoted energy development and thus should be abolished. According to Reagan, "marketplace magic" would cure not only the temporary energy glitch but all the nation's ills. As Reagan enthusiastically put it, "When the free market is permitted to work, millions of individual choices and judgements will produce the proper balance of supply and demand our economy needs."[23]

These ideas were embodied in Reagan's 1981 National Energy Plan. Guided by cornucopian values, the Reagan White House attempted a massive giveaway of public wealth to private interests. Like Albert Fall, his predecessor of sixty years earlier, Interior Secretary James Watt got the nation's petroleum reserves transferred from the Defense Department to the Interior Department, then proceeded to sell off as much of it as possible to huge oil corporations. Unlike Fall, Watts took nothing more than the excitement that ideologues experience when they act on their ideals. And what more symbolic target could a cornucopian attack than the petroleum reserves that were supposed to be conserved for a future emergency. In addition, Watts leased 100 million acres of Alaska's public lands to oil developers and an estimated 1.5 billion tons of coal from the Powder River region to coal developers. Perhaps most controversial was Watts's 1981 announcement that within five years he would lease off for unrestricted development all 1.1 billion acres of outer continental shelf (OCS), which may hold 710 billion barrels of recoverable crude oil and 1,640 trillion cubic feet of natural gas.[24] The total amount of OCS lands leased over the previous three decades was only 40 million acres! As a result of these giveaway Reaganite policies, mining corporations acquired rights to billions of dollars in wealth at the expense of the US Treasury, taxpayers, and future generations. Having been sold, the leases cannot be reversed without lengthy, expensive court battles and compensation to the corporate "owners."

There was an unreconcilable contradiction in Reagan's policies between his pledge to boost energy supplies and his cornucopian obsession with destroying any governmental conservation, efficiency, and alternative-energy programs whose purpose was to decrease demand and increase supply. Cornucopianism got the better of Reagan and the nation. Reagan dumped Carter's goal of boosting solar power to 20 percent of the nation's total energy consumption by 2000, and revealed his antipathy to renewable, clean energy sources by having solar panels ripped from the White House. CAFE standards were relaxed rather than strengthened.

Comprehensive planning and policy, symbolized by the Energy Department, was also targeted by market zealots. In 1982, Energy Department Secretary James Edwards declared his most important goal was "to close down [his Department], bury it once and for all, and salt the earth over it so it will not spring up again."[25] Reagan and Edwards later backed off from this promise. In fact, in 1983, Reagan submitted his own "National Energy Policy Plan," which would be "based on less federal regulation, lower taxes, reduced federal expenditures, and maximum reliance on the private sector to make decisions about the production and consumption of commodities, including energy."[26] Although Reagan seemed to be abandoning energy policy to market whims rather than forging it with long-term, comprehensive planning, the government continued to pick winners and losers. The Reagan White House completely reordered the government's spending priorities. While Reagan slashed R&D funding for alternative energies and conservation measures, he boosted it for nuclear energy.

In 1986, Reagan stepped up his attack on alternative energy and conservation practices. That year he finally got Congress to accept his longstanding demand that the synfuels program be terminated. The program had received a sharp blow three years earlier when Exxon dropped out of the joint government–business effort after investing $500 million. Now it was completely abandoned. Also in 1986, Reagan waived the fuel-efficiency standard for the nation's automobile fleets required by a 1975 law; instead of reaching an average 27.5 miles per gallon for their automobile fleets by 1986, manufacturers could get by with only 26 miles per gallon. This lower standard was extended throughout the Reagan and Bush years.

In justifying his decision, Reagan argued that "only market forces, not government controls, will bring about significant economic improvements in automobile efficiency."[27] The statement was ideologically rather than empirically correct. In fact, automobile producers, like all other manufacturers and businesses, do not pollute less or build more efficient, safe products unless government regulations force them to do so. Reagan's ruling hurt the one automobile producer, Chrysler, which had complied with the law. Chrysler had invested in and achieved the standard; Ford and General Motors failed to invest enough to fulfill the regulation. Chrysler thus complained that it was being punished for its achievements while Ford and General Motors were rewarded for their failure to obey the law.

The energy crisis eased throughout the early 1980s as global oil prices declined steadily from their peak of $34 a barrel in 1981 to $24 by early 1986. Then in the spring of 1986, global oil prices plunged from $24 to $11 a barrel. Inflation dropped accordingly and economic growth increased. What explains this extraordinary turnabout in oil prices?

The oil glut that washed over the world by the mid-1980s resulted from a decade of greater conservation, efficiency, production, and alternative-energy policies pursued by virtually

every government in the world in response to the rise of oil
prices from $2.50 in 1973 to $34 in 1980. Households and
businesses alike invested in energy conservation devices. With
oil prices at exorbitant levels, oil fields could be exploited
which formerly were too expensive to develop, such as in
the North Sea and Alaska's north slope. Oil from new sources
and increased production from old sources flooded global
markets, which swelled further as OPEC members cheated
on their quotas. As a result, OPEC's percentage of global
oil exports plunged from two-thirds to one-third within a
dozen years. Thus, over a fourteen-year period, as supply
steadily increased and demand steadily fell, OPEC's power
and oil prices declined and finally plummeted.

What effect, if any, did Reagan's policies have on this drop
and then collapse of oil prices? In fact, very little, if any –
this remarkable turnabout occurred despite rather than
because of Reagan Administration policies. Reagan's public
land giveaway did not significantly boost production in the
short term, while his anti-conservation policies stimulated
greater energy demand and lower supplies. Of all four presidents' policies which confronted the energy crisis, perhaps
Carter's conservation policies contributed the most to the
eventual oil price drop.

The oil price collapse was not an unqualified blessing for
the United States. It may have boosted America's economy
and the pocketbooks of its citizens, but it depressed the
"oil patch" in Texas, Louisiana, and Oklahoma, and other
states in which energy production was an important economic sector, which had become dependent on high prices.
Awash again in cheap gasoline, the public became increasingly complacent and profligate, bringing the inevitable future
energy crisis closer. A 1985 poll revealed that only 1 percent of Americans considered energy among the nation's
most pressing problems.[28]

Reagan's cornucopian policies were continued by the Bush
Administration, which took power in 1989. As an ex-oil man,
President George Bush celebrated fossil fuels and disdained
alternative energies. His initial policies reflected his preju-
dices. He tried to open 1.5 million acres of the 19 million-
acre Arctic National Wildlife Refuge to oil exploitation.
Environmentalists blocked that initiative. Although stymied

in his effort to increase domestic oil supply, Bush did nothing to decrease demand through conservation and efficiency measures. America continued to import 7 to 9 million barrels of oil every day. Meanwhile, OPEC's share of global oil exports, which had dropped as low as 31 percent in 1985, had risen to 40 percent by 1990.

The vulnerability of the United States to foreign oil finally dawned on the Bush White House in the summer of its second year. On August 2, 1990, Iraqi forces overran neighboring Kuwait, bringing as much as 11 percent of known global oil reserves under Baghdad's control. On August 5, British Prime Minister Margaret Thatcher finally pressured President Bush into declaring that Iraq must withdraw from Kuwait. Over the next half-year, Bush forged international and domestic coalitions to pressure Iraq. When the United Nations' deadline of January 15, 1991, passed with Iraqi forces still occupying Kuwait, the Coalition forces began a six-week bombing campaign against Iraq which culminated with a five-day ground war. Baghdad agreed to a ceasefire, withdrawal from Kuwait, and dismantlement of its nuclear, chemical, and biological weapons programs. This success cost the Coalition partners about $53 billion. Fortunately for the United States, its allies picked up most of the cost.

During the crisis, oil prices jumped from a low of $12.79 in June 1990, increased to $30.86 in October 1990, and peaked at $41.00 on January 16, 1991, when the Coalition bombing campaign began. Two days later, on January 18, prices plummeted ten dollars to $31.00 and then were halved to $15.55 by June 1991 and $13.98 in February 1992.[29] This rapid rise and fall of oil prices reflected fears about the future more than actual shifts in supply and demand.

Following the war, Bush did attempt to reduce America's vulnerability. The 1992 Energy Policy Act took limited steps to reduce America's growing dependence on imported oil, including incentives for the electricity industry to spur innovation and reduce costs, further tax cuts for oil and gas wildcatters, measures to promote energy conservation and efficiency, subsidies and tax cuts for alternative energies including electric cars, reduced paperwork for licensing nuclear plants, and more money for energy research and development. Although generally pleased with the bill, environmentalists rued that it did not require greater miles-per-gallon for new vehicles or hike oil taxes to promote conservation and increase revenues. In that year's presidential race, independent candidate Ross Perot went so far as to call for 50 cent oil-tax hike. Bill Clinton became president in 1992, but has largely continued the energy policies of his predecessor.

Despite all the disruptions since 1973, global oil reserves – the extractable amount known to be underground – are actually higher today than before the first oil crisis, while America's oil reserves have remained roughly constant. The trouble for the United States is that over the past half-century, whether oil prices rose or fell, America's oil security has become increasingly vulnerable. By the mid-1990s, the United States imported half of all its petroleum needs, with nearly 10 percent of that coming from the unstable Persian Gulf region. By the year 2000, the United States may be importing 60 percent of its oil-consumption needs. Within a generation, OPEC's share of global oil reserves will again reach two-thirds. Once that happens, unlike during the late 1970s and early 1980s, OPEC's share will continue to increase as oil fields elsewhere diminish. The Persian Gulf states in particular will enjoy an increasingly powerful oil weapon, whether they choose to wield it or not.

More sophisticated oil-detection and drilling technology will stretch America's oil reserves. However, those reserves will inevitably drain away. The most effective means of increasing the oil supply is by decreasing demand. West European countries and Japan have proved that conservation is the best means of reducing dependence on foreign oil and boosting economic growth. Those countries average twice America's energy efficiency. Despite or because of the range of policies, America's energy efficiency did double from 1973 through to today. CAFE standards after 1975 (notwithstanding the Reagan White House's relaxation) have doubled the average fuel efficiency of an American car to 28 miles-per-gallon, an achievement which means the United States is 4 million barrels of oil less dependent on foreign sources than it otherwise would have been. If Americans increased CAFE standards and reduced driving by 25 percent, they could eliminate their dependence on foreign oil.[30] While it might be in America's long-term interests to use cheap foreign oil now, and Conserve America's reserves, that is not happening. Only progressive conservation measures including much higher taxes on oil use (comparable to that imposed by other democratic industrial countries) could stretch America's reserves well into the next century and thus enhance American security.

Most Americans are either ignorant of or indifferent to this reality. A decade of high oil prices failed to shake the American public's cornucopian belief in a bottomless petroleum pool. All the while, the petroleum industry has promoted public-relations campaigns and lobbied government to ensure that public ignorance and the policies it reflects remain unshaken.

NATURAL GAS POLICY

Natural gas and oil are often found together in the same underground stratum. Despite their relationship, they are governed by different policies and regulatory regimes. Although originally both natural gas and oil were controlled by the same powerful groups of companies, the government separated the two industries. The petroleum industry acquiesced in losing natural gas to entrepreneurs because, at the time, oil was much more profitable and extensively used.[31]

Natural gas is a chemical cocktail of methane, propane, ethane, and other hydrocarbons. Although it burns at 1,100 BTUs per cubic foot, a much lower intensity than oil, natural gas also spews far fewer pollutants into the air and thus contributes much less to pollution and the greenhouse effect. Natural gas has contributed about one-third of America's energy for the last decade. There is much more natural gas than oil in the United States, about 167 trillion cubic feet (tcf), enough to last thirty years at current consumption rates. Geologists suspect there may be another 600 trillion cubic feet to be discovered. World reserves are estimated at 3.9 quadrillion.

During the petroleum industry's first half-century, oilmen treated natural gas as a nuisance, venting it into the air or burning it off to get at the oil. Natural gas was too dangerous to transport or store since it could not be compressed and it seeped out of the screw-threaded, jointed pipes of that time. Eventually oilmen stopped wasting natural gas when they realized they needed the pressure of natural gas underground to force the oil to the surface.

Then in the 1920s, compression and improved welding techniques created pipelines which both contained and transported natural gas. However, natural gas did not become marketable until a pipeline was completed from its Oklahoma fields to Detroit. Pipelines eventually webbed the country and with them natural gas became a viable alternative to oil or coal for heating buildings and food.

Unfortunately for consumers, there was an oligopoly among the corporations Standard Oil, Columbia Gas and Electric, Electric Bond and Share, and Cities Service that dominated the natural gas market and extracted windfall profits from consumers. In 1935, Congress passed the Public Utility Holding Company Act, which authorized the newly created Securities and Exchange Commission (SEC) to break up those trusts. To regulate the new entrants to the natural gas market, Congress then created the Federal Power Commission (FPC) as part of the 1938 Natural Gas Act. The FPC's five appointed commissioners regulated the rates and facilities of the natural gas industry. Henceforth, companies had to justify any expansion of facilities or rate hikes to the FPC, which could veto the change.

Not surprisingly, the industry fought the FPC. The Supreme Court upheld the FPC's powers in *FPC* v. *Hope Natural Gas* and *FPC* v. *Colorado Interstate*. Unable to win in court, the industry tried to get a law passed stripping the FPC of its power. In 1947, Oklahoma Senator Robert Kerr introduced and fought for such a bill. While Congress debated the Kerr bill, President Truman nominated Leland Olds to a third term on the FPC. Olds advocated strict regulation of the industry and blasted the Kerr bill. Proponents of the Kerr bill retaliated by smearing Olds with the unsubstantiated charge that he was a communist. Even if the charge were true, communism certainly would have been allowed under the Constitution. Unfortunately, during the 1940s and 1950s, groups and individuals as powerful as they were extreme succeeded in suspending the Constitution for thousands of innocent Americans, by persecuting them as alleged communists. Olds was rejected. Truman vetoed the Kerr bill.

The industry shifted back to the courts and once again, in the 1954 *Phillip* v. *Wisconsin,* the Supreme Court ruled in the FPC'S favor. In 1956, another bill cleared Congress which would have stripped the FPC's powers. Eisenhower would have signed the bill had not a scandal arisen over the industry trying to buy congressional votes. To avoid giving the appearance of encouraging corruption, Eisenhower reluctantly vetoed the bill. Two years later yet another FPC-busting bill came close to passing Congress, but once again charges of vote-buying torpedoed it.

The decades of attacks and lobbying gradually turned the FPC in the industry's favor. In 1959, the FPC approved El Paso Natural Gas's takeover of the Pacific Northwest Pipeline Corporation. Consumer groups sued. In 1962, the Supreme Court ruled that the FPC had acted improperly in approving the merger before the Justice Department gave the go ahead. El Paso then lobbied Congress to pass a bill allowing the FPC the power to grant merger permission without Justice Department approval. The efforts failed.

In April 1973, President Nixon claimed that the FPC had contributed to natural gas shortages by overregulating the industry. Although increasing numbers of businesses and households wanted to convert to natural gas, there was not enough supply. With OPEC's oil embargo and six-fold increase of oil prices from October 1973 to early 1974, there was increased pressure to deregulate natural gas prices and production. Prices were raised and production increased steadily throughout the mid-1970s. The 1978 Natural Gas Policy Act established a range of natural gas prices from different fields, which would gradually rise until all prices were deregulated in 1985. It also abolished the FPC and placed the natural gas industry under the jurisdiction of the Federal Energy Regulatory Commission (FERC).

The two biggest lobby groups in battles over FPC regulations are the American Gas Association (AGA) of producers and American Public Gas Association (APGA) of city-owned utilities. Less important in the conflict have been environmentalists, who favor natural gas over other fossil fuels because it is much cleaner. All three groups want to expand the supply of natural gas; they differ, of course, over the price rate. Deregulators justified lifting price controls for natural gas because the vast pipeline network across the United States created enough competition to allow prices to be shaped by free market forces rather than monopoly. Regulators counter that the industry remains too concentrated for genuine market forces to work; because of "market imperfections" the government had to continue to regulate prices and the industry. Eventually the deregulators won. Natural gas prices have remained relatively competitive with other energy prices. Given the relatively large reserves, natural gas will become an increasingly important part of America's energy pie.

NUCLEAR ENERGY POLICY

The nuclear industry is perhaps the best example of the "Frankenstein syndrome," in which scientists can more easily create than control new technologies. Proponents once heralded a nuclear age in which energy would be so cheap utility companies would not bother to meter it. But the inability of scientists to overcome technological and political obstacles to the safe running of nuclear plants and disposal of nuclear wastes has meant that, nuclear weapons aside, the United States has not and probably never will experience a nuclear age. No new nuclear plants have been commissioned in the United States since 1973. Nuclear power peaked at around 7 percent of total energy needs and 20 percent of electricity needs in the 1980s. This amount will diminish steadily in the decades ahead as, one by one, existing nuclear plants reach the end of their life and are decommissioned.

The nuclear age formally began on December 2, 1942, when scientists in Chicago achieved the first controlled nuclear explosion. The goal, however, was to create nuclear weapons rather than energy. In its race to produce nuclear weapons to end World War II, the United States employed over 150,000 people and expended $1.5 billion. At Los Alamos, New Mexico, in June 1945, the United States exploded the world's first nuclear bomb. Atomic bombs dropped on Hiroshima and Nagasaki in August 1945 forced the Japanese to surrender, thus saving the hundreds of thousands and perhaps millions of lives that would have been lost in an American invasion of Japan.

President Truman realized that strict controls had to be imposed on this terrible new weapon. The Atomic Energy Act of 1946 created the Atomic Energy Commission (AEC) of five appointed commissioners to regulate what was intended to be nuclear energy for the military. Congress insisted on oversight by creating the Joint Committee on Atomic Energy (JCAE). In 1947, the AEC began building an experimental nuclear reactor but gave up in 1950. In 1951, however, Dow Chemical and Monsanto Chemical applied to the AEC for a license to develop a reactor to generate electricity for civilians. The White House agreed and authorized the AEC to create the Industrial Participation Program for private entrepreneurs. In 1953, Congress appropriated money and authorized Westinghouse and Duquesne Lighting Company to build a nuclear plant at Shippingport on the Ohio River 35 miles from Pittsburgh. The 1954 amendment to the Atomic Energy Act formalized its initial steps in allowing private firms to participate in the nuclear industry. Henceforth, corporations could own nuclear power plants while leasing the uranium which fueled them, and had to accept strict AEC oversight. Between 1955 and 1963, Washington guided America's nascent nuclear industry with its Power Demonstration Reactor. Public and private utilities constructed their own reactors based on the government design. The private nuclear energy industry received a major boost with the passage in 1957 of the Price-Anderson Act, which limited the insurance liability for the owners to $560 million for one accident. The liability has risen to only $660 million since then; taxpayers would pay for any damage above that amount.

By the 1950s, nuclear energy policy was shaped by a classic iron triangle embracing the AEC, the JCAE, and the nuclear energy industrial associations and power companies. All along, this cozy, mutually beneficial political group failed to address the profound safety, health, and economic issues raised by concerned observers; long-term economic and environmental costs were sacrificed to short-term political benefits. The nuclear triangle, however, did succeed in creating nuclear energy.

In 1959, the Shippingport plant became the first privately owned venture to generate nuclear electricity. Yet, despite massive direct and indirect government subsidies, the investment and operating costs of the Shippingport plant and several others which began operations in the following years were not competitive with coal and petroleum plants. America's allies, Britain in 1956 and France in 1962, were actually the first to create commercially viable nuclear energy plants. They did so, however, with massive technology transfers from the United States and higher prices for other energy sources, which made it easier for nuclear energy to compete.

In 1960, AEC announced its intention to guide the industry to a commercially viable reactor by 1968. Two years later, the AEC increased its already heavy subsidies to the industry by announcing that henceforth it would cover all design costs. With this massive government support, America's nuclear energy industry finally took off in the mid-1960s with utility firms ordering nine nuclear power plants in 1965, twenty-two in 1966, and twenty-four in 1967. Increasing concerns about pollution further boosted the promise of nuclear energy. The 1967 Air Quality Act severely restricted the emissions of oil- and coal-fired plants in cities. Utility firms increasingly looked to nuclear energy as the solution to pollution.

More regulatory changes occurred. In 1974, the AEC was renamed the Nuclear Regulatory Commission (NRC) and created the related Energy Research and Development Administration (ERDA). That year, the NRC cheerfully asserted that the probability of a nuclear accident was once in ten million years. In 1977, there was a further bureaucratic shakeup when FEA, ERDA, FPC, and ten smaller agencies were combined to form the Department of Energy (DOE). In Congress, JCAE was abolished and its duties split among other committees in both the Senate and the House.

Despite these successes, nuclear power's promise as a panacea to energy and pollution problems was short-lived. In 1974, 239 nuclear reactors with 237 megawatts of capacity were either already operating or being constructed; in 1978, there were only 219 reactors with 215 megawatts of capacity.[32] Over 100 nuclear power plants ordered since 1972 have been cancelled outright or indefinitely delayed.

Why did the promise of nuclear power fade so quickly? The first two major blows occurred in 1971 when a US Court of Appeals ruled that in licensing the Calvert Cliffs nuclear plant near Baltimore, the AEC had not upheld the National Environmental Policy Act. Later that year, the court ruled similarly for the AEC licensing of a nuclear plant at Quad Cities in Illinois. This regulatory crackdown raised licensing, building, and operating costs from an average $345 million in 1971 to $3.2 billion or ten times more in 1980. Utilities began to reconsider the nuclear option. In 1978, Congress passed the Nuclear Non-proliferation Act, in which the United States abandoned its breeder-reactor project and would no longer supply or process plutonium for its allies. Then, on March 28, 1979, America's nuclear energy industry was doomed when the Three Mile Island nuclear plant near Harrisburg, Pennsylvania, almost experienced a nuclear meltdown and actually released radioactive steam into the air. Across the country, citizen groups began protesting and suing utilities that planned to build nuclear plants nearby. Construction and operating costs skyrocketed through court delays and higher insurances rates. Although, by 1980, Washington had poured $18 billion into nuclear energy, the increasingly obvious dangers caused costs to soar and drowned support for the industry.

Congress responded to Three Mile Island by creating the Federal Emergency Management Agency (FEMA) in 1979 and giving it responsibility for addressing nuclear and other industrial or natural disasters. FEMA attempts to work together with state and local governments, and the nuclear facility, to prepare plans for dealing with a crisis. As always, it proved easier to pass than implement such laws. Four years after Three Mile Island, an NRC investigation of the ability of those responsible to deal with another nuclear disaster concluded that "preparations for an emergency response to a nuclear accident in the industry, the NRC, and the states are incomplete, untried, haphazard, or nonexistent."[33] More specifically, the federal and state governments have yet to devise joint plans for dealing with nuclear disaster. Within the federal government alone, twelve agencies have some jurisdiction in case of a catastrophe. Although the major responsibility for dealing with a disaster rests on the state and local governments, they lack the necessary money or facilities. Thus, many state and local governments have refused to participate in FEMA planning.

As if the danger of a nuclear meltdown were not enough, Americans face a more insidious threat that lurks in the ever growing mountains of nuclear waste in dumps scattered across the country. In 1980, Congress addressed the nuclear-waste problems by passing two bills. The Uranium Mill Tailings Act authorized the NRC to identify and remove highly radioactive mine tailings or building materials. The Low Level Waste Policy Act addressed the disposal of nuclear waste from medical and other industrial uses. The Act divides the country into regions whose states must agree on one site in which to dump their waste. If all do not agree, each would then be responsible for disposing of its own low-level waste.

The following year, in 1982, Congress passed yet another law which attempted to manage the worsening nuclear-waste problem. The 1982 Nuclear Waste Policy Act created the Office of Civilian Radioactive Waste Management within the DOE to manage the problem. The DOE would investigate five geologically sound sites, of which three would be recommended to the president by January 1985. The president then would narrow the list to one and recommend it to Congress by March 31, 1987. Meanwhile, the DOE would investigate five further sites, of which three could not be on the original list, and had to recommend three to the president by July 1, 1989. Once again, the president would choose one site and recommend it to Congress by March 31, 1990.

The DOE fulfilled the law by recommending sites at Deaf Smith County, Texas, Yucca Mountain, Nevada, and Richland, Washington. The states of all three designated sites immediately protested and exerted enormous pressure to be removed from consideration. Fearing that the Republican Party would be hurt by pushing the issue, Reagan suspended the selection process in 1986; Congress ratified Reagan's decision the following year.

Any headway nuclear energy advocates may have made during the Reagan years died with the 1986 Chernobyl nuclear reactor explosion that devastated a swath of Ukraine and spewed a radioactive cloud that eventually encircled the world. Meanwhile, if rising oil prices between 1973 and 1986 failed to spark a nuclear-energy revolution, plunging oil prices since then along with safety concerns and expensive regulations have all but killed the industry in the United States.

America's nuclear energy industry is dying. As of 1994, there were 113 nuclear power plants across the United States. All of these plants will be shut down within the next generation. No new ones are under construction or even licensed. The average cost of electricity from a nuclear-powered plant remains about 50 percent higher than that from a coal-powered plant; the electricity from any future nuclear plants built may cost twice as much.

Politics rather than technology or science will determine the future of nuclear energy. Despite recent advances in safety and efficiency, there is no significant support for nuclear energy. Private utilities cannot afford nuclear energy's ever increasing insurance and regulatory costs. Only government can assume the risks. Only a few governments have invested in the enormous costs of developing the industry, of which France and Japan have been the most successful in steadily increasing the amount of energy generated by nuclear power. By 1995, nuclear power contributed about 45 percent of France's and 25 percent of Japan's electricity.

Nuclear energy is not a natural-resource-intensive industry. Overall, far less of nuclear energy's raw material, uranium, is required to create electricity than the raw materials for a plant generated by fossil fuels. The same amount of electricity generated from a coal-fired plant which burns 2 million tons of coal a year could come from 35 tons of uranium in a nuclear plant. The United States has an estimated 277,000 tons of uranium oxide, and the fuel is relatively abundant elsewhere around the world. The expense for a nuclear plant comes from insurance and construction premiums, and its short operating life.

Nuclear energy is based on the ability to split a uranium

atom's nucleus, which, when controlled, produces energy and, uncontrolled, an explosion. Current nuclear energy technology is based on "light water reactors," in which the nuclear heat creates steam power which in turn drives turbines and generates electricity. Theoretically, there are perfectly safe forms of nuclear power which could supply virtually all of our energy needs forever. Nuclear breeder technology is based on nuclear fusion, in which atoms are fused rather than split. Unfortunately, nuclear breeder technology remains in the realm of science fiction. In 1984, Congress killed the Clinch River breeder reactor, the government's only pilot program.

Unlike breeder-reactor technology, nuclear fusion uses non-radioactive materials such as seawater. But this technology remains a gleam in the eyes of certain scientists. The financial, technological, and political constraints to nuclear fusion remain seemingly insurmountable. The fuel must be heated hundreds of millions of degrees before it fuses, the fuel particles must be made dense enough before they can fuse, and the process must be continued long enough for fusion to occur.

Yet no matter where and how it is generated, nuclear power can never be just another form of energy. The potentially catastrophic danger of nuclear energy puts it in its own category. An accident in a coal-powered electric plant will affect only those immediately involved; a meltdown in a nuclear plant can damage a region and its inhabitants for tens of thousands of years. Three million Americans live within ten miles of a nuclear facility.

Those who cry "not in my backyard" do so with good reason. Plutonium has a half-life of 24,000 years, which means it will only be half as deadly at that time. It would take yet another 24,000 years for the plutonium to become a quarter as deadly, and so on. At some point after hundreds of thousands of years had passed, the plutonium would become harmless. While plutonium-238 has a half-life of 24,000 years, some transuranic wastes have half-lifes of 200,000 years, which means it would take tens of millions of years before it became harmless. That is a long time geologically, let alone politically.

Preventing meltdowns is the least difficult part of regulating the nuclear industry. Decommissioning plants is highly expensive. The Shippensport, Pennsylvania, nuclear plant, the nation's first to operate, became the first to shut down in 1982. The plant was entombed in cement while the 770-ton reactor was extracted, conveyed all the way to Hanford, Washington, and buried. Eventually, every nuclear plant now operating will be decommissioned at an enormous expense. But decommissioning a plant is not the end of the problem.

A chronic worsening problem is what to do about the twenty-six metric tons of plutonium at thirteen sites and the thousands of tons of low-level radioactive waste being stockpiled in cooling tanks and concrete tombs across the country in scores of different sites awaiting ultimate disposal. While political gridlock impedes a decision, radioactivity is slowly but persistently eating away the containers. Initial policy toward nuclear waste involved reprocessing it into plutonium for additional use. Carter canceled all government subsidies for nuclear reprocessing in 1977. While many regions enjoy the benefits of nuclear-powered energy, none wants a radioactive storage facility in its backyard. Meanwhile, millions of tons of radioactive waste sit in temporary dumps which are highly unreliable. Between 1956 and 1976, half a million gallons of highly radioactive liquid wastes leaked at the government's Hanford, Washington, facility. Lesser leaks have been reported elsewhere. Others have undoubtedly been covered up. The possibility of nuclear meltdowns and chronic problems of nuclear waste do not just loom over the United States. Today, twenty-four countries have nuclear energy industries, of which the United States produces about 36 percent of all the world's nuclear-powered energy.

ELECTRICITY POLICY

Electricity can be generated from diverse sources.[34] In 1992, coal accounted for approximately 55 percent of electricity produced in the United States, nuclear 22 percent, falling water 10 percent, natural gas 9 percent, petroleum 4 percent, and wind, geothermal, and biomass 0.5 percent. The conversion of fossil fuels into electricity is inefficient, with three Btus burned for every one Btu of electricity generated.

Prices for fossil fuels have shifted widely over the past two decades. In 1973, fossil fuels cost an average $0.50 per million Btus, in 1981 prices peaked at $2.26, then dropped to $1.61 by 1992. In 1992, the United States generated 2.8 trillion kilowatt hours, one-quarter of the world's total electricity.

Since electricity can theoretically be produced anywhere, there are no regions, states, or cities which have more electricity clout than others. Some areas, however, enjoy far cheaper fuels for electricity. Hydroelectricity is obviously the cheapest and most stable. As long as the rivers run, hydroelectricity runs. Greater demand can be satisfied through greater efficiency and conservation of electricity use.

The electricity industry arose in the late nineteenth century out of Thomas Edison's inventions of generators, light bulbs, and conducting wires. At first, dozens of urban entrepreneurs competed to supply electricity to customers. The electricity industry, however, is a natural monopoly since it favors the largest economies of scale possible. As the industry concentrated, cities established regulatory commissions. In 1907, New York became the first state to regulate the electricity industry; other states soon followed. By 1922, forty-seven states and the District of Columbia had established state electricity commissions. In some states and cities, the government agencies regulated the industry for the public good. In most, however, the industry captured the agencies through corruption and used them to gouge the public. In response to public outcries against the industry's corruption and high prices, cities and states increasingly began buying out and running the electricity utility corporations.

As New York governor, Franklin Roosevelt made regulating the electricity industry central to his policies. In 1931, he pushed through the Assembly a bill creating the New York State Power Authority, which was authorized to tap the hydroelectric power of Niagara Falls and the St Lawrence Seaway. Although the St Lawrence turbines did not begin to turn until 1957, and Niagara Falls' until 1961, the agency became a model for others across the nation.

More importantly, Roosevelt entered the White House in 1933 determined to electrify the nation literally and figuratively. He pushed through the Tennessee Valley Authority (TVA) in 1933, and championed other vast hydroelectric systems across the United States. In 1935, Roosevelt created by executive order the Rural Electrification Administration (REA) whose hundreds of Rural Electrification Cooperatives (REC) transformed the countryside. That same year, Congress passed the Public Utility Holding Company Act to regulate the electricity and energy industries. The Securities and Exchange Commission (SEC) was created to regulate the financial dealings of all corporations, including those providing electricity.

These institutions and projects became the centerpiece of his New Deal. They put millions of people to work transforming poor, backward regions with modern systems of roads, dams, canals, electricity grids, railroads, refrigeration, power stations, and bridges. This infrastructure and billions of dollars in investments in turn stimulated other economic activities and unleashed entrepreneurship. Agriculture in particular was modernized as farmers were given access to such labor-saving and productivity-enhancing implements as power tools, incubators, and milking machines. And these regulatory and developmental agencies also ensured that electricity and energy monopolies would not exploit consumers who were hooked up to the grid.

This electricity grid dramatically boosted America's socio-economic development. By the 1960s, however, problems arose which indicated reforms were necessary. A massive blackout of the northeastern states and Canada in 1965 and smaller brownouts and blackouts elsewhere prompted demands that the nation's fragmented electricity grid be comprehensively unified. The existing linkages from one grid to the next were too weak. The system was eventually modernized.

The composition and costs of electricity sources changed significantly in the 1960s and 1970s. Starting in the 1960s, nuclear power captured a larger share of electricity generation. A 1972 law required all utilities to install scrubbers to reduce pollution. Laws in 1974 and 1978 encouraged utilities firms to switch from oil to coal; the later National Energy Act actually forbade new utilities from using either of those fossil fuels. The 1977 Public Utilities Resources Policy Act (PURPA) allowed states to determine their own electricity rates, while encouraging greater energy efficiency and conservation, and allowing emissions pollution trading. As the dangers of nuclear power became increasingly evident, particularly after the Three Mile Island disaster of 1979, even more utilities diverted to coal energy sources.

The rise in oil barrel prices from $2.50 in 1973 to $36 in 1980, and less dramatic, yet still painful, price increases for other energy sources, did slow annual electricity usage increases from 7 percent to 2 percent from 1973 to 1983. But as energy prices dropped in the mid-1980s and stayed low, electricity usage has increased an average 4 percent each year from 1984.

The electricity industry, whether publicly or privately owned, remains heavily regulated. John Davies points out that in

> the number of utilities, government ownership predominates. There are 2,000 state and municipal utilities and nearly 1,000 cooperatives. Ten national government entities generate power, including TVA, the Army Corps of Engineers, and the Bureau of Reclamation. The large number of state, municipal, and cooperative utilities contrasts with only 259 private companies. On the other hand, private investor-owned utilities generate 79 percent of the total electricity. State and municipal utilities generate 9 percent, the national government 7 percent, and cooperatives 5 percent.[35]

The decisive role of the government in providing and regulating electricity for Americans will not change for the foreseeable future.

ALTERNATIVE ENERGY POLICIES

The United States remains dependent on fossil fuels for 90 percent of its energy needs. Fossil fuels are not only finite, but their burning contributes to pollution, acid rain, and the greenhouse effect, all of which exact enormous and worsening economic and environmental costs.

Because the United States cannot provide for all its fossil fuel needs, it must import the remainder. Imported oil in particular comes from unstable areas like the Persian Gulf. The United States and world economies were hit hard by

OPEC's quadrupling of oil prices in 1973 and further doubling in 1979. Although, for a variety of interrelated reasons, oil prices have dropped since the mid-1980s, they will inevitably rise again within a decade as the world's supply diminishes and becomes ever more concentrated in the hands of a few countries, none of which have an undying love for the United States.

The cheapest way to reduce American dependence on fossil fuels is through greater conservation and efficiency. Many would agree with Rosenbaum that "conservation should be considered another source of energy – the fifth energy alternative after petroleum, natural gas, coal, and nuclear fuel."[36] Investments can yield enormous energy and economic savings over the long term. For example, the universal usage of the most efficient light bulbs could reduce the nation's electricity consumption by one-third.

Unfortunately, only the Carter and Clinton administrations recognized the importance of alternative energies and conservation. Even then, they had trouble getting Congress to pass their legislation and the bureaucracies to implement it. Washington has refused to pour the financial and technical resources into developing environmentally friendly and virtually endless energy sources like solar, wind, and geothermal power that it has into the nuclear, oil, coal, and natural gas industries. Those four renewable energy sources contribute less than 1 percent of America's energy supplies. The primary reason for this neglect is political rather than technological. The fossil fuel and nuclear energy industries have vastly more political power and destroy any attempts to divert government programs and subsidies from themselves to alternative energy industries.

No energy resource has more potential than that from the sun. Every thirty minutes the amount of solar energy hitting the earth exceeds all the energy consumed by the United States in one year.[37] By some estimates, solar energy could supply as much as one-quarter of the nation's energy needs. Passive solar-energy systems include using better insulation in building materials so that less energy is dissipated, along with better designs and siting of buildings so that more of the sun's rays can heat buildings in cold climates or less rays will strike buildings in hot climates. Active solar-energy systems gather sunlight and convert it into electricity. The initial costs for homeowners to invest in various forms of solar energy are steep – $2,000 to $3,000 for a solar water system and $5,000 to $13,000 for a space- and water-heating system.[38]

Despite the enormous potential, no significant government policy toward solar power emerged until Jimmy Carter took office. In 1977, the Carter White House increased funding and tax credits for solar energy. This stimulated a massive household investment in solar energy. Between 1977 and 1984, 924,000 American households claimed the solar-technology tax credit; in 1984 alone, Americans installed about 150,000 solar-energy water systems and 9,000 solar space-heating units.[39] Then, in 1985, in accord with its cornucopian agenda, the Reagan White House succeeded in getting Congress to eliminate tax incentives for households and businesses investing in solar energy.

Cornucopian federal policies are not the only obstacle to solar-energy development. There are over 3,000 different building codes in communities across the United States. Few of these encourage the installation of passive solar energy or other energy-saving devices; many discourage such practices.

Despite the hostility of the Reagan and Bush years, the solar-energy industry has made significant technological strides. Successive generations of photovoltaic cells have made solar-energy prices competitive with those of fossil fuels. A joint venture between Southern California Edison and Texas Instruments unveiled a photovoltaic cell in 1992 that cost only one-fifth the price of then existing ones. Imbedded in aluminum siding, the cells could replace existing house shingles for about $3,000 and would produce about one-third of that home's energy.

As with solar energy, technological advances have reduced the price of wind power to one competitive with fossil fuel sources. The seven cents to produce a kilowatt hour of wind power is actually cheaper than nuclear power and only slightly more than coal power. Yet, while solar energy has the potential to become a major source of energy, wind can never be more than a supplement. The potential to harness the wind varies enormously from one region to the next. Mountain passes and the Great Plains are primary sources. Of the 17,000 wind turbines currently operating across the United States, most are in California, mainly because of generous state investment incentives. Those incentives, and the political will and power that provide them, are largely lacking elsewhere.

The only alternative-energy policy the federal government has significantly supported is hydroelectricity. Bureaucracies such as the Army Corps of Engineers, Bureau of Reclamation, and Tennessee Valley Authority have dammed scores of rivers with hundreds of dams. Federal subsidies have encouraged state and local governments, and private investors, to build thousands of other hydroelectric dams. The 1978 Public Utilities Regulatory Policies Act (PURPA) boosted the hydroelectric industry by forcing utilities to buy electricity from those plants at an "avoided cost rate," which was calculated at how much the utilities would have had to pay if they had produced the energy themselves. As a result, applications for small hydroelectric plants soared from a hundred in 1976 to over 4,500 in 1979. In 1981, Washington further targeted the industry with provisions of the Crude Oil Windfall Profits Tax that allowed an 11 percent tax credit for small hydroelectric plants. Although Reagan slashed direct subsidies for hydroelectric power from $720 million when he took office in 1980 to $115 million when he left office in 1989, he never succeeded in killing the programs. Bush and Clinton have maintained these relatively low spending amounts.

Like solar energy, hydroelectric power has enormous energy potential but feeble political support. Hydroelectric power in the 1990s contributed less than 5 percent of America's energy pie, a percentage unchanged since the 1960s. A study by the Corps of Engineers concluded that hydroelectric dams built at 656 sites in the northeastern United States could generate around 6,000 megawatts of electricity, the equivalent of 40 million barrels of oil at 1980 prices, while boosting the amount of electricity available to New England and New York by 300 percent.[40]

Biomass, the burning of wood or plant-derived ethanol and methanol, is yet another renewable energy source. In the pre-industrial era, Americans relied on wood for heating and cooking, and on charcoal derived from wood to run their forges. Altogether, Americans used about half of all cut wood for fuel; wood supplied nearly 95 percent of all fuel. As an energy source, wood diminished both as a percentage and in absolute volume over the next century and a half as other energy sources like coal, oil, natural gas, and nuclear power became technologically and economically viable. Woodpulp for paper and lumber for buildings became the dominant uses of trees.

In the last half-century, wood and other biomass has made a slight energy comeback. As early as 1944, Washington extended the first subsidies to biomass and synfuels. The low cost of oil, coal, and nuclear energy kept the synfuel research on the political and technological backburner until the late 1970s. The quadrupling of oil prices in 1973 and further doubling in 1979 encouraged many Americans to invest in wood-burning stoves. In 1979, President Carter pushed through the Energy Security Act, which among other things created the US Synthetic Fuels Corporation and subsidized it with $20 billion. The synfuels program investigated biomass as one of several energy sources. The Reagan White House succeeded in killing the program in 1986.

The best way to increase energy resources is to constantly find more efficient and alternative ways of using them. President Carter made this point very well in a speech to Congress in 1977:

> The cornerstone of our policy is to reduce demand through conservation. Our emphasis on conservation is a clear difference between this plan and others which merely encouraged crash production efforts. Conservation is the quickest, cheapest, and most practical source of energy.[41]

Unfortunately, conservation and efficiency have been squeezed aside by powerful energy interest groups which enrich themselves by encouraging high and reckless consumption.

One of the largest areas for energy savings is co-generation. Factories consume enormous amounts of energy to produce goods. Co-generation is the process by which that energy is tapped for generating additional steam or electricity beyond merely running machinery. Half of all energy consumed in the United States produces steam. If that steam were harnessed rather than released, it could produce enormous energy savings. Co-generation is relatively cheap – 50 percent of the cost of nuclear power and 20 percent less than coal-generated electricity.

Co-generation has only positive effects. Yet co-generation is a prisoner of market forces. It reached its height in the 1920s when it supplied 30 percent of America's electricity. That percentage declined to about 15 percent by 1950 and then 5 percent by 1973 as fossil fuel prices dropped. As those prices rose through the 1970s and into the 1980s, increasing numbers of factories and businesses harnessed co-generation. But the investments in co-generation have dropped with the oil and coal gluts of the 1980s and 1990s. Unfortunately, industries lack the tax incentives to invest in co-generation technology that would save them considerable money and reduce America's energy consumption over the long term. As with other alternative energy sources, the fossil-fuel and nuclear-power industries have squelched any attempts to boost co-generation.

Some state and local governments have attempted to fill the conservation policy void. For example, California passed a law requiring that at least 2 percent of the cars whose producers annually sell more than 5,000 vehicles in the state be electric. With the nation's worst air pollution, Los Angeles has imposed strict regulations on vehicle, business, and household emissions that far exceed the national standards. In order to retain access to California's 37 million mass market, industries must create more environmentally sound products.

California's electric-car law could, particularly if emulated by other states and cities, significantly reduce fossil fuel consumption and pollution. Every vehicle fueled by electricity could save from ten to twenty oil barrels annually. With their limited range and small size, they would make great commuting cars. Electric cars could significantly reduce urban air pollution. The pollution would be generated at the power station where it could be controlled with scrubbers, rather than from each vehicle.

Unfortunately, electric cars are trapped in a vicious economic cycle. They are expensive because they are not mass produced and they are not mass produced because they are expensive. Electric vehicles remain unpopular because of their high price of from $20,000 for a car to $100,000 for a mini-van, along with their limited cruising range of about 100 miles. An electric car's batteries cost between $3,000 and $5,000 each and must be replaced every two or three years – a sizable investment for middle-class buyers. They also take six to eight hours to recharge.

The government can break this vicious cycle by creating demand for electric vehicles in two ways. First, national, state, and local governments have huge vehicle fleets. If they bought electric vehicles they would create more mass production and lower prices. The government could also promote electric vehicles by giving tax rebates to those who use them. California's regulations alone have led to significant technological advances. Each of the Big Three American manufacturers and several Japanese and European automobilemakers have unveiled electric cars which run on nickelcadmium, nickel-iron, or sodium-sulfur batteries, can run as far as 120 miles between recharges, and can obtain speeds of 65 miles per hour.

LEGACY

As in all other natural-resource industries, the government has promoted energy and other mineral industries through massive subsidies, tax favors, protection from foreign competition, and public land giveaways. But it has been very selective in picking winners and losers. Those industries with political power used it to extract vast direct and indirect subsidies from the system. No energy industry has received more government support than nuclear energy – Washington literally built the nuclear energy industry from the ground up. Alternative energies arose recently; they have little political influence and even less government support.

Until 1973, there was little perceived need for a comprehensive energy policy. Policies for each energy source had developed independently over time from their unique arrays of political and economic forces. OPEC's boycott and fivefold increase in oil prices caused a decade-long crisis. In response, three presidents tried a range of policies designed to increase and diversify supply and decrease demand. In contrast, the Reagan and Bush White Houses abandoned a comprehensive, long-term policy to diversify America's energy resources in favor of short-term market forces.

The most enduring legacy of the attempts to deal with the energy crisis is the Department of Energy (DOE), which Congress created in 1977 to formulate and implement a comprehensive energy policy that would reduce America's dependence on imported oil, promote alternative energies, and regulate the nuclear-power industry. In 1994, the DOE had 19,000 employees and a budget of $2.5 billion. By most accounts, the DOE has not only failed miserably to fulfill its duties but has been accused of gross mismanagement, misallocation of resources, and squandering of funds. Bureaucratic politics inhibited the DOE's mandate to create and implement a comprehensive energy policy. Other bureaucracies, most notably the Nuclear Regulatory Commission, the Agriculture Department, and the EPA retained vast powers over segments of the diverse energy industry. Any comprehensive plan could only occur after extensive consultation and compromise among the DOE and the other bureaucracies. As if these constraints were not enough, President Reagan tried to abolish the DOE. Although he failed to destroy the DOE, he weakened it through budget cuts and imposing ideologues as administrators with the mission of gutting the department.

The United States still lacks a comprehensive energy policy, let alone one that embraces all minerals. Meanwhile, the United States is becoming increasingly dependent on foreign sources of oil. But with oil prices at all-time lows in real (adjusted for inflation) prices, there is no political or popular pressure to act. Even when a calamity strikes, as with the nuclear meltdown at Chernobyl of April 26, 1986, the Exxon Valdez oil spill of March 24, 1989, or Iraq's invasion of Kuwait on August 2, 1990, policy makers address that particular crisis while avoiding a comprehensive approach that could prevent such a disaster from happening again.

There are alternatives to our present reliance on petroleum. The United States is self-sufficient in natural gas. Each increase in natural-gas consumption of a trillion cubic feet generates 50,000 to 70,000 new jobs.[42] Yet natural gas will eventually dwindle as well. As it does, coal will inevitably become more important unless there are technological break-throughs in alternative energies such as solar power. The United States possesses about one-third of the world's coal reserves, an amount that may last as much as three hundred years. Coal contributes more than half of America's electricity and about one-quarter of total energy needs. In 1991, coal generated 54.8 percent of electricity, followed by 21.8 percent for nuclear power, 9.9 percent for hydroelectricity, 9.3 percent for natural gas, 3.8 percent for oil, and 0.4 percent for other sources.[43]

Coal does not have to be the heavily polluting energy it currently is. Coal gasification is experiencing a technological revolution that may herald a new era of cleaner, abundant energy. Simply burning coal in a furnace converts only 32 percent of it to electricity. In contrast, coal gasification is 53 percent efficient. The technology involves steaming coal with a mix of biomass materials such as wood chips, sugar cane, and sludges.[44]

Federal mineral policies have largely subsidized a range of industries with varying degrees of direct and indirect subsidies. None of these policies has been more outrageous than the 1872 law which is essentially a vast giveaway of public wealth and land to huge and largely foreign mining conglomerates. Although it was written by mining corporations, the law was sold to the public as a means of helping small-scale prospectors gain and exploit a stake. There were not all that many small-time prospectors when the law was written; today there are virtually none. Since 1872, mining corporations have taken over and dug hundreds of billions of dollars worth of wealth from public lands.

There have been periodic attempts to reform the law. In 1873, the year after it was enacted, Congress passed a law separating coal mining from all other mining and overseeing its activity on public lands. The 1920 Mineral Leasing Act separated fossil-fuel (gas, oil, and oil shale) and fertilizer (sodium, phosphate, potassium) minerals from others, and imposed royalties on their extraction from public lands. Since then, the 1872 Mining Law has applied only to "hardrock" minerals like silver, gold, and copper.

While the hiving off of specific minerals from the 1872 law proved possible although difficult, rewriting that law has proved politically impossible. Presidents Harding, Truman, Nixon, and Clinton proposed overhauls of the 1872 Mining Law. Corporations exploiting these minerals crushed all those reform attempts. The 1954 Multiple Mineral Development Act reinforced the 1872 Mining Act by confirming all existing and future permits or leases on public lands, while the 1970 Mining and Minerals Policy Act was largely a statement of principles concerning the value of mining on public lands. Neither law contained any enhanced regulations of mining, imposed royalties, or forced miners to clean up their toxic messes. Fortunately, the 1872 law does not apply to all public lands. About 8 percent of existing public lands were bought from private owners. On those lands, miners are required to apply for a permit, curb construction, clean up environmental damage, and pay royalties.

Mining of all kinds has devastated ecosystems across the nation. Varying aspects of the following description of the impact of coal mining in Appalachia could apply to mining operations nearly anywhere:

> pockmarked by strip mines, [it] has been transformed into a moonscape. This denuded terrain easily floods, rapidly erodes, and loses its ability to sustain agriculture. Dangerous landslides rumble down degraded slopes and bury homes. Mine drainage, soaked with toxins and sediments, clogs rivers, kills wildlife, and contaminates drinking water. Unattended standing ponds threaten the safety of unsuspecting children who use the areas as playgrounds. As a result, vital ecosystems, human lives, and livelihoods are destroyed.[45]

Lawrence MacDonnell points out that:

> metal and nonfuel mining in the United States generated over fifty billion metric tons of waste material by 1985, and that over one billion tons of waste are now generated each year. Only five percent of those wastes are estimated to be toxic, but that equates to about sixty million tons of material requiring special management each year.[46]

Superfund lists over sixty mostly abandoned mining sites for priority cleanup – at taxpayer expense. The cleanup costs for the Berkeley Pit Copper Mine on the Clark's Fork River are over $1 billion![47]

The first environmental regulations on mining did not emerge until the 1970 Clean Air Act and 1972 Clean Water Act, which required that high-altitude mining must conform to the "best available technology" for cleanup of discharge waters. These preliminary measures were reinforced by the much tougher environmental regulations of the 1976 Federal Coal Leasing Amendment Act and 1977 Surface Mining Control and Reclamation Act. These laws have slowed rather than reversed mining pollution.

Hardrock mining remains an industry that leaches far more than it enriches the American economy. According to historian Thomas Watkins, miners extracted only $20 billion between 1849 and 1970, yet left behind little more than environmental destruction:

> If gold and silver mining created cities and states where none had been before, it remained for less romantic enterprises to settle and develop them for the future; the mining itself left little more than the memory of rape, for it took as much as it could as fast as it could, and it gave back as little as possible.[48]

In 1910, mining peaked at 2.5 percent of the economy; by 1994, mining accounted for only 0.5 percent of GNP. Despite its diminishing power, the hardrock mining industry will remain as powerful as ever, in asserting its interests, as its fossil-fuel counterparts.

4 Dams, Irrigation, and Faucets

There is no more precious and essential natural resource than water. Humans are nine-tenths water; death will follow those who go more than several days without drinking it. Like us, all the plant and animal life upon which we survive also depends on water. Prolonged droughts can wither crops and decimate livestock. Every civilization's survival – from the most ancient to recent – has depended on taming rivers and tapping aquifers. Wells, irrigation, aqueducts, pipes, canals, plumbing, dams – the means of supplying the demand for water have not changed much over the past seven thousand years, only their scale and technological sophistication.

Americans take water for granted. A slight twist of the taps and they can be soothed under long hot showers, run the sprinklers all day across carefully cropped lawns, wash the car, and fill backyard swimming pools. The average American daily consumes 90 gallons directly, an additional 600 gallons to process all that day's manufactured goods and services, and yet another 800 gallons to put food on the table! America's demand for water has soared with its population and affluence. America's population was 4 million in 1790, 75 million in 1900, and 260 million in 1995.[1]

Theoretically, America's water supply is vast and virtually inexhaustible. The current demand for water is only one-fourteenth the supply. Groundwater within 2,500 feet of the earth's surface will last fifty years at current consumption rates.[2]

In reality, there are severe and growing water problems. America's water supply is grossly maldistributed. The Mississippi River roughly divides the United States into two great realms unequal in climate or topography. The lands from a couple of hundred miles west of the Mississippi all the way to the Atlantic Ocean are lush in foliage, water, and people. The further west one journeys from the Mississippi River, the dryer and more sparsely populated the lands become. Among the thirty-one eastern states, precipitation annually averages 42.5 inches and runoff 15.0 inches. Except for the West Coast states, precipitation diminishes across the West. The Plains states of North Dakota, South Dakota, Nebraska, Kansas, Oklahoma, and Texas receive an average of 25.4 inches of precipitation and 4.5 inches of runoff. Precipitation averages 13.3 inches and runoff 1.8 inches across the western states of Montana, Utah, Colorado, New Mexico, Wyoming, Nevada, and Arizona. In the rainy northwest states of Washington and Oregon, precipitation averages 32.1 inches and runoff 20.8 inches. No states are more divided into wet and dry regions than California and Idaho whose precipitation averages 22.3 and runoff 9.0 inches.[3] Precipitation extremes are even greater. While portions of the southeast might get 60 inches of rain annually, portions of the southwest might receive an inch. One-third of the United States receives less than 20 inches of rainfall a year.

Traditionally, although eastern farmers relied on rainfall, households and businesses everywhere across the nation and western farmers drew their water from streams. Until the 1930s, aquifers supplied a tiny fraction of the nation's water since most wells drew water from no more than 25 feet below the surface. But the widespread use of the vertical turbine pump in the late 1930s revolutionized groundwater's use. Water could now be drawn relatively cheaply from 300 feet down. By 1970, groundwater supplied 35 percent of all water in the western states. The most important groundwater source is the Ogallala Aquifer, which runs under most of the Plains states and supplies 40 percent of that region's water.

Everywhere across the United States, particularly in its dryer regions, American civilization is imperiled. Water is life's foundation, and to varying degrees everywhere, the waters from which Americans draw sustenance are being fouled and depleted. Over the centuries, as the population has exploded in number and affluence, the demand for water and the life it spawns has led to aquifers and rivers poisoned by chemicals and drained by overuse. America's population and its diverse thirsts for water continue to expand. Aquifers that took tens of thousands of years to fill will be poisoned by chemicals filtering down from fields, homes, and factories above, and drained within a century by people tilling fields, washing cars, and watering lawns.

One source of pollution is made by nature but spread by humans. Increasing numbers of the nation's rivers and farmlands are dying from salt saturation. Whenever water percolates through soil it picks up salts and other minerals; the more water is recycled from river and aquifer, to land and back again, the more salty that water becomes. Water taken from the average western rivers will have 200 parts of salt per million, when it returns to the river its salinity has soared to 6,500 parts per million.[4] At some point that water becomes so salt-saturated that it kills rather than sustains life. In many regions, a veneer of arable soil sits atop a hard, thick, impermeable clay base. As increasingly salty waters are dumped on the soil and percolate through it, they are trapped above that clay level. The salt builds up steadily through the soil until it can no longer sprout plant life. For example, a vast network of government-subsidized dams and irrigation projects transformed California's San Joaquin Valley into one of the world's most productive farm regions. But salinity is steadily transforming large stretches of that valley to desert. To varying degrees, Washington's water policies have created or worsened all of these catastrophic problems.

WATER POLICY-MAKING

Too many people, demanding too much water, and creating too much pollution have caused the ever more severe water crises afflicting ever more regions across the United States. But why has this occurred? The answers are rooted in American culture, history, and federal policy.

Water's relative abundance or scarcity shapes the culture of those people living off it. Marc Reisner contrasts eastern and western values with regard to water:

In the West, lack of water is the central fact of existence, and a whole culture and set of values have grown up around it. In the East, to "waste" water is to consume it needlessly or excessively. In the West, to waste water is not to consume it – to let it flow unimpeded and undiverted down rivers.[5]

Government policy toward those two vast regions is as different as the regions themselves and has both reflected and shaped regional attitudes toward water. The nation's wet and dry lands operate under different water-rights systems. "Riparian rights," in which those adjacent can use the nearby water, largely govern the eastern United States with its abundant rainfall. "Appropriative rights," in which those who claim a water source first own it, govern the dry western lands. Appropriative rights encouraged entrepreneurs to settle the region.

The American frontier experience started with the first settlements of Europeans and Africans on the continent's east coast and continued for the next three centuries. And the further west those people went, generally the dryer those lands became. In the popular imagination, the American frontier remains largely the austere, dry, dramatic landscapes starting somewhere west of the Mississippi River and stretching across the continent to the Pacific Ocean. In countless novels and films, a colorful procession of characters playing their respective roles transformed that land from wilderness to civilization – mountain men, farmers, miners, sheriffs, preachers, loggers, and so on.

Yet the one occupation that did more to transform the West than any other somehow escapes that colorful parade – dambuilders. Throughout the twentieth century, the Bureau of Reclamation and Army Corps of Engineers constructed dozens of dams across nearly all the West's great and minor rivers, thus extending drinking water, electricity, and irrigation to tens of millions of people who otherwise could not have survived in those dry lands. As Reisner puts it, civilization across the American West:

> depends on the manipulation of water – on capturing it behind dams, storing it, and rerouting it in concrete rivers over distances of hundreds of miles. Were it not for a century and a half of messianic effort toward that end, the West as we know it would not exist.[6]

Water policy is essentially about dams – and the irrigation, drinking water, and hydroelectricity that they provide,
and the people to whom they are provided. The Bureau of
Reclamation and Army Corps of Engineers did not just tame
western rivers – Washington literally dammed all of America.
The nation's waterways are plugged with over 60,000 dams
over 25 feet high, and 2.5 million smaller dams. Virtually
all of those dams were built within the twentieth century.
In the early twentieth century, technological advances creating new and better concrete, pumps, turbines, generators,
power transmission lines, and earth-moving equipment enabled engineers to build ever bigger and safer dams, which
in turn transformed vast regions from poverty to prosperity.
Of course, not all of those dams were built directly by the
government. By 1900, there were only 2,661 dams across
the country. Between 1900 and 1982, federal bureaucracies
built over 60,000 dams retaining over 860 million acre-feet
of water. These water works transformed every region on
which they were imposed – none more so than the arid
Western lands. Even if Washington did not directly build a
dam, federal, state, and/or local government subsidies, tax
cuts, expertise, and other services certainly inspired the creation of most of the nation's dams, as well as the wells that
provide drinking water and irrigation for most farmers and
other rural residents.

The benefits of these policies have been as maldistributed
as the population and rainfall. Throughout the West, government dams and canals benefit mostly farmers, and then mostly
those who raise cattle fodder such as hay and alfalfa. In
some places farmers pay as little as 1 percent of the water's
cost. Urban and suburban dwellers subsidize farmers by paying
higher water rates and taxes. Hydroelectricity supplies 5
percent of America's electricity needs. The nation's taxpayers subsidized the costs of building the dams which supply
hydroelectricity, which is relatively cheaper than electricity
supplied by fossil fuels or nuclear energy.

These huge government water projects have transformed
entire regions from poverty to prosperity, a reality not ap-
preciated by everyone who has benefited. All too often, it
seems the greater an individual's ideals, the greater the gap
between his ideals and actions. Call it hypocrisy if you will

but it is certainly an ingrained aspect of human nature. For example, many of the people living in the Tennessee River watershed deplore "big government." Yet, had it not been for the government-owned and operated Tennessee Valley Authority (TVA) that region might well still be mired in intractable mass poverty and isolation. The TVA is not the only example of "big government" overcoming entrenched economic backwardness that was impervious to private enterprise. All across the nation, regions, states, and localities have been transformed – usually for the better – by public works projects that, in principle, most of its inhabitants deplore – at least for others. But these projects have imposed enormous socioeconomic and environmental costs.

There are few issues which are more governed by special-interest politics than water policy. It is difficult to overestimate the importance of water projects to Congress: "water projects are the grease gun that lubricates the nation's legislative machinery. Congress without water projects would be like an engine without oil; it would simply seize up."[7] The water lobby includes not only agribusiness that is enriched by the subsidized water, but construction firms which build and maintain the dams, canals, and pipes. Like other special interests, water interests control the relevant congressional committees, such as the Senate Water Resources and House Water and Power Resources committees, that control water projects and laws. Those Congressional committees and subcommittees are packed with representatives from districts in which farmers and ranchers hold the money and votes vital for gaining and keeping political power. Most water projects are targeted for the West and South, from which come about three hundred Congressional representatives and sixty-six senators. For example, 288 water projects were funded in the 1980 Public Works Appropriation bill, of which all but 8 were in the South or West. Of those 288 projects, all but 8 cost less than $25 million.[8]

Four government bureaucracies battle both to shape and to implement water policy. The US Army Corps of Engineers and the Bureau of Reclamation are the two national water titans that build the nation's dam, hydroelectricity, and irrigation systems. The Tennessee Valley Authority does the same within one region. Finally, the Soil Conservation Service concentrates on small projects for farmers.

The Corps and Bureau mostly fight and sometimes coop- erate over water policy. To promote their respective interests, Corporations and politicians have learned how to play the Bureau and Corps off against each other. With its roots in the American Revolution, the US Army Corps of Engineers was founded to assist navigation and defense. Throughout the nineteenth century, the Corps largely shed its defense responsibility and expanded its navigation duties to dam- building, irrigation, and eventually hydroelectricity and rec- reation. Today, although the Corps is still attached to the Defense Department, over 98 percent of its employees are civilians. The Bureau of Reclamation was founded a cen- tury after the Corps. Although its mission was to provide irrigation to small farmers, it was soon captured by huge agribusiness, state, and regional interests. Like the Corps, its duties have expanded to include irrigation, hydroelec- tricity, flood control, navigation, fisheries, and recreation. Theoretically, the Bureau's expenses are to be paid by sell- ing irrigation rights to farmers; in practice, the Bureau loses money to subsidize agribusiness.

As in other industries, water policy is shaped by an iron triangle of government agencies, private corporations, and politicians with a stake in the issue. Thus do special interests prevail over national interests.

EARLY WATER POLICIES

Throughout America's colonial and early Republic eras, water policy was mostly a local concern. It was only after a town or city had polluted or drained their local sources that they coveted more distant waters. As the cities and their water needs expanded, shortages became acute. The solution was for the local and state governments to build reservoirs to hold water, and vast canals to transport it to consumers.

From American Independence, the federal government has subsidized the development of water resources, at first primarily through improving navigation. The US Army Corps of Engineers is one of the nation's oldest and most dis- tinguished military units. General George Washington created it as a unit within the Continental Army to build roads, bridges, and fortifications. In 1794, it was officially designated the US Corps of Engineers and divided into a military branch, which concentrated on building fortifications, and a civilian branch, whose duties extended to promoting navigation in the nation's harbors and rivers. At first, the Corps attempted to fulfill its navigation duties largely by charting the nation's waterways and building lighthouses. Throughout the nineteenth century, the Corps was increasingly authorized to improve navigation by building canals, locks, and dams. The turning point came in 1824 when the Supreme Court ruled that the interstate commerce clause allowed the Corps of Engineers to improve navigation on the nation's rivers. The Corps contributed significantly to the proliferation of canals in the eastern United States in the early nineteeth century – there were 1,300 miles of canals by 1830 and 3,300 by 1840.[9] Canals diminished in importance as the railroad network expanded steadily around this time.

In the mid-nineteenth century, Washington passed several laws designed to encourage the West's settlement. Many of these laws were explicitly water policies. The Swamp Acts of 1848 and 1850 allowed the transfer of federal lands to states which drained and converted wetlands. The 1862 Homestead Act granted a quarter-section, or 160 acres, to any settler who stayed on and improved that land for five years, or paid $1.25 an acre for it. The Desert Lands Act of 1877 provided 640 acres at $1.25 an acre if settlers irrigated it within three years. The Timber Culture Act of 1873 granted 160 acres of semi-arid land to homesteaders who planted and sustained trees on 40 acres for at least ten years. The law was designed to encourage not only settlement but soil and water preservation. The Carey Land Act of 1894 gave arid lands to states that developed irrigation projects. Unfortunately, abuse of these settlement laws was common. Birdhouses were built to prove "erected domiciles"; barrels of water were poured on desert land to prove "irrigation."

Those were the least serious consequences of the public-lands giveaways. The men who made these laws knew little or nothing about the conditions in the semi-arid western lands. The Timber Law provides the most glaring example of a policy based on ignorance. Those who devised it believed the theory that "rain follows the plow," that foliage, whether it be crops or trees, attracted moisture, which allowed more foliage, which in turn attracted more moisture. The theory was wrong. The arid regions are ruled by natural cycles of wet and dry years which are little affected by human activity. West of the 100th meridian, rainfall averages less than 20 inches annually. Only dryland farming can possibly work in such an environment. Of course, the land speculators who helped write those land giveaway laws did not care whether the theories upon which the laws were justified worked or not.

Thus, many of these federal policies encouraged millions of people optimistically to abandon their homes and jobs to head west and settle lands that should have been left alone. More often than not, heartache, tragedy, and waste were the result. For example, of the 1 million people who tried to homestead the high plains in the late nineteenth century, only 400,000 remained there permanently.

Survival in those dry lands depended on cooperation and close social ties, things many settlers had hoped to leave behind. Untypical of the pioneers were the Mormons, who were the first settlers to irrigate dry regions, and they did so independently of any government assistance. Between 1850 and 1880, the Mormons had succeeded in irrigating 1 million acres of semi-arid land, and by 1900 7.5 million acres.[10] The Mormons succeeded because they were ruled by a strict theocracy that promoted communalism, not the semi-anarchy with which most frontier Americans lived.

Throughout the late nineteenth century, only one prominent and lonely voice argued that Washington's land policies were grossly wrong – and he was largely ignored. Virtually all Americans are familiar with the Lewis and Clark expedition of 1804–6 across the West to the Pacific Ocean and back. Far fewer have heard of John Wesley Powell's expedition down the Colorado River in 1869. In his subsequent study, *A Report on the Lands of the Arid Region of the United States, with a More Detailed Account of the Lands of Utah*, Powell argued that because the West was so dry and its lands so barren, it could support only isolated pockets of civilization, and only then with expensive irrigation projects. Without irrigation, a settler needed much more than 160 acres upon which to run enough livestock to survive – Powell recommended increasing the homestead land allotment to 2,560 acres for the West's dryest regions west of the 100th meridian. He also argued that water rights should revert to the state after five years if they had not been developed, to prevent water barons from gaining a stranglehold over them and thus inhibiting the expansion of towns.

Powell became a national hero for his Colorado expedition. His report won the praises and association of many of the nation's leading scientists. In 1881, Powell became head of the Geologic Survey and Bureau of Ethnology. Powell conducted an extensive water survey of the West to determine the most viable areas for irrigation, and expanded his ideas and arguments in subsequent reports. But Washington failed to heed his advice. The public-land laws remained unchanged.

By the late nineteenth century, several incidents and political forces pressured Washington to initiate a policy of dam-building. The homestead laws had been successful in encouraging the settlement of regions with abundant rainfall. The drier the lands, however, the less successful the homesteading. The challenge for homesteaders was even greater because often others owned the local waters upon which their subsistence depended. Perhaps as many fights in the West have been over disputed water rights as over card games. Western values and laws accord the right to water to those who own its source. Thus anyone whose property extends over a watershed can dam those streams and control the access to anyone downstream. Most water barons did not hesitate to exploit their monopoly at the expense of local settlers.

Toward the nineteenth century's end, progressives lumped water barons along with other monopoly capitalists who owned the nation's railroads, oil fields, and steel mills. The monopoly capitalists impeded development by charging exorbitant prices for basic services like water and transportation. The more the monopolists charged, the less money farmers and city folk had to spend on other goods and services. The result was a stunted, impoverished economy. Break up the monopolies, progressives argued, and the middle class and the entire economy would expand with new, dynamic wealth. Although the 1890 Sherman Anti-trust Act targeted for breakup the huge national monopolies, it had no effect on regional monopolies. Progressives believed that only government could pry the small farmers and ranchers loose from the water barons' grip.

Just as troubling was the incompetence of the private firms that built and operated thousands of dams across the country. Countless dams were so structurally weak that they would not hold water, or eventually burst from hard rains or swelling spring runoffs. On May 31, 1889, a privately built dam above Johnstown, Pennsylvania, burst. The 16 billion gallon wall of water surging down the valley wiped out the town and at least 2,200 people. Outraged political and private voices demanded governmental regulation of dams.

Yet, the political balance remained in the state capitals rather than in Washington. In 1894, Senator Joseph Carey of Wyoming submitted a bill whereby Washington would cede a million acres of public lands to any state government that promised to irrigate it. The bill passed. Progressives lauded the Carey Act as the solution to the exploitation of impoverished, exploited farmers, ranchers, and town-dwellers by the water barons. The Carey Act did lead to 288,553 acres of new irrigated farmland across the West. But critics soon saw the Carey Act as a half-way measure to the West's water problems. Many of the states had trouble raising enough money to build the dams and irrigation canals, and then managing them when they did.

President Theodore Roosevelt was a progressive and conservationist. Having ranched in North Dakota during the 1880s, Roosevelt understood the political and technological problems behind irrigation. In December 1901, shortly after assuming the presidency, Roosevelt declared that the "Western half of the United States would sustain a population greater than that of our whole country today if the waters that now run to waste were saved and used for irrigation."[11] Only the federal government had the financial and technological expertise to transform the West from desert to a patchwork of irrigated Edens.

Roosevelt's views were shaped by John Wesley Powell's *Report on the Arid Lands* and the more recent proposals of Nevada Senator and dambuilder Francis Newlands. Roosevelt encouraged Newlands to write and submit a bill into Congress that would create a new federal water policy and agency based on Powell's report. Newlands' bill was voted down, with many opponents decrying it as "socialistic." Wyoming Senator Francis Warren introduced his own bill whereby the federal government would have simply aided the state legislatures in water policy rather than completely taking it over as Newlands' bill would have required. Roosevelt said he would support Warren's bill with some "minor changes." The House version was essentially a revival of Newlands' bill. In the conference to reconcile the two bills, Roosevelt was able to force through the House version by enlisting the support of key eastern senators and representatives by threatening to withhold federal funding of their harbor and river improvement programs. Roosevelt signed the bill into law on June 17, 1902.

The Reclamation Act of 1902 was a revolutionary step in federal water policy. The Act created the Reclamation Service (renamed the Bureau of Reclamation in 1923) with the legal duty of ensuring water for all those who owned 160 acres or less within 17 western states. Under the Act, a husband and wife could each own 160 acres and thus receive water for their combined 320 acres. Projects were financed by a Reclamation Fund, which was in turn supplied by revenues from the sale of public lands and later by irrigation purchases by farmers. The Act exempted farmers from paying any interest on water purchases and allowed them up to ten years for repayment; taxpayers have subsidized such farmers ever since. The Reclamation Act of 1914 extended the repayment period to twenty years.

Fearful of losing out to the Bureau, the Corps of Engineers pressured Congress to grant it additional duties. The Inland Water Commission's 1908 Report called on the Corps to improve the nation's waterways for navigation so that bigger ships could operate. The Flood Control Act of 1917 gave the Corps increased powers to improve and build dams, and levies necessary to prevent flooding on the nation's rivers. The Federal Water Power Act of 1920 created a Federal Water Commission composed of representatives of the Agriculture, Interior, and War Departments to coordinate the nation's range of water policies.

With the 1902 Reclamation Act and subsequent laws, the federal government had taken the lead in water policy. Yet local special interests still determined the specifics of policy. The only difference was that now those special interests had greater government resources at their command.

EARLY BATTLES

Roosevelt and his successors fought hard to get those water bills passed, over the objections of cornucopians who did not directly benefit from the projects. "Socialism!" cried the benefitless cornucopians. Those who protested against the dams were joined by others with a different objection — "Desecration!"

The late nineteenth-century alliance between conservationists and environmentalists died in the battle over Hetch Hetchy Valley in Yosemite. As early as 1882, the valley was first identified as a potential dam site that could provide drinking water for an ever growing San Francisco. In 1890, however, the valley was designated part of Yosemite National Park and thus theoretically off limits to development. San Francisco's ability to supply water to its rapidly expanding population became increasingly strained. In 1901, Mayor James D. Phelan applied to the Interior Department to build a dam in the valley. Interior Secretary Ethan Hitchcock rejected the application. The mayor reapplied following the devastating earthquake and fire on April 18, 1906. Despite the water shortage's urgency, the application languished for another two years until Interior Secretary James Garfield approved it on May 11, 1908.

Environmentalists like John Muir, Robert Underwood Johnson, and others immediately protested at the decision and launched a national campaign to overturn it. In the struggle, the Sierra and Appalachian Mountain Clubs allied and created national organizations. Predictably, Muir equated the proposed dam at Hetch Hetchy with barbarians destroying a sacred site: "Dam Hetch Hetchy! As well dam for watertanks the people's cathedrals and churches for no holier temple has ever been consecrated by the heart of man."[12]

The Hetch Hetchy controversy tore Roosevelt between his conservationist and environmentalist inclinations, with Pinchot and Muir perched on opposite shoulders and streaming arguments into his ears. In 1908, he asked engineers to look for alternative sites. Learning that there were no feasible alternatives, Roosevelt reluctantly chose to support the proposed dam. Then, he reversed his decision later that year, declaring during his annual message on December 8, 1908, that Yellowstone and Yosemite "should be kept as a great national playground. In both, all wild things should be protected and the scenery kept wholly unmarred."[13]

Both the House and Senate held hearings on the issue in 1909. The battle over Hetch Hetchy split the nation along regional lines with most of the public in western states for, and most of those in eastern states against the dam. Environmental arguments got through in the House, which voted to reject San Francisco's application. Yet, the issue did not die because the dam's economic potential grew. Engineers now proposed that the dam would provide San Francisco not only with water but also with hydroelectricity. Once again environmentalists succeeded in bottling up any petitions.

Four years later, the issue reemerged with the newly installed Woodrow Wilson Administration. Franklin Lane, the new Interior Secretary, was from San Francisco and favored the dam. He did admit that Congress held the final say on the issue. San Francisco Representative John Raker introduced a bill to allow the dam. Once again, conservationist and environmentalist forces joined battle in Congress. Appearing before the House Committee on Public Lands, Gifford Pinchot reported that "the fundamental policy of the whole conservation policy is that of use, to take every part of the land and its resources and to put it to that use which it will serve the most people."[14] Pinchot's carefully reasoned conservationist argument carried the day. The Committee unanimously approved the application and sent it to the floor for a vote on August 29, 1913. After a few days of fierce debate, the House approved the bill on September 3 by a vote of 183 to 43, with 203 abstentions. The Senate took up the bill on December 1 and on December 6 voted 43 for and 25 against, with 29 abstentions. President Wilson signed it into law on December 19, 1913.

Although the environmentalists lost the Hetch Hetchy battle, they gained enormous political skills and organization at the national level. "Remember Hetch Hetchy!" became a rallying cry for a generation of environmental activists. As Rod Nash put it, "the most significant thing about the controversy over Hetch Hetchy was that it occurred at all. One hundred or even fifty years earlier a similar proposal to dam a wilderness river would not have occasioned the slightest ripple of public protest."[15]

Despite its sweeping technological and financial power, the Reclamation Service did not prevail everywhere. In some places, local entrepreneurs remained powerful enough to elbow aside the Service and build their own dams and irrigation projects. One of the first big projects that the Reclamation Service considered targeted the waters of California's Owens Valley for diversion to Los Angeles. Politics derailed the Service's proposal.

Northern and southern California differ greatly in climate and values. North and south have competed fiercely for business, immigrants, and government handouts ever since the United States conquered California and the rest of the southwest from Mexico in 1848. The two great cities of northern and southern California, San Francisco and Los Angeles, respectively, exemplify the regional differences. Until well into the twentieth century, San Francisco vastly overshadowed Los Angeles in economic dynamism, population, and culture. The transcontinental railroad linked San Francisco with the eastern United States in 1869. San Francisco's magnificent natural harbor became one of the Pacific basin's busiest. In contrast, Los Angeles lacked a viable port, the transcontinental railroad did not reach the city until 1885, and the population was one-tenth of San Francisco's at the century's turn. Like other western cities, Los Angeles experienced a series of booms and busts of business and population. Northern California enjoys relatively abundant waters from rainfall and snowpack in the Sierra Mountains; southern California receives virtually no rainfall let alone snow, and its aquifers are steadily diminishing.

As southern California's population expanded throughout the twentieth century, it demanded that ever more waters be diverted from the north. The north protested, resisted, and would have prevailed had not Washington stepped into that regional war, which was not just over water but economic, population, and political power as well. The water lobby in

Washington threw its massive political weight behind southern California's demands for northern water, and in so doing decisively and forever tipped the power balance. Los Angeles has become southern California's population, economic, and pop-cultural capital. Yet the ever expanding population of Los Angeles and southern California exists amidst a vast desert. The only reason why such a huge population can survive there is because all their water needs are pumped in from the Colorado River and relatively water-abundant northern California. America's taxpayers have underwritten that development.

But at the century's turn, few could have foreseen those incredible developments. Then the city's survival was at stake. The population was rapidly draining the basin's groundwater reserves. Geologists feared that the groundwater and thus the city would dry up within years. Most local water resources were owned and operated by the privately owned Los Angeles City Water Company. In 1904, the company began shutting down wells in the San Fernando Valley north of Los Angeles which had lost their artesian pressure. Farmers protested bitterly. Later that year, Los Angeles City bought out the private water company and renamed it the Los Angeles Department of Water and Power. The Department's first report studied in depth the water crisis and concluded that the only solution was to bring in water from elsewhere. But from where and how?

Two hundred and fifty miles and several mountain passes north of Los Angeles, the Owens River gushes out of the Sierra Mountains into Owens Lake in the Great Basin. Owens Lake is four thousand feet higher than Los Angeles, which sits just above sea level. Throughout the 1890s, Fred Eaton, a former Water Company superintendent and then Los Angeles mayor began proposing to dam the Owens Valley and canal its water south to Los Angeles residents and San Fernando Valley farms. He won over to his scheme several of Los Angeles' leading entrepreneurs, including newspaper editor Harrison Gray Otis, newspaper circulation king Harry Chandler, and engineer William Mulholland. This coalition would eventually be joined by the talents and fortunes of many of the wealthiest men of Los Angeles and California. The coalition formed a consortium to underwrite and develop the project.

The coalition was not the only group which aspired to build that project. In 1903, Frederick Newell, the Reclamation Bureau's first Commissioner, dispatched a surveying team led by Joseph Lippincott to Owens Valley to investigate its dam potential. The Reclamation Bureau drew up a plan to dam the river and convey the water to Los Angeles.

News of the Reclamation proposal alarmed the consortium, who decided to derail it and develop their own project. Reisner argues that to acquire that water, "Los Angeles employed chicanery, subterfuge, spies, bribery, a campaign of divide-and-conquer, and a strategy of lies to get the water it needed. In the end, it milked the valley bone-dry, impoverishing it, while the water made a number of prominent Los Angeleans very, very rich."[16]

The first step was to bribe Lippincott to scuttle the federal project. Having accomplished that, the coalition began buying up land along the Owens River. Buying land was easy for those wealthy men, but even they lacked the money to finance the vast dam and canal system to bring the water to Los Angeles. To get the finance, they launched a massive public-relations campaign to convince Los Angeles' voters to support the city's takeover of the project. In 1905, a city referendum authorizing the city to fund the project passed by a fifteen-to-one margin.

Another vital step was to get Congress and the president to cancel the moribund Reclamation Bureau project and grant permission for the canals to pass over public lands between Owens Valley and Los Angeles. By 1906, the coalition had succeeded in gaining congressional approval. But would President Roosevelt sign off on the measures? Mulholland traveled to Washington to confer with Roosevelt and his key resource policy advisor Gifford Pinchot. Roosevelt gave his blessing to the project. In July 1907, the Reclamation Bureau officially annulled its own project. In order to assert legal dominion over those lands, Roosevelt then included Owens Valley in the newly created Inyo National Forest.

The aqueduct took six years to build, and extended 223 miles, of which 53 were in tunnels. To supply the workers on this project, Los Angeles had to:

build 120 miles of railroad track, 500 miles of road and

trails, 240 miles of telephone line, and 170 miles of transmission line.... [T]he whole job would be done with
hydroelectricity; therefore, two hydroelectric plants would
be needed on the Owens River to run electric machinery
that a few months earlier had not even been invented.
The city would have to maintain, house, and feed a work
force fluctuating between two thousand and six thousand
for six full years.[17]

On November 5, 1913, the project was completed and
the first waters flowed toward Los Angeles. Five years later,
the amount of irrigated acres in San Fernando Valley had
expanded 2,500 percent from 3,000 to 75,000! Los Angeles'
population shot up from 200,000 in 1905 to 1.2 million by
1925. But southern California's flowering meant the wither-
ing of Owens Valley. By the 1920s, the once thriving farms
and towns there had largely disappeared.

During the 1920s, a drought afflicted Los Angeles so severely that even the aqueduct could not overcome it. San
Fernando Valley's farmers were hard-hit. The consortium
agreed to build another dam in Owens Valley and send even
more water down the aqueduct. Some in Owens Valley resisted the new project and actually dynamited several dams
and aqueducts. Eventually, however, the consortium was able
to crush the resistance and develop its project. By the 1930s,
Los Angeles owned 95 percent of the farmland and 85 percent of the towns in Owens Valley. And the Los Angeles
basin's population soared.

DAM-BUILDING BETWEEN THE WARS

The loss of the Owen's Valley project to the Los Angeles
syndicate was not the Reclamation Service's only defeat. The
Reclamation Service had a rocky start across the West. The
biggest problem was Section 9 of its charter, requiring the
Reclamation Service to provide water to homesteaders anywhere, no matter how dismal the chances of creating a viable irrigation system for them. Senators and Representatives
jockeyed to bring home the pork to their respective states
and districts without regard to a project's viability. The

Reclamation Service plunged into debts and a backlog of projects. In 1910, Congress simultaneously pumped a $20 million loan into the Reclamation Service's coffers to prevent its collapse and eliminated Section 9. Henceforth, Reclamation projects would theoretically be initiated from scientific study rather than political pressure. Unfortunately, congressmen sidestepped this rule by attaching porkbarrel riders to other laws. In 1914, Congress agreed to extend the repayment period for farmers from ten to twenty years. Complaints about competition and overlap between the Reclamation Service and the Corps of Engineers led to the 1920 Water Power Act, which created a Federal Power Commission to oversee all the federal government's various water policies.

By 1924, the newly renamed Reclamation Bureau had started or completed twenty-seven projects across the West. Yet severe problems remained. Sixty percent of farmers were defaulting on their water payments. The value of crops grown on Reclamation lands had dropped from $152 million in 1919 to $83.6 million in 1922. Only 10 percent of all money loaned from the Reclamation Fund had been returned. Although many small-scale farmers could not reap a viable financial return from their efforts, the Bureau's improvements had boosted their lands' value. Many defaulted on their payments and sold out their land to speculators. Once again, the Fund teetered at insolvency's brink.[18] To encourage farmers to stay, Congress extended the repayment period to forty years in 1924. Two years later, Congress passed the Omnibus Adjustment Act, which attempted to curb land speculation by requiring those with excess lands to register them with the government and sell them within a certain period at prices prevailing before the Bureau's improvements. The repayment period was then extended to fifty years.

Political pressure rather than potential economic payback forced the Reclamation Bureau to build hundreds of dams across the West. For example, by 1907 the Reclamation Service had started nine projects on the Missouri River. None of those projects would repay itself within the forty years required by the amended Reclamation Act. Over their first forty years, those nine dams cost taxpayers $55,755,000 to build and operate them but reaped only $17,518,000 from irrigation and hydroelectricity users.[19]

The first vast project that the Bureau tackled was taming the Colorado River. In the 1890s and into the early twentieth century, various entrepreneurs had tried and failed to dam and divert the Colorado. Although California contributed virtually nothing to the Colorado River's flow, its politicians and business elite lobbied Washington for rights and Bureau projects to tame the waters. The other states in the Colorado River watershed – Wyoming, Utah, Colorado, Nevada, New Mexico, and Arizona – united to resist California's effort to monopolize the waters.

In 1922, Commerce Secretary Herbert Hoover sat down with political and business representatives of all seven states to forge a compromise. The negotiations lasted eleven months. In November 1922, the representatives signed the Colorado River Compact, in which the watershed was divided into an Upper Basin of Utah, Wyoming, and Colorado and a Lower Basin of Nevada and California, with parts of New Mexico and Arizona in both basins. Each basin was allocated 7.5 million acre-feet of water. One acre-foot is the amount of water one foot deep that covers an acre of land, or 325,851 gallons. The Upper- and Lower-Basin states would have to divvy up their respective shares among themselves.

Hailed as a masterpiece of compromise, the Compact was severely flawed. The agreement was based on the Service's estimation that the Colorado River's annual flow averaged 17.5 million acre-feet. The Service had overestimated by one million acre-feet, but that flaw would not be evident until each state and Mexico began to demand its full portion. Ironically, California, the state which contributed the least flow to the Colorado, had by far the largest population and agricultural potential of all the Compact states. The Upper-Basin states contributed the most waters to the river, yet had limited populations and agricultural potential. Political and economic power rather than environmental reality divided the Colorado River's waters. The Compact's politics resulted in some bizarre economic tradeoffs. The government subsidized farmers in the Upper-Basin states to grow crops that farmers in the Lower-Basin states were paid not to grow because they could grow them cheaper and more abundantly and thus lower income for farmers everywhere.

The Compact would not take effect until the voters in

each state ratified it. California's government declared it would not submit the Compact for ratification unless the others agreed to build Boulder Canyon Dam and the All-American Canal to divert its waters to southern California's Imperial Valley. California justified the diversion because its population and agricultural potential far outstripped those of the other states combined. The other states rejected California's bid. For six years, the Compact lay in limbo.

Then, in 1928, Congress broke the deadlock by authorizing Boulder Dam and the All-American Canal if six of the seven states ratified the Compact and California limited its annual diversion to 4.4 million acre-feet. All the other states reluctantly agreed to sign except for Arizona, which resented receiving only 2.8 million acre-feet under the allocation agreement. Construction on Boulder Dam began in November 1932. Three years later on September 30, 1935, President Roosevelt dedicated Boulder Dam. The world's largest dam had cost only $50 million. Construction began on the All-American Canal linking the Colorado River and California's Imperial Valley in 1934 and was completed in 1942.

Franklin Roosevelt aspired to be a progressive president like his distant cousin Teddy. His New Deal programs attempted to bring jobs, roads, water, and electricity to impoverished regions of the nation through massive public-works policies. In 1933, Roosevelt got Congress to enact the National Industry Recovery Act (NIRA), which empowered the federal government to promote industries. Under the NIRA, Roosevelt created the National Planning Board to coordinate America's industrial and natural resource policies. The National Planning Board mostly targeted natural resources for development, and thus was renamed the National Resources Board (1934–5), the National Resources Committee (1935–9), and the National Resources Planning Board (1939–43) before Congress abolished it.

The most important of Roosevelt's public-works projects involved water. During Roosevelt's twelve years in office, more than 5,000 dams were completed, a rate of 1.2 per day. Of these new dams, 37 percent were for recreation, 21 percent for stock or farm ponds, 17 percent for water supply, and 12 percent for irrigation.[20] These projects greatly enhanced the powers of the government's two existing dam-building bureaucracies, the Corps and Bureau. Roosevelt created two more, the Tennessee Valley Authority (TVA) in 1933 and the Soil Conservation Service (SCS) within the Agriculture Department in 1935. The Army Corps of Engineers' duties and powers were enhanced by the River and Harbor Act of 1935 and the Flood Control Acts of 1936 and 1944; with its greater money, personnel, and responsibilities for taming rivers, the Corps built ten large dams annually for the next half-century. The Water Facilities Act of 1937 empowered the Agriculture Department's SCS to help farmers cope with a drought, that started in 1934 and persisted for several devastating years, by building dams to control floods and irrigate fields. The Reclamation Project Act of 1939 expanded the Bureau's already generous irrigation subsidies to farmers, including a ten-year grace period and fifty years to repay.

Throughout this era, the Bureau and Corps engaged in an orgy of dam-building that would continue for several generations. By 1936, six vast dam complexes – Hoover in Arizona, Shasta in California, Grand Coulee in Oregon, Bonneville in Wyoming, and Fort Peck in Montana, along with the independent Tennessee Valley Authority in Tennessee – and dozens of smaller projects, were nearing completion. By the end of World War II, the Bureau or Corps had together launched or completed the creation of thirteen huge "main-stem" dams.

The most successful project of them all was not touched by the Bureau or the Corps. For nearly a decade, Senator George W. Norris had fought for the conversion of the Tennessee River Valley into a vast complex of dam, irrigation, flood-control, and hydroelectric projects. Republican presidents and cornucopians in Congress continually rejected his proposal. Upon taking office, Franklin Roosevelt championed it as part of his New Deal. On May 18, 1933, Roosevelt signed into law Norris's bill creating the Tennessee Valley Authority (TVA). Never before had the federal government attempted such a vast project designed to transform an immense region from poverty to prosperity. In doing so, the TVA forged a new relationship between government and business in which they acted as partners for the public good. Government agencies with their technical experts and long-term plans managed markets and private enterprise.

Meanwhile, the Corps and Bureau battled shamelessly to build dams across the country, perhaps nowhere more so than on the Missouri River and its tributaries. The Missouri River is America's largest; its watershed sprawls across one-fifth of the country. Both water bureaucracies lusted for control over the Missouri watershed. The catalyst for the Missouri's conversion from a free to a government-controlled river was the 1943 flood, which caused $50 million in damages and flowed across 2.4 million acres of farmland. In 1944, the Corps unveiled a plan, named after its district engineer Lewis Pick, which included five main-stem dams, six dams on tributaries, and hundreds of miles of levies. The Bureau presented its own plan, named after its regional director Glenn Sloan, which proposed over ninety dams which would irrigate 4.7 million acres. Each bureaucracy wanted to control a TVA-type empire across the Missouri River Basin.

The Roosevelt White House and Congress were torn between whether to choose the Corps or the Bureau plan. On September 21, 1944, Roosevelt attempted to resolve the stand-off by rejecting both plans and by creating an independent Missouri Valley Authority. The possibility inspired the Corps and Bureau to combine to save their common interests. After two intense days of negotiations in Omaha over October 16 and 17, 1944, Corps and Bureau representatives emerged to announce the Pick–Sloan Plan, which simply combined the two plans except for one dam proposed by the Corps. The Pick–Sloan plan called for creating a vast network of 100 dams on the Missouri watershed, including six huge dams, which would control flooding, irrigate 5 million acres of farmland, create hydroelectric power, and promote navigation. Along 750 miles of the Missouri River, the project would drown 1.2 million acres of rich farmland, displace thousands of people, and destroy Indian shrines, burial grounds, and ancient villages. As a local farmer commented on one stretch of "improved" river: "I never could understand why they flooded 20,000 acres of bottomland so they could irrigate 12,000 acres of rocks."[21] Although the $1.9 billion compromise was billed as saving the taxpayers money, it actually cost them $250 million more than if only one of the plans had been chosen. The plan would eventually cost taxpayers $6 billion.[22]

Opposition to the expanding system did not arise until the 1970s in response to a Bureau of Reclamation proposal to build the Garrison and Oahe dams, which would divert waters toward Canada and the James River. Environmentalists rallied against the project's destruction of wildlife refuges while farmers feared that their fields would become salinated and they would be saddled with enormous debts like elsewhere across the West. The United Family Farmers succeeded in getting the Bureau to axe the Oahe Dam proposal in 1982. The Audubon Society led the charge against Garrison Dam, and was able to delay the project. However, in 1986, Congress broke a decade-long moratorium on dam construction by approving the $1.2 billion Garrison Dam project for North Dakota. The amount of acreage targeted for irrigation was reduced from the 1 million of the original proposal in 1960 to 130,000.

What were the benefits and costs of all this dam-building? The benefits were many. The government-led dam-building sharply boosted America's economic development, wealth, living standards, and industrial power. The hydroelectric power produced by these dams brought electricity to huge regions of the United States. The amount of irrigated acres tripled from 2.7 million in 1930 to 7 million in 1960, and farm production rose accordingly. Reisner goes so far as to argue that America's victory in World War II was accelerated by the construction of these dams:

> No one knows exactly how many planes and ships were manufactured with Bonneville and Grand Coulee electricity, but it is safe to say that the war would have been seriously prolonged at the least without the dams.... By 1942 ... we possessed something no other country did: a huge surplus of hydroelectric power. By June of that year, 92 percent of the 900,000 kilowatts of power available from Grand Coulee and Bonneville Dams ... was going to war production.[23]

All of these successes came at an immense cost. With two major and two minor dam-building institutions, the bureaucratic politics of one-upmanship, turf battles, duplication, and wasted resources became endemic. Goals conflicted;

bureaucracies would build dams to manage flooding while simultaneously draining wetlands and channeling rivers, which exacerbated flooding. Irrigation silted the dams which had been created for irrigation. Since the government picked up virtually all of the bill, local governments tended to ask for as much as they could get in terms of water projects, whether they were necessary or not. If they were forced to match federal funds evenly, local governments might be much more judicious in the projects they promote. Vast numbers of farmers, ranchers, construction firms, towns, and cities, along with their political representatives, became increasingly dependent on taxpayers' dollars to survive.

Congress not only tolerated this corruption and waste, it encouraged it through misguided laws. Although both the 1936 Flood Control Act and 1939 Reclamation Act required projects to be approved only if they demonstrated that the benefits exceeded the costs, this "river-basin accounting" criterion was fulfilled largely with creative number-crunching. When Congress abolished the National Resources Board in 1943, it divided the responsibilities for the nation's water policies among several Senate and House committees and subcommittees. In doing so, Congress essentially conceded the nation's water-resource policy to special interests. Not surprisingly, a disproportionate number of Corps of Engineers projects accumulated in the congressional districts of committee and subcommittee Chairs.[24]

POSTWAR WATER POLICIES

If anything, the dam-building became even more frenzied amidst the postwar prosperity. Between 1945 and 1969, an additional 35,000 dams were created, or 3.9 new dams daily. Although only 5 percent of these dams were built and owned by a federal agency, almost all received some public subsidies.[25] Bureaucratic and special-interest politics rather than economic necessity launched many of these projects.

The political backlash to the water lobby and its wasteful, destructive, and self-serving policies built slowly over the postwar era. During the 1950s and 1960s, as dams destroyed one wild river after another, environmentalists increasingly questioned whether the long-term costs of these dams exceeded the benefits. In the half-century since Hetch Hetchy, the environmentalists had steadily built up their strength. In 1905, there were only 7 national and 2 state environmental organizations; by 1955, there were 78 national and 236 state organizations.[26] For the first time, serious political opposition arose to specific Bureau or Corps projects and sometimes derailed them.

A proposed dam at Echo Canyon on the Green River provided a rallying point for environmentalists during the 1950s similar to that of Hetch Hetchy a half-century earlier. In 1915, President Wilson had designated Dinosaur National Monument. In 1938, President Roosevelt enlarged the monument to 200,000 acres, many of which encompassed parts of Echo Canyon. Then, during the late 1940s, the Bureau of Reclamation unveiled plans to build a ten-dam Colorado River Storage Project, of which one dam would drown Echo Canyon. Not just Echo Canyon's fate hung in the balance. Proposed dams threatened other protected national lands including the Grand Canyon, King's Canyon, and Glacier national parks. If the Bureau succeeded in building a dam at Echo Canyon, it would have established a precedent for erecting dams and exploiting any national park or monument.

Ironically, the Echo Canyon dam was proposed because of a lack of demand for those waters. In the 1950s, the increased demand on Colorado River waters caused increasing strains on Compact participants. Of the seven compact states, only California drew its full allotment. By 1952, California was diverting 5.3 million acre-feet annually from the Colorado, far exceeding its entitled allotment of 4.4 million acre-feet. All the other states had various schemes to use their allotment, they simply lacked the population and economy to exploit them. The Reclamation Bureau proposed building an Echo Canyon dam to allow the Upper-Basin states to claim some of their allotted waters.

The Interior Department held the first public hearing on the Echo Canyon dam proposal on April 3, 1950. Advocates for and against the dam presented their arguments. Among other reasons, the Bureau justified the site by claiming that it would hold 165,000 acre-feet of water, more than any alternative site on that stretch of the Green River. The Sierra

Club investigated and discovered that the Bureau's statistics were terribly wrong – at most, the proposed dam would hold 19,000 acre-feet while drowning a beautiful canyon which theoretically was protected by its national monument status. Unmoved by the environmentalist appeals, in June 1950 Interior Secretary Oscar Chapman announced his approval of the project.

The environmentalists then focused their efforts on Congress. Although the Interior Secretary could approve any plan he wanted, only a congressional appropriation could realize it. As in the Hetch Hetchy battle, that over Echo Canyon pitted western mining, farming, logging, grazing, and chamber of commerce interests, and their national and state representatives, against east and west coast environmentalists. The Wilderness Society and Sierra Club led the attack against the proposed dam. America's leading environmentalists made eloquent testimonies before congressional hearings. Wilderness Society Chair Howard Zahniser argued that wilderness is essential for civilization's survival because in its midst "we sense ourselves to be dependent members of an interdependent community of living creatures that together derive their existence from the sun."[27] Sigmund Olsen provided one of the more powerful anti-dam statements when he asked rhetorically whether "in our mad rush to dam every river, chop every tree, utilize all resources to the ultimate limit . . . [we] might not destroy the very things that have made life in America worth cherishing and defending?"[28] To this, the cornucopians could provide no adequate reply.

The environmentalists reinforced their efforts before Congress with a nation-wide public-relations campaign. They produced and distributed pamphlets with titles like "What is Your Stake in Dinosaur?" and "Will You DAM the Scenic Wild Canyons of Our National Park System?" The novelist Wallace Stegner edited the powerful book *This is Dinosaur: Echo Park Country and its Magical Rivers.*[29] Articles championing the anti-dam perspectives appeared in the *New York Times, Reader's Digest, Collier's, Life,* and *Newsweek.* Funding poured into the coffers of environmental organizations.

The Colorado Storage Project reached the Senate floor in April 1955. Oregon Representative Richard Neuberger offered an amendment striking the proposed Echo Canyon dam from the list. A bloc of all but three western senators voted down the amendment. The environmentalists' disappointment dissipated on July 8, 1955, when the House Committee on Interior and Insular Affairs released a report on the Colorado Storage Project which excluded the Echo Canyon dam. The coalition of Colorado basin corporate interests and their governors, senators, and representatives fiercely lobbied the House Committee to restore Echo Canyon dam to the list. Despite these efforts, the Committee released onto the floor a Colorado Storage Project bill which stated specifically that "no dam or reservoir under the authorization of the Act shall be within any National Park or Monument."[30] The House voted in favor of the bill, which then went to conference for a compromise with the Senate version. The final bill approved by both Houses included the sentence forbidding dams in any national park or monument. President Eisenhower signed the bill into law on April 11, 1956.

The Echo Canyon battle was the environmentalists' greatest victory to date. In their fight against the proposed dam, the environmentalists used virtually every means available including direct lobbying of key politicians and bureaucrats, fundraising and contributions, barrages of books, articles, and editorials across the mass media. The momentum gained by this victory carried environmentalists into a range of ambitious battles in the decades ahead.

But environmentalists paid a terrible price for their victory. While they fought and won the battle for Echo Canyon between 1950 and 1956, they abandoned the struggle for an even more spectacular region that was not protected as a national park or monument – Glen Canyon. The Bureau eventually agreed to drop its proposed dam at Echo Canyon only in return for the Sierra Club agreeing not to challenge a different dam down the Colorado River at Glen Canyon. It was a Faustian bargain. After tremendous soul-searching, the Sierra Club eventually made it. In 1963, the National Reclamation Bureau completed its Glen Canyon dam as part of the Colorado River Storage Project. The following year, David Brower wrote the commentary and Eliot Porter took the photographs for the book *The Place No One*

Knew: Glen Canyon on the Colorado. In the book, Brower admitted that "Glen Canyon died in 1963 and I was partially
responsible for its needless death."[31]

The chagrin over losing Glen Canyon helped galvanize
opposition to yet another proposed dam project. Emerging
from seven years of battle over wilderness protection and
Echo Canyon, environmentalists immediately found themselves embroiled in yet another struggle. A clause in the
1919 law creating Grand Canyon National Park enpowered
the Interior Secretary to allow "reclamation projects." On
January 21, 1964, Interior Secretary Stewart Udall published
his Pacific Southwest Water Plan, which included a network
of new dams and irrigation projects throughout the region,
including one at Marble Gorge which would flood forty miles
of Grand Canyon National Monument, and one at Bridge
Canyon which would flood thirteen miles of Grand Canyon
National Park.

Although environmentalists had skirmished against the
project for several years, the full-fledged battle to stop the
proposed Grand Canyon dams commenced with a full-page
advertisement in the *New York Times* on June 9, 1966, entitled, "Now only You can Save the Grand Canyon from Being Flooded . . . For Profit." Later that summer, another
advertisement, which appeared in numerous newspapers and
magazines, was pointedly titled, "Should We Also Flood the
Sistine Chapel so Tourists Can Get Nearer the Ceiling,"
thereby countering arguments by dam advocates that a reservoir would allow easier access to the canyon for boaters
and fishermen.

The Johnson Administration played hardball against the
environmentalists. The day after the anti-dam *New York Times*
advertisement, the Internal Revenue Service informed the
Sierra Club's shocked leadership that it had lost the organization's tax-exempt status for donations. The government
harassment backfired. Although Johnson's action financially
hurt the Sierra Club, the Club continued to speak out.
National environmental organizations, led by the Sierra Club,
launched a mass letter-writing campaign against the dams.
When criticized for standing in the way of progress, Zahniser
replied, "We are not fighting progress, we are making it."[32]
The Sierra Club's mass media campaign successfully rallied

public opinion against the dam projects. Sierra Club membership trippled from 39,000 in June 1966 to 135,000 in 1971. Other prominent voices took up the cry, including such national magazines as *Life* and even the highly conservative *Reader's Digest.*

Faced with overwhelming public animosity toward the proposed dams, the Johnson Administration finally threw in the towel. On February 1, 1967, Interior Secretary Udall announced that the projects would be deleted from the Pacific Southwest Water Plan. The plan's bill passed both congressional Houses that year without including the proposed Grand Canyon dams. The following year, on July 31, 1968, a Congressional conference produced the Colorado River Basin Project Act, which explicitly forbade any Colorado River dams between the Hoover and Glen Canyon dams. President Johnson not only signed that bill into law on September 30, 1968, but within days, on October 2, 1968, Johnson signed the National Wild and Scenic Rivers Act, which created a protection system similar to that for wilderness. The Johnson Administration had seemingly made a stunning political and philosophical conversion.

Yet, there was a catch to the Colorado River Basin Project Act. While excluding any Grand Canyon dams, the law allocated $1 billion for five new projects throughout the region. Within two decades, the project's costs had risen to $5 billion, making it by far the most expensive watershed development project yet authorized. Throughout the 1950s and 1960s, conflict among the Colorado River Compact participants had grown along with the region's population and economy. Arizona went so far as to sue California for diverting waters from its quota. The case appeared before the Supreme Court. In *Arizona* v. *California,* the Court ruled in 1963 that California had illegally diverted over 600,000 acre-feet of Arizona's allocated waters and would have to give it back. Other than California, no state had more ambitious plans for its portion than Arizona. Since 1912 when he first went to Washington, Arizona Representative Carl Hayden had lobbied for the Central Arizona Project, which would pump Colorado River water into the households of Tuscon and Phoenix, and desert valleys across central Arizona to convert them to farmland. When Congress finally authorized the Central Arizona Project, Hayden triumphantly retired at the age of 92.

Nonetheless, the 1968 Colorado River Basin Project Act proved to be a watershed in water policy. Before then, the water lobby enjoyed the policy initiative, and gained most of what it demanded. Ever since then, the water lobby has been on the defensive. The reasons for this power shift are fairly clear. Most of the viable dam sites have been either developed or protected. Dam-building costs soared along with an array of interrelated problems such as crime, drug abuse, homelessness, poverty, and unwed mothers, while America's growth rate and prosperity faltered. The United States had fewer financial resources with which to address ever worsening socioeconomic crises.

Congress imposed a decade-long moratorium on new dam construction starting in 1976. In those ten years, the Corps construction budget shrank 34 percent and its personnel dropped by 15 percent, while the Bureau's construction budget was cut 28 percent and its personnel fell 10 percent. In 1984, for the first time, maintenance exceeded construction in both bureacracies' budgets. Although Congress voted for the Garrison Dam project in 1986, no other major projects have been approved since.[33]

Nonetheless, even through the present, the political instincts of presidents lead them to succumb to the water lobby's enormous power. Conservationist Lyndon Johnson only conceded to the environmentalists after years of battle. Until President Jimmy Carter took office, no president has ever dared to challenge the water lobby directly. Although he came from a state whose districts benefited from water projects, Carter was determined to cut out wasteful porkbarrel spending and limit water policy to essential projects. Carter had promised to balance the budget by the end of his first term. Water projects were an obvious target for cuts.

The White House drew up a "hit list" of nineteen water projects that it would cull from the federal budget. Politically, Carter's strategy was akin to Don Quixote tilting at windmills. All of the key senators and representatives chairing key committees had their own special projects for their states and districts. In throwing down the gauntlet to those projects, Carter jeopardized his entire legislative agenda, which could be bottled up in committee.

Rather than retreat and compromise, Carter reacted to the initial congressional uproar by expanding the hit list to eighty projects! On June 13, 1977, the House Appropriations Committee sent to the floor a bill which appropriated funds for all but one of the water projects on Carter's hit list. Under the threat of a Carter veto, the bill passed the House and Senate. But when the bill appeared before Carter, he reluctantly signed it. Carter had thus succeeded in alienating his opponents and allies alike on the issue.

Similar battles were fought the following year. This time, however, Carter vetoed the pork-laden appropriations bill when it appeared on his desk. The President was aided by the California popularist Howard Jarvis's campaign to cut taxes and spending. On the morning of October 5, 1978, when the override vote was scheduled, the *Washington Post* and *New York Times* carried full-page advertisements by Jarvis entitled, "The Public Works Appropriations Bill is the Big Tax, Big Government, Big Spending, Big Waste Bill of the Year." Congress failed to override the veto.

Carter's campaign against the water lobby had received another boost earlier in 1978 from a different source, the Supreme Court. In June 1978, the Supreme Court ruled that the proposed Tellico Dam on the Tennessee River violated the Endangered Species Act and thus should be stopped. At stake was the snail darter, which had been listed as endangered. The proposed $100 million Tellico Dam was a perfect example of pork-barrel politics. It would have produced only 23 megawatts of electricity, only 2 percent of the capacity of the nuclear and coal plants the TVA was producing elsewhere, and it provided no additional flood control and few recreational benefits. Unfortunately, if the Supreme Court's ruling had been heeded, it would have saved the taxpayers few dollars; the dam was 90 percent complete when the ruling was handed down.[34]

In fact, the water lobby was unfazed by the Supreme Court ruling. To a bill going before the House of Representatives, they attached a rider which allocated all funds necessary to complete the Tellico Dam and absolved the dam from all laws. The House and Senate passed the bill with the rider attached. Everyone assumed that Carter would veto the bill. But Carter's Panama Canal Treaty would soon be debated and voted on by the Senate. The head count revealed a very close vote; one he would lose if he vetoed the bill. Carter signed it.

It was a return to water politics as usual under Ronald Reagan. Like most westerners, Reagan at once deplored government subsidies yet eagerly grabbed what he could from the system. And like most westerners, he was oblivious to his own hypocrisy. His presidential policies were just as contradictory. Initially, the Reagan White House spoke of cost-sharing with the states and cutting back the number and expense of dam projects. In fact, Reagan initially proposed that the states pay 33 percent of the costs compared with only 10 percent that Carter had demanded. Then, like his predecessor, Reagan ran into the water lobby's congressional wall. Reagan threatened to veto the 1984 $20 billion water appropriations bill, which funded more than 300 projects. Like Carter, he ended up signing it.

In 1986, the federal government finally succeeded in imposing a relatively equitable cost-sharing formula for water projects that the Corps of Engineers shares with state and local governments. The Corps now requires local governments to supply 100 percent of the costs for the construction, operation, and maintenance of hydropower for municipal and industrial uses; between 25 and 50 percent of the construction costs and 100 percent of the operation and maintenance costs for flood control; and 25 percent of all costs for water-quality and fish and wildlife promotion.[35] The Bureau of Reclamation, however, remains opposed to similar cost-sharing schemes for its projects because it fears losing potential clients and thus projects and prestige.

CONTEMPORARY BATTLES

The age of dam-building is over. Virtually any river spot that could be dammed has been. The rest are protected by various federal laws. Even if those protected stretches of river were vulnerable, the water lobby would have difficulty finding funds in the present age of cost-cutting. Yet, the war for water will continue as long as regions continue to experience population and economic growth amidst fixed water supplies.

To varying degrees each of the states has its own water-politics issues, nowhere more so than California with the nation's largest state population. The "California dream" of endless sunshine, suburbs, and opportunities, remains an irresistible magnet for many around the world. In one decade alone, from 1980 to 1990, California's population rose from 23 million to 31 million. If California were a country, its economy would be the world's seventh largest. That huge and ever-growing population and economy lives mostly on a desert. No desert of the world is more productive. California produces one-third of the nation's food. Those huge farms in the Central, Imperial, and Napa valleys and elsewhere are exremely thirsty – they drain 81 percent of all water pumped from the state's 1,190 reservoirs. The success of California's agribusiness also depends on massive injections of pesticides and herbicides – more than 30 percent of all consumed in the United States.

Despite its productivity and importance to the nation's dinner tables, agribusiness is a relatively small part of California's diverse economy – in 1992, only $18 billion of a $350 billion economy. And the composition of the state's agribusiness is puzzling considering that California is mostly semi-desert. Among California's most important crops are water-intensive crops like alfalfa, cotton, and rice. None of these crops would be possible without massive federal and state subsidies and irrigation works.

What is the source for all that water which spills across California's cotton fields, trimmed lawns, and putting greens? Over the past century, most of the state's aquifers have been pumped dry. For sustenance, hydrologists have dammed and diverted the rivers pouring through the canyons of the state's spine, from the Sierra Mountains, or taken waters from the Colorado River.

With the demand for water ever rising and the supply relatively stable, battles over its ownership have inflicted enormous economic, political, and environmental carnage. Water wars have pitted farmers against cities and suburbs, northern against southern California, valley against valley,

Washington against Sacramento, bureaucracies against each other, and environmentalists against nearly everyone.

The federal government's premier water agencies – the Bureau of Reclamation and Corps of Engineers – have played leading roles in transforming the state from a desert supporting at most several hundred thousand people to one rising toward 40 million. During the 1930s, the Bureau's Central Valley Project converted that region of semi-desert and wetlands into the world's most productive farmland.

Although the Bureau's legal mandate is to supply irrigation only to poor farmers with no more than 160 acres of land, in the Central Valley, as elsewhere, huge landowners found plenty of ways around those restrictions. Land titles to vast estates were divided up in "paper farms" among relatives and friends, sometimes fictitious. Throughout the twentieth century, the Bureau prosecuted only one case of fraudulent use of its water in the Central Valley. In 1982, the agribusiness lobby pressured Congress to raise the maximum acreage allowance for access to Bureau water from 160 acres to 960 acres. By 1985, farmers had repaid only $50 million of the $931 million of accumulated loans for access to the Central Valley System.[36] Rather than raise water rates, the Bureau continued to subsidize agribusiness by wringing more appropriations from Congress.

Over the decades, the Central Valley's development, which made a handful of corporate farmers very rich, exacted an ever harsher tribute from the environment. In 1983, media reports of massive waterfowl die-offs at the Kesterson National Wildlife Refuge in California's San Joaquin Valley sparked a reappraisal of water policy toward the region. Scientists soon determined that the chemical selenium had wrought the devastation, and the chemical had seeped into the wildlife refuge by the San Luis Drain, a Bureau of Reclamation irrigation system which watered much of the southern valley.

Cowed by the negative publicity, Interior Secretary Donald Hodel announced that the San Luis Drain would be diverted by June 30, 1986. The deadline was reached but the political pressure had built on the Interior Department to reorient the Bureau of Reclamation's mission. In 1987, the Interior Department announced that henceforth the Bureau of Reclamation would concentrate on managing water resources rather than constructing new, expensive systems. The policy shift represented a power shift from small numbers of farmers and ranchers to urban dwellers and environmentalists.

The environmental disaster in Kesterson is a well-publicized example of a widespread phenomenon across the West. In many regions, the soils were once the bottom of vast seas. Over tens of millions of years, sea life died and merged with the soils to create a thick, hard clay. After the seas receded, more porous and richer soils built up upon that clay base. But that surface soil is quite shallow, in many places only a few feet thick. As farmers irrigate the soil, the water percolates down, picking up natural salts as it goes, and becomes trapped or "perched" above the clay layer. Thus, over time, the surface soil becomes salinated from that clay layer all the way to the surface, rendering once-productive soil lifeless. The price tag for solving this drainage problem for the Central Valley alone is estimated to be between $4 and $5 billion.

For nearly fifteen years, another battle in California has been waged over the fate of Mono Lake. Mono Lake is California's second largest body of fresh water, and a beautiful jewel within the Great Basin high desert. As its population and economy expanded, southern California's tentacles of canals and reservoirs crept further north along both sides of the Sierras. By the 1940s, Los Angeles's Department of Water and Power (DWP) demanded and received state permission to divert the flow from four of the five streams feeding Lake Mono. Los Angeles eventually received about 15 percent of its total water from Mono Lake. Ever since then, Los Angeles has been steadily killing Mono Lake. Five decades of diversion dropped the water level to 45 feet below its natural level and raised the salinity level just as steadily. Within two decades, the water will be too salty to use.

Conservationists and environmentalists alike have united to stop Mono Lake's destruction. In 1983, the National Audubon Society sued Los Angeles for the degradation caused by the diversion of Lake Mono's waters. Subsequent court battles were inconclusive until 1989 when the California Supreme Court saved Mono Lake by upholding a ruling by the state Water Resources Control Board directive that Los Angeles's diversion of Mono Lake's waters violated the fish and game code. The Court issued an injunction against further diversions until Mono Lake rose two feet above its present level. The state legislature then established an Environmental Water Fund, with $36 million earmarked to help Los Angeles develop alternative sources.

Unless it finds new sources, by 2010 southern California will only be able to supply 70 percent of its water needs.[37] The result could be exorbitant prices for meager water rations. But the consequences of Los Angeles finding alternative water sources could be even worse. Unlimited population growth will accelerate the domino effect of unquenchable water demands degrading a succession of ecosystems. So far, northern Californian political interests have limited those advances.

As if huge aqueducts draining the Colorado River, Owens Valley, and Lake Mono were not enough, southern Californians have used every political, economic, legal, and extralegal tactic possible to capture still more distant sources. Throughout the late 1950s into the 1960s, the Metropolitan Water District of Southern California (the Met) proposed the California Water Plan, which coveted the far waters of the Feather River in the northern Sierra Mountains, and Klamath River meandering through parts of Oregon and northern California. According to the $1.75 billion plan, those rivers would be tamed with huge dams and diverted south through aqueducts hundreds of miles long which would, along the way, cross earthquake faults and the Techahapi Mountains. Early northern resistance caused the Met to drop linking the Klamath River with their scheme, but they insisted on rights to the Feather River. All those monied interests backing the Met plan convinced Governor Pat Brown to champion the project. In 1960, a state bond issue of $1.75 billion which would finance the scheme passed a state referendum by 174,000 votes.

Work began on the project the following year and would continue for nearly two more decades through governors Ronald Reagan and Jerry Brown. The price soared throughout these years. Yet the project's backers could always count on the state legislature, which was dominated by agribusiness and southern Californian interests, to bail it out. Over time, however, increasing numbers of Californians wearied of the project's expense and environmental damage. Northern Californians were increasingly aware that water was power; in allowing the transfer of their water to the south, they were simultaneously transferring jobs, wealth, and votes, thus building up their rival region's power at their own expense. It just did not make political or economic sense for northern Californians, nor did it make environmental sense for increasing numbers of people from across the state. When a bond issue to complete the Peripheral Canal linking north and south came before voters in 1982, it was defeated by nearly a two-to-one margin. To date, the uncompleted project remains a monument to water politics.

Rather than build immensely expensive new dams and canals far to the north, much of southern California's expanding water needs could be met by more efficient use of the waters it now receives. When it is completed, at a cost of $3.6 billion, the Central Arizona Project and the Colorado River Aqueduct linking it to the Colorado River will divert 650,000 acre-feet annually, which is now consumed by 1.5 million southern Californians. Conservation measures such as lining the canals and ditches with cement would reduce the amount of water lost and salts acquired from the soil. For example, the Imperial Valley alone drains 2.5 million acre-feet annually from the Colorado River. Lining the Imperial Valley's plumbing could save an estimated 440,000 acre-feet annually, enough to supply water to 1.2 million people.[38]

Contemporary water wars are not limited to California. Damming the Columbia River has created great benefits for many and imposed enormous costs on others. For Indian tribes in the Columbia River basin, the salmon was as important to their livelihood as buffalo had been to tribes on the Great Plains. The salmon catch at the time of Lewis and Clark was estimated at 18 million pounds; in 1980 it was only 6.8 million pounds.[39] A treaty of 1855 between the US government and the Nez Perce, Warm Springs, Umatilla, and Yakima tribes in the central plateau guaranteed the latter's fishing rights on the Columbia River.

There was no trouble until the mid-twentieth century when each new dam on the Columbia and its tributaries reduced the salmon catch for native and other Americans who depended upon it for their livelihood. The Warm Springs Indians sued for damages from the devastation of their salmon fishery. In 1969, US District Court Judge Robert Belloni ruled in *US* v. *Oregon (Belloni)* that the tribes were "entitled to a fair share of the fish produced by the Columbia River system."[40] The ruling was reinforced in a 1974 decision in *US* v. *Washington (Boldt)*, which allowed Indians to catch up to half the state's off-reservation salmon yield. In 1977, the treaty tribes created the Columbia River Inter-tribal Fish Commission (CRITRC) to lobby government. In alliance with environmental groups, their efforts were instrumental in pressuring Congress to pass three laws in 1980: the Northwest Power Planning Act, which mandates that salmon fisheries be given equal weight with hydroelectricity in the Columbia River basin; the Salmon and Steelhead Conservation and Enhancement Act; and the Pacific Northwest Electric Power Planning and Conservation Act, which reordered the local utility's (Bonneville Power Administration) policies from more dam construction to enhanced conservation and efficiency.

The Act created a Fish Passage Center to allow more fish to bypass the dams during their annual migrations. The dams regularly killed 15 percent of migrating fish and up to 90 percent during drought years. Between 1960 and 1980, the dams killed an estimated 44 million salmon and steelhead worth $6.5 billion.[41] The installation of fish ladders helped more salmon survive the gauntlet of turbines and spillways along the Columbia River.

But the battle for the Columbia fisheries was not over. In 1983, a federal judge ordered Oregon and Washington to cooperate on a long-range management plan for the Columbia River basin fishery. In 1985, the upstream tribes the Shoshone and Bannock sued in federal court for a portion of the catch. Their legal basis was a treaty of 1868 with the US government which guaranteed them access to their traditional hunting and fishing grounds. Judge Edwar Leavy ruled that the two Upper-Basin tribes and Idaho also be admitted to the pact. Into the 1990s, the salmon catch continued to dwindle despite this spate of laws, agreements, and legal rulings.

America's water wars have not only pitted state against state and region against region, but at times, the United

States against both its neighbors. The initial Colorado River Compact left out Mexico altogether. Since the water allocation was based on an overestimation of the river's flow, the amount Mexico received diminished steadily as the seven states tapped into their quotas. By the early 1940s, Mexican diplomats were complaining bitterly about their "stolen waters." Normally, the northern giant could have ignored its weak neighbor's pleas and complaints. But Washington was eager to enlist as many allies as possible during World War II, so it agreed in 1944 to allocate 1.5 million acre-feet to Mexico, and set up the International Boundary Water Commission to ensure it got there.

Here again, an agreement that initially seemed satisfactory to all parties proved flawed over the long term. The treaty said nothing about water quality. As human activities upstream proliferated, the water reaching Mexico became increasingly salinated and polluted, and eventually unfit for agricultural or household use. The salt content of water in the Colorado River headwaters is virtually nil; when it reaches Mexico the salt concentration is 2,500 parts per million, enough to destroy a field. Although most of the river's ever growing salinity is natural, an estimated 37 percent is caused by irrigation. After Colorado River waters are diverted to farms often hundreds of miles away, some eventually dribbles back to the river. It is not the same water. En route, the water steadily picks up salt from the soil over which it runs – 4.7 million tons of salt![42] Altogether the salt inflicts an estimated annual damage of $490 million by withering crops and corroding pipes and equipment in the United States and Mexico.[43] The salt damage to crops in Mexico was estimated to be $3.7 million annually across the 500,000 irrigated acres or $370 for the average 50-acre farm.[44]

For years, Mexico protested at the Colorado River's growing salinity, but the United States ignored its pleas. However, on June 15, 1972, the Mexican President addressed the US Congress, declaring that

> Imperial and Mexicali valleys belong both to the same basin, that of the mighty Colorado River; the only possible explanation of the 1944 treaty is that riparian nations should work out solutions based on sincerity and

equity. . . . We can't understand why the same spirit and imagination the United States deploys to unravel intricate problems with his enemies are not used to solve very simple matters with friends.[45]

The arguments worked. Diplomats met and negotiated. Under a 1973 treaty, the United States agreed that the water allocated to Mexico actually be "usable." The following year, Congress attempted to implement the treaty by passing the Colorado River Basin Salinity Control Act, whose centerpiece was a proposed desalting plant at Yuma, Arizona.

It would have been difficult to find a more economically costly way to lower the Colorado River's salinity. Farmers upstream pay only $3.50 per acre-foot for waters that may eventually return salt-laden to the river. The desalting plant would cost $210 million to build, and through reverse osmosis would produce annually 67,000 acre-feet of water with 295 parts per million of salt at a cost of $333 per acre-foot.[46] That bill does not include a $250 million project to line canals that lead to 70,000 acres of farmland with cement, which might reduce 143,000 tons of salt that leach from the waters, and a much more cost-effective $35 million project to line ditches and improve farming practices, which might prevent a further 230,000 tons of salt from mixing with the waters. That total raises the amount spent to over $3,000 an acre, far above that farmland's market value.[47]

It would have been far cheaper for the government to simply buy out the most inefficient farmers being subsidized by Colorado River water and allow those waters to flow unimpeded to Mexico. But no state, no matter how fervently its residents pontificate about getting the government off their backs, the evils of welfare mothers, and virtues of states' rights and rugged individualism, would give up any federal subsidies. So America's taxpayers forked out hundreds of millions rather than tens of millions of dollars to fulfill their country's legal and moral obligation to Mexico. Today, the Colorado River dwindles to mud flats as far as twenty miles from the sea.

LEGACY

Water politics was traditionally shaped by an iron triangle of politicians, bureaucrats, and special interests. Reisner offers a succinct summary of the politics behind the federal water projects:

> the dams created jobs (how efficiently is another matter) and made the unions happy; they enriched the engineering and contracting firms, from giants like Bechtel and Parsons to small-time cement pourers in Sioux Falls, and made them happy; they subsidized the irrigation farmers and made them happy; they gave free flood protection to the real estate developers who ran the booming cities of the West out of their pockets and made them happy; and as a result of all this, the politicians were reelected, which made them happy. No one lost except the nation at large.[48]

And just what has been lost? Throughout the twentieth century, Washington has squandered tens of billions of dollars on projects with little or no economic payback, which have destroyed magnificent canyons and fragile ecosystems, and ultimately poisoned with salts and heavy metals the very fields that it tried to irrigate. Reisner argues that the cost "was a vandalization of both our natural heritage and our economic future, and the reckoning has not even begun."[49]

The much vaunted independence of the West's farmers, ranchers, miners, loggers, and others is a cultural myth. The reality is that no one is more dependent on government handouts to survive than the West's traditional residents. The Bureau of Reclamation is to the West's farmers and ranchers what the Department of Health and Welfare is to unemployed, single mothers. Although they represent less than 5 percent of the West's population, ranchers and farmers receive water at a fraction of its market value, low-interest loans, free technical advice, cheap access to public lands, and elaborate irrigation systems – all subsidized at the taxpayers' expense. To pile irony upon irony, it seems federal water policy not only enables but encourages those with the least naturally available water to use the most:

in a wet state like Minnesota, the average family of four consumes only 0.44 acre-feet of treated water in a year, and in Oregon it's all of 0.34 acre-feet. But in dry Colorado, it's 0.93 acre-feet, arid Wyoming, 0.96 acre-feet, thirsty Arizona, 0.99; desert Nevada, 1.12; and parched Utah, 2.46.[50]

Like an addictive drug, water projects make the politicians as dependent as the farmers, households, and others. The ability of a politician to remain in Congress depends on many things, of which perhaps the most important is to bring federal projects and money back to his district and state. Congressional logrolling over water projects is rampant; "You support my dam project and I'll support yours," seems to be the prevailing ethic.[51]

The rivalry between the Corps of Engineers and the Reclamation Bureau has contributed to much of the economic waste, corruption, and environmental devastation. With their overlapping duties, the logic of bureaucratic politics drives each agency to compete fiercely for as much money, employees, projects, and prestige as it can wring from Congress. Reisner says it is impossible to "know how many ill-conceived water projects were built by the Bureau and the Corps simply because the one agency thought the other would build it first."[52]

Although both the Bureau and Corps are beholden to presidential directives and congressional appropriations, in fact both bureaucracies are virtual empires unto themselves. As Reisner put it,

> most presidents have not been able to control it any better than they could control the weather or the press. . . . Jimmy Carter lost the momentum of his presidency, and a chance at a second term, through a hapless effort to bring the Bureau and the Corps of Engineers under control. Eisenhower, Johnson, Nixon, and Ford all tried to dump or delay a number of projects the Bureau and Corps wanted to build, and failed in almost every case. Congress simply tossed the projects into omnibus public-works bills which would have required that the president veto anything from important flood-control projects to fish hatcheries to job programs in order to get rid of some misbegotten dams.[53]

Why did so many Bureau and Corps projects fail miserably to fulfill their grandiose economic projections? Former Bureau Commissioner Bill Dominy could have been speaking for either bureaucracy when he admitted that:

> Reclamation made some bad mistakes – we miscalculated water availability, we laid out canals that didn't work right, we had drainage problems we should have anticipated. Soil, altitude, crop prices, markets – they all made a difference. On top of that there were no requirements . . . any idiot [could] get into a Reclamation project. You didn't have to demonstrate that you had capital, farming skills, anything. Any fool could sign up and get on a Reclamation farm and use whatever intelligence he had cheating the government. When the projects began to go bankrupt [they] were afraid to expose them. They covered the goddamn things up and that got us in a hell of a lot of trouble with Congress. We were illegally delivering water all over the place. Payments were way in arrears and no one was doing a damn thing about it. I think we were violating the law at least as often as we were not violating it.[54]

There are several reasons for the decline of these bureaucracies. First, there are just not that many canyons left to plug; the costs of managing a project are far less than building it. Second, after the national debt quadrupled between 1981 and 1993, there is simply not enough money left in the public till to finance any more big projects. Third, people today have a much more sophisticated understanding of the economic and environmental costs of those vast projects. Finally, shifting coalitions of those whose interests are adversely affected by local projects, whose ranks might include urbanites, suburbanites, environmentalists, and even certain farmers and economists, have arisen to challenge the water lobby's power monopoly.

Meanwhile, the Environmental Protection Agency (EPA) has increasingly become a major player in water policy. The 1968 Wild and Scenic Rivers Act and 1973 Endangered Species Act arm the EPA with considerable powers to impede economically costly and environmentally destructive projects. By January 1989, 119 rivers were designated for protection under the Wild and Scenic Act and hundreds more were being evaluated for inclusion. In 1989, the EPA temporarily halted the proposed construction of the Two Forks Dam on the South Platte River, pending a review. By November 1990 the review was complete; EPA head William Reilly vetoed the project as environmentally destructive and economically wasteful.

The golden era of plumbing the country with dams, canals, and irrigation has long passed. Few rivers continue to run free, and most of those are now protected by environmental laws. The environmental and economic costs of all those dam and irrigation projects is obvious to increasing numbers of interest groups, common citizens, and even engineers who dream of participating in such schemes.

All of those thousands of dams, huge and small alike, are steadily silting up. Their lifetimes vary, but obviously their usefulness as reservoirs and hydroelectric plants diminish with their holding capacity. Siltation is an insidious problem that afflicts all dams. Some dams are so poorly constructed that they are timebombs waiting to crumble. On June 5, 1976, the 310-million-gallon earthen Teton Dam collapsed, and the flood killed eleven people and damaged $1.17 billion in property. And then there is the ever-worsening problem of the salinization of increasing areas of once productive farmland. So, what then will be the fate of all the water and electricity users currently dependent on those dams?

Having been the major contributors to the troubled legacies behind most of the nation's dam systems, the Bureau and Corps are extending their missions to cleaning up the disasters. In the decades ahead, both the Bureau and Corps will continue to manage existing projects and attempt to reverse the enormous environmental damage unleashed by different projects. For example, the Corps transformed the Everglades of south Florida into a checker-board of agribusiness empires. While the Corps' water system temporarily boosted the nation's food supply and enriched some agribusiness corporations, it devastated the region's ecology and poisoned its water. Today, the Corps is trying to "meander" rivers flowing south from Lake Okechobee that it had formerly straightened in the name of progress. In the future, the Bureau and Corps may end up systematically tearing down one silted dam after another that they had once so proudly built.

That will be the future for all natural resource policies. To varying extents, generations to come will pour hundreds of billions of dollars into cleaning up the environmental and economic disasters created by past policies. But formulating and implementing those restoration projects for the nation's soil, forests, grasslands, canyons, watersheds, aquifers, and wildlife will not be easy. Special interests like ranchers, farmers, loggers, miners, chemical makers, and so on will fight every step of the way to cling to their taxpayer-financed handouts or corporate welfare. Will national environmental and conservationist interests eventually prevail over the special cornucopian interests? Only time will tell.

5 Natural Resource Policy into the Twenty-first Century

Cornucopian values dominated America's first two and a half centuries. Throughout that time, Americans viewed stumps, mine shafts, canals, factory smokestacks, and dams as symbols of progress. Nature's bounty was useless beyond its conversion into products to serve mankind's material needs. And that conversion best takes place if everyone is free to pursue their narrow self-interests; in helping themselves, people inadvertently help others. Slogans such as "a rising (economic) tide lifts all boats," the "magic of the market-place," "live today, for tomorrow ye shall die," and "the public be damned!" remain central to the cornucopian creed.

Cornucopianism is intellectually and emotionally rooted in three perspectives – a literal interpretation of the Biblical demand that humans "multiply and subdue the earth," a classical economic belief in "market magic," and the realities and mythologies that emerged as Americans struggled to survive amidst wilderness and convert it to civilization. The religious-like intensity with which cornucopians saw and exploited natural resources is thoroughly understandable in the context of early American history. Environmental historian Rod Nash vividly explains the early-day virulence of cornucopianism:

Safety and comfort, even necessities like food and shelter, depended on overcoming the wild environment. For the first Americans, as for Medieval Europeans, the forest's darkness hid savage men, wild beasts, and still stranger creatures of the imagination. In addition, civilized man faced the danger of succumbing to the wilderness of his surroundings and reverting to savagery himself. The pioneer, in short, lived too close to wilderness to appreciate it.[1]

Freedom is a relative rather than an absolute reality. As someone once put it, "Your freedom to swing your fist stops an inch from my nose." In the late nineteenth century, increasing numbers of prominent people began arguing that the freedom to exploit America's natural resources was steadily diminishing the freedom of future generations to enjoy those same material and aesthetic riches. Conservationists and environmentalists share the belief that natural resources should be used on a "sustained yield" basis. Natural resources such as forests, grasslands, soil, water, and air are renewable only if they are exploited at a rate that nature can replenish them. And as for those resources that are non-renewable, such as ores and fossil fuels, they should be exploited in ways that do not harm other natural resources like water and air. Conservation, energy efficiency, and substitutes can stretch out the use of those non-renewable resources with the inevitable day when they will run out.

Of course, any natural resource can be exhausted if there is too much demand for its use. Contrary to the cornucopian belief that all problems are temporary and can be solved by "market magic," conservationists and environmentalists alike would agree that the United States and the world face enormous, worsening, and interrelated environmental crises such as over-population, the depletion of the ozone layer, global warming, desertification, deforestation, toxic pollution, and species depletion. The world's natural resources – forests, soils, water, air, and others – are threatened by ever-more overwhelming demands for them. The world's current population of 5.6 billion people has already exploited more resources than nature can replenish. The world's population is expected to double within a half century. As Lester Brown put it,

> by many measurements, contemporary society fails to meet this criterion [of sustainability]. . . . Nothing short of fundamental adjustments in population and energy policies will stave off the host of costly changes now unfolding, changes that could overwhelm our long-standing efforts to improve the human condition.[2]

Although allied on most issues, conservationists emphasize managing the sustained yield of natural resources for the long term, while environmentalists seek additionally to set aside large tracts of "nature for nature's sake." They also differ on how far policies and people must change to rein in the world's environmental crises. Throughout the twentieth century, the alliance between conservationists and environmentalists has splintered and re-formed over countless issues.

Then, in the late 1960s, the environmental ranks cleaved between mainstreamers and radicals. This split, too, was over values and strategies. Mainstreamers attempt to achieve their goals through the existing political system. Success at the federal, state, and local levels of American government demands organization, finance, expertise, skills at pressuring politicians, bureaucrats, interest groups, and the media, and a willingness to cut deals. Radicals not only reject any political compromise, but largely reject the political system as hopelessly corrupted by special interests, and they also reject society itself as hopelessly mired in consumerism. While mainstreamers might go to the relevant media, politicians, bureaucrats, and courts to stem, say, the clear-cutting of an old-growth forest, radicals might spike that forest's trees, pour sugar in the gas-tanks of bulldozers, and lay their bodies on logging roads. Mainstreamers embrace Thoreau's idea that human wholeness and development depend on marrying the best of civilization and nature; radicals attempt to achieve those same dreams by living as closely in harmony with nature as possible.

As we have seen, until the late nineteenth century, America's natural resource policies largely consisted of giving away public wealth to private individuals and corporations. Although influential voices from George Perkins Marsh on had championed "conservation," the movement was boosted by its most articulate and influential supporters such as Muir and Underwood during the "progressive era" at the turn of the century. Likewise, environmentalism was rooted in the transcendentalist perspective in literature and art of early that century, but did not become a cohesive, national movement that shaped policy until around the same time as conservationism. Working together, these new movements were able to wrest victories amidst the prevailing cornucopianism – Yellowstone National Park (1872), Adirondack Park (1886), National Forest Reserves (1897), and others. Important as this succession of acts was in slowly reversing public land use policy, most of the first regulatory policies were intended to arrest and hopefully reverse urban rather than rural or wilderness decay – waters were chlorinated, sewage systems built, garbage hauled far away.

Then, during his eight years as president (1901–9), Theodore Roosevelt solidly rooted conservation within natural resource policy by vastly expanding the national forests, parks, wildlife refuges, and monuments. He promoted a greater public awareness on the practical and moral imperatives to use America's natural wealth wisely so that future generations would also benefit. Ironically, it was during Roosevelt's Administration that the growing tensions between many conservationist and environmentalist goals and values resulted in a break between the two. Nonetheless, ever since then both have steadily strengthened in the three-way policy tug-of-war among them and cornucopians.

As a result of those political struggles, with the passage of the 1964 Wilderness Act, the hodgepodge of public-land laws had come to designate five categories of use. For a minimal fee, ranchers can graze their livestock on national "grasslands" and loggers can clear-cut "national forests." "National wildlife refuges" are ecosystems supposedly immune from economic exploitation, yet hunting, fishing, mining, and logging are allowed in many. "National Parks" are largely for recreational use, although business concessions and infrastructure are included. "Wilderness" areas theoretically are immune to any development but can be grazed and mined and hunted.

There are as many agencies responsible for managing the 658 million acres of public lands as there are designated uses. With 270 million acres, the Bureau of Land Management (BLM) is the largest, followed by the Forest Service (191 million acres), US Fish and Wildlife Service (92 million), National Park Service (80 million acres), and Defense Department (25 million acres). To complicate matters further, over 3,000 federal laws, many ambiguous or contradictory, shape natural resource policy. Scores of congressional committees wrote and rewrote these laws – twenty congressional committees have some power over water policy alone.

Not surprisingly, natural resource conservation is often entangled in red tape and bureaucratic turf battles. For example, the "roughly 28,000 square miles of land in the Greater Yellowstone Ecosystem are divided among two national parks and a national parkway, seven national forests in three administrative regions, three states, at least twenty counties, and many thousands of private landowners."[3]

There is a paradox to contemporary natural resource policy – the public overwhelmingly supports environmentalism while the policies mostly cater to cornucopian interests. Most Americans have become environmentalists – at least in awareness if not politically. Recent *New York Times* polls consistently reveal that three out of every four Americans agreed that "protecting the environment is so important that requirements and standards cannot be too high, and continuing environmental improvements must be made regardless of cost."

Despite this shift in national consciousness, cornucopians continue to enjoy immense political power out of all proportion to their number of supporters. Any analysis of American natural resource policy must agree with historian Bernard Shanks that:

> Public lands are the source of the largest welfare program in America. Laws subsidize livestock grazing and timber harvesting, in turn encouraging overgrazing and overcutting. Federally financed and built, water projects obliterate fishing, wildlife habitat, freeflowing rivers, and community resources for the profit of a few people or agribusiness. Under mining and mineral-leasing laws, national mineral resources are transferred into the hands of a few people with negligible benefits to the public. The American people have been losing not only their wealth, but the freedom to use the land.[4]

This was not supposed to happen. According to such laws as the 1960 Multiple Use, Sustained Yield Act, the 1964 Classification and Multiple Use Act, the 1976 National Forest Management Act, and the 1976 Federal Land Policy and Management Act, bureaucracies must make "multiple use" and "sustained yield" the guiding principles for managing most public lands. In other words, the government only allows the exploitation of forest, grass, water, and other resources to the extent that it can be naturally renewed.

Tragically, the bureaucracies charged with managing public lands more often seem to mismanage them. The US Forest Service sets minimum bids at below market rates without calculating its own costs of building logging roads and other services. The BLM is derisively called the Bureau of Livestock and Mining not only because it allows ranchers and miners to exploit public lands for minimal, below-market fees, but also because it allows them to leave devastated ecosystems in their wake. The 1872 Mining Law continues to allow those with registered claims to withdraw as much wealth as they can from public lands without paying a penny in royalties. By 1994, the BLM and its predecessors had leased for mining alone over 30 million acres, a region as large as New York state. The Agriculture Department promotes policies that protect agribusiness at an enormous cost to taxpayers and consumers. As in other industrial sectors, most government handouts for agriculture go to those who least need it – the wealthiest. In 1989, 56 percent of all subsidies went to farmers making net annual profits of over $100,000. A mere 18 percent of the nation's farmers received 90 percent of all direct government payments, while another 18 percent received 10 percent of all handouts, and the remaining 64 percent of farmers got no money at all.[5] The Bureau of Reclamation and Corps of Engineers provide water to ranchers and farmers at rates sometimes one-hundredth that paid by households. On their own land, Americans can draw water freely from streams or aquifers, and then discharge the waste back; the government charges nothing for the privilege even if others depend on that same water source. The EPA cuts deals with polluters which are often little more than a financial slap on the wrist.

What explains cornucopianism's virulence amidst ever-growing environmental awareness and support? Iron triangles are political alliances of interest groups, congressional committees, and government agencies which share common goals and benefits. Politicians need funds and votes to win office; special interest groups in their districts can provide both in return for favorable policies. Bureaucrats meanwhile implement the laws passed by Congress; hoping to gain a lucrative job or other kickbacks, many bureaucrats provide even more favorable benefits to an industry. Thus, each triangle side depends on the others to achieve its goals.

Nearly every natural resource policy is shaped by an iron triangle. Farmers, ranchers, loggers, miners, and others are organized into powerful local and national organizations. By freely distributing financial contributions and through adept use of the mass media, these special interests can easily bottle up in committee or defeat on the floor conservation or environmental bills. Even if a bill is passed, the special interest group can arm-twist bureaucrats into not fully implementing it. In local issues, the average industry group is probably far more powerful than, say, the average neighborhood group protesting the siting of a factory, feed lot, or waste dump.

How do regulatory agencies so often become the handmaidens of special interests? David Davies notes the "malfunction of regulatory bodies" which "go through a life cycle":

> In the early days, the agency was oriented toward the consumer. It strived to serve the citizens whose demands brought it into being. As time passed the public lost interest. Popular apathy allowed the industry being regulated to assert itself. The consumers no longer devoted time and attention to seeing that the regulatory agency served their interests, so the agency ceased to do so. It oriented itself toward the industry. The industry lobbied for pro-industry members to be appointed. It argued its cases at length to persuade the agency members and particularly the staff. Eventually the regulated became the regulator.[6]

Despite its continued entrenched political power, in light of the knowledge about ourselves and the world upon which we live, cornucopianism has become an anachronism. Cornucopians still act on the misguided belief that you can have economic growth or a cleaner environment, but not both. Yet, natural resource policy is not about "owls v. people" as cornucopians assert. Numerous recent studies have clearly proved that improving the environment and developing the economy are interrelated. The World Commission on Environment and Development proclaimed in 1987 that "the 'environment' is where we all live and 'development is what we all do in attempting to improve our lot within that abode."[7] The Commission's very name reveals its sophisticated understanding that environmental and developmental concerns are inseparable.

Cornucopians, for example, object to any energy conservation or efficiency measures. Let free markets prevail, they argue; the faster we consume one type of energy the faster we'll invent a new and better one. In the real world, the more energy efficient an economy, the more dynamic and prosperous it is. A 1992 study by the Union of Concerned Scientists revealed that to lower carbon emissions by 70 percent over the next 40 years would cost the economy $2.7 trillion but generate $5 trillion in additional income, for a net gain of $2.3 trillion.[8] A carbon tax could encourage industries, vehicle owners, and households to invest in energy-efficient technologies. The additional revenues would help government at the local, state, and national levels to deal with other worsening problems. Meanwhile the greater efficiency reduces pollution and its attendant costs. Everyone wins.

In a country whose culture celebrates individualism and liberty, Washington alone owns one-third of the land. The federal government acquired land from the Atlantic to the Pacific and beyond by negotiation and conquest. Over the centuries it has given away most of those public lands, while allowing individuals and corporations to exploit natural resources on most of the remaining land.

Although cornucopians demand that those lands be "privatized," there are excellent reasons to retain those lands for the public good. As Zaslowsky and Watkins put it, "the public land systems compensate for the chief shortcoming of free enterprise – which is its inability to respond to any but its own pressing demands, all of them originating, understandably, in the need to maximize profits as quickly as possible."[9] Theodore Roosevelt put it even more succinctly: "In the past we have admitted the right of the individual to injure the future of the Republic for his present profit. The time has come for change."[10]

Unfortunately, Roosevelt's assertion that the future of American civilization and power depended on abandoning cornucopianism and embracing conservationism and environmentalism remains unheeded. Nonetheless, conservationists and environmentalists have much to cheer about in their impact on natural resource policy. Much of their respective agendas have been achieved, especially where they overlap. For over a century they have managed to set the exploitation of most of the country's natural resources on a sustainable basis and preserve many of America's natural wonders.

Yet, all those efforts may have simply slowed rather than reversed America's environmental decay. The National Biological Survey concluded in 1995 that every one of the 126 ecosystems identified across the United States were "imperiled," with 58 "endangered" (having declined by 85–98 percent of its original range) and 38 others "threatened" (having lost from 70 to 84 percent). One of the participants, biologist Dr Reed F. Noss, pointed out that, "We're not just losing single species, we're losing entire assemblages of species and their habitats."[11]

So, what of the future? Throughout much of American history, the population problem was a case of "too few rather than too many." But this is no longer the situation. Today, like the rest of the world, the United States faces a worsening crisis of too many people demanding too many natural resources. While the United States remains among the least crowded of the industrial democracies, the populations of increasing numbers of cities and entire regions are grinding against the surrounding lands' ability to sustain them. The problem is acute in the nation's more arid regions. Yet, to varying extents, all metropolitan areas struggle with the problem of living well within their respective environmental carrying-capacities as landfills close, water tables drop and foul, and natural lands dwindles. These crises will worsen as America's population continues to soar. In 1992, America's official population surged past 255 million and, at the present pace, will reach 380 million by 2050, an increase of 50 percent. Tragically, even if those future Americans chose to use their diminishing natural resources wisely, it may be too late to do so.

From the mid-1960s through 1981, a political consensus held that environmental problems were serious, getting worse, and had to be systematically addressed. That consensus was held by moderate Republicans and Democrats, and conservationists and environmentalists alike. No president since Republican Theodore Roosevelt has passed more sweeping, progressive environmental laws than Republican Richard Nixon.

This consensus disintegrated during the twelve years of power held by the cornucopian Reagan and Bush administrations. Cornucopianism staged a sweeping comeback, fueled by the so-called "wise use" and "property rights" banners that first emerged in the 1970s. By the 1990s, more than 600 "property rights" groups had formed under the umbrella group "Alliance for America." Most of these groups were simply front organizations for industrial associations. The American Forest and Paper Association has been particularly active in funding, organizing, and training these groups to lobby and sue government. Other cornucopian groups like the fundamentalist Christian Coalition and National Rifle Association (NRA) joined the Alliance for America in generating grassroots support and pressuring local and state governments into accepting their agenda. By 1995, ten states had written laws requiring compensation to property owners when regulations diminish that land's real or potential value.

In 1992, however, the election of conservationist Bill Clinton to the presidency and environmentalist Al Gore to the vice presidency, along with a Democratic Congress, seemed to suggest the nation was once again turning its back on cornucopianism. The Clinton White House, however, failed to push through any major environmental programs in their first two years. Then, in the November 1994 election, cornucopians succeeded in capturing both houses of Congress and swore to destroy the laws that slowed and in some cases reversed centuries of environmental degradation. Perhaps no Congress since the "robber baron" era of the late nineteenth century has been more blatantly in the pocket of cornucopian industrial and agribusiness interests. The Republicans openly invited logging, mining, ranching, farming, petrochemical, and other environmentally destructive industries to help them write laws that would gut virtually all environmental laws.

Over the next two years, the Republicans mounted an all-out assault on a century of environmental laws and policies. Formidable as their power seemed, the cornucopians succeeded in pushing only one measure into law. Clinton refused to veto an especially destructive logging bill that opened virtually all public forests to logging, but allowed loggers to "salvage" trees from forest fires, thus encouraging them to commit arson to get their chain saws at currently protected forests. Cornucopians cleverly and ironically attached it to a relief bill for victims of the Oklahoma City federal building, which was destroyed by cornucopian terrorists.

Congressional logjams and Clinton vetos, however, derailed most other cornucopian efforts. One bill would have cut EPA spending by one-third, place a moratorium on new regulations, require cost–benefit analyses for all existing health, safety, and environmental regulations, and prevent the EPA from enforcing the law. Another would have eliminated the requirement that businesses publicly disclose the amount and type of pollution they emit, as well as strike hundreds of chemicals from the EPA disclosure list. An oil-drilling bill would have opened the Arctic National Wildlife Refuge and all coastal areas to exploitation. A property "takings" bill would have required the government to indemnify owners whose property loses real or potential value because of regulations. Another bill would have eliminated the Endangered Species Act which has done more to preserve fragile ecosystems than any other law. A revision of the Clean Water Act would have essentially destroyed existing standards, opened all wetlands to development, and let businesses pollute as they wish. A mining bill would have sold off public lands to miners and confirm existing claims. An amendment to the superfund toxic clean-up bill would have eliminated the requirement that businesses are liable for the pollution they cause and halted most current clean-ups. A pesticide bill would have prevented the EPA from barring certain chemicals. A "self audit" bill would have prevented the EPA from enforcing regulations against any business that admitted it violated standards. A grazing law would have lower fees and allow ranchers to run even more cattle on public lands. Another bill would have prevented the EPA from fulfilling its own laws to issue regulations for the petroleum industry, which is the twelfth worst on a list of 174 types of polluters defined by the Clean Air Act.[12] Although bitter at their defeats, cornucopians cherish a wish list that includes these and a range of other measures.

What will the future bring? Conservationists and environmentalists alike were heartened by Bill Clinton's re-election. Yet while most battles may tilt against cornucopians, a final victory will prove to be elusive. The war for America's natural resources is never-ending.

Notes

Notes to the Introduction

1. For the classic study on this theme, which has strongly influenced the following discussion, see Roderick Nash, *Wilderness and the American Mind*, 3rd edn (New Haven, CT: Yale University Press, 1982).
2. God and His scribes, *The Holy Bible*, Revised Standard Version (Grand Rapids, MI: Zondervan Publishing House, 1952), Genesis 1:26, p. 2.
3. For contemporary neoclassical economists, see: Jagdish Bhagwati, *Lectures: International Trade* (Cambridge, MA: MIT Press, 1983); Jagdish Bhagwati, *Protectionism* (Cambridge, MA: MIT Press, 1988); Jagdish Bhagwati and Hugh Patrick (eds), *Aggressive Unilateralism* (Ann Arbor: University of Michigan Press, 1990); Jagdish Bhagwati, *The World Trading System at Risk* (Princeton, NJ: Princeton University Press, 1991).
4. See such classic environmental works as: Henry David Thoreau, *Walden and Other Writings* (New York: Barnes and Noble, 1993); Ralph Waldo Emerson, *Self-Reliance* (New York: Bell Tower, 1991).
5. Lester R. Brown and Sandra L. Postel, "Thresholds of Change," *The Futurist*, 21 (September/October 1987), p. 11.
6. Gifford Pinchot, *The Fight for Conservation* (Garden City, NY: Harcourt, Brace, 1910), p. 42.
7. Gifford Pinchot, *Breaking New Ground* (New York: Harcourt Brace and Jovanovich, 1947), p. 322.
8. Cornucopians have recently appropriated the term "wise use" to help sell their own attempts to destroy environmental regulations and gain unhindered access to exploit the earth's resources.
9. Walter Rosenbaum, *Energy Politics and Public Policy* (Washington, DC: Congressional Quarterly Press, 1987), p. 205.
10. Edward R. Tufte, *Political Control of the Economy* (Princeton, NJ: Princeton University Press, 1978), p. 142.
11. Bernard Shanks, *This Land Is Your Land* (San Francisco: Sierra Club Books, 1984), pp. 286–7.
12. Ibid., pp. 7–8.

Notes to Chapter 1: Farming, Grazing, and Hunting

1. Unless otherwise indicated, statistics in this section come from Nancy A. Blanpied, *Farm Policy: The Politics of Soil, Surpluses, and Subsidies* (Washington, DC: Congressional Quarterly, 1984).
2. Steven Holmes, "Fewest U.S. Farms since 1850: 1.9 million," *New York Times*, November 9, 1994. According to the Census Bureau, a farm

is anything which produces more than $1,000 a year in agricultural products whether it be grains, vegetables, livestock, or fibers.

3. "New Farms Represent a Lifestyle," *Omaha World Herald*, August 23, 1992. Willard W. Cochrane and C. Ford Runge, *Reforming Farm Policy: Toward a National Agenda* (Ames: Iowa State University Press, 1992), p. 4.
4. Blanpied, *Farm Policy*, p. 104.
5. Pierre Crosson, "Cropland and Soils: Past Performance and Policy Changes," in Kenneth Frederick and Roger Sedjo (eds), *America's Renewable Resources: Historical Trends and Current Challenges* (Washington, DC: Resources for the Future, 1991), p. 174. Blanpied, *Farm Policy*, p. 105.
6. Crosson, "Cropland and Soils," p. 174.
7. Kenneth D. Frederick and Roger A. Sedjo, "Overview: Renewable Resource Trends," in Frederick and Sedjo (eds), *America's Renewable Resources: Historical Trends and Current Challenges* (Washington, DC: Resources for the Future, 1991), pp. 9, 13.
8. Bernard Shanks, *This Land Is Your Land* (San Francisco: Sierra Club Books, 1984), p. 75.
9. Crosson, "Cropland and Soils," pp. 178, 179, 182.
10. Hugh Hammond Bennett, *Soil Conservation* (New York: McGraw-Hill, 1939), p. 13.
11. Crosson, "Cropland and Soils," p. 182.
12. Ibid., p. 186.
13. Ibid., p. 187.
14. Keith Schneider, "The Farm Economy is Fine and Can Expect More Aid," *New York Times*, February 4, 1990.
15. Ronald Smothers, "U.S. Shutting 1,274 Farm Field Offices," *New York Times*, December 7, 1994.
16. Douglas Frantz, "Reports Describe Widespread Abuse in Farm Program," *New York Times*, October 3, 1994.
17. Steven Holmes, "Fewest U.S. Farms since 1850," *New York Times*, November 9, 1994.
18. Philip Hilts, "Substance Abuse is Blamed for 500,000 Deaths," *New York Times*, October 24, 1993; Philip Hilts, "Children of Smoking Mothers Show Carcinogens in Blood," *New York Times*, September 24, 1994; Shirley J. Hansen, *Managing Indoor Air Quality* (Lilburn, GA: Fairmont Press, 1991), p. 6; US Public Health Service, "The Health Consequences of Involuntary Smoking," *Surgeon General's Report* (Washington, DC: Government Printing Office, 1986); Richard Kluger, *Ashes to Ashes: America's Hundred-Year Cigarette War, The Public Health and the Unabashed Triumph of Philip Morris* (New York: Alfred A. Knopf, 1996).
19. Philip Hilts, "Sharp Rise Seen in Smokers' Health Care Costs," *New York Times*, July 8, 1994.
20. John Darnton, "Report Says Smoking Causes a Global Epidemic of Death," *New York Times*, September 21, 1994.
21. If not otherwise indicated, most of the information in the following paragraphs came from "The Price of Tobacco," *New York Times*, March 22, 1993; Philip Hilts, "Clinton Says Government Needs to Combat

Smoking by Youths," *New York Times*, August 4, 1995; Michael Wines, "Proposal on Tobacco Gets Some White House Backing," *New York Times*, July 14, 1995.

22. Jonathan Hicks, "Tobacco Industry Fights New York Óver Smoking Bill," *New York Times*, September 26, 1994. See also Ronald Smothers, "After Years of Despair, Tobacco Farmers Enjoy Prospect of Better Times," *New York Times*, December 15, 1994.
23. Marc Reisner, *Cadillac Desert: The American West and its Disappearing Water* (New York: Penguin, 1993), pp. 437–8, 11. See also, Wilbur R. Jacobs, "The Great Despoilation: Environmental Themes in American Frontier History," *Pacific Historical Review*, 47 (1978), p. 6.
24. "Agriculture Department Hails Plant Scientists," *New York Times*, October 16, 1994.
25. B. Delworth Gardner, "Rangeland Resources: Changing Uses and Productivity," in K. D. Frederick and R. A. Sedjo (eds), *America's Renewable Resources* (Washington, DC: Resources for the Future, 1991).
26. George Wuerthner, "The Price is Wrong," *Sierra*, 75, no. 5 (September–October 1990), p. 39; George Wuerthner, "How the West was Eaten," *Wilderness*, 54, no. 192 (Spring 1991), p. 36.
27. Karl Hess and Jerry Holechek, "Subsidized Drought," *New York Times*, December 12, 1994.
28. Gardner, "Rangeland Resources," pp. 129, 130.
29. Quoted in Gardner, "Rangeland Resources," p. 133.
30. William D. Rowley, *US Forest Service Grazing and Rangelands* (College Station, Texas: Texas A. & M. Press, 1985), p. 54.
31. Samuel Dana and Sally Fairfax, *Forest and Range Policy: Its Development in the United States* (New York: McGraw-Hill, 1980), p. 135.
32. Quoted in Dyan Zaslowsky and T. H. Watkins, *These American Lands: Parks, Wilderness, and the Public Lands* (Washington, DC: Island Press, 1994), p. 127.
33. Gardner, "Rangeland Resources," p. 138.
34. Kenneth Frederick and Roger Sedjo, "Overview: Renewable Resource Trends," p. 9.
35. Gardner, "Rangeland Resources," p. 128.
36. Ibid., p. 147.
37. Ibid., p. 138.
38. Timothy Egan, "Wingtip 'Cowboys' in Last Stand to Hold on to Low Grazing Fees," *New York Times*, October 28, 1993.
39. Ibid.
40. Keith Bradsher, "'Strategic' Goats Gobble up Trade Subsidy," *New York Times*, February 24, 1993.
41. Ibid.; Katherine Seelye, "Aid to Mink Ranchers: Pork or Priority?" *New York Times*, July 20, 1995.
42. Theodore Roosevelt, *African Game-Trails: An Account of the African Wandering of an American Hunter-Naturalist* (New York, 1910), p. 4.
43. Zaslowsky and Watkins, *These American Lands*, p. 178.
44. Ibid.
45. Timothy Egan, "Strongest U.S. Environment Law May Become an Endangered Species," *New York Times*, May 26, 1992.

46. Timothy Egan, "Ranchers Balk at U.S. Plans to Return Wolf to the West," *New York Times*, December 11, 1994.
47. Marguerite Holloway, "High and Dry," *Scientific American*, 265 (December 1991), pp. 16–17.
48. US Department of the Interior, US Fish and Wildlife Service, *Wetlands Status and Trends* (Washington, DC: US Government Printing Office, 1991). For other works on wetlands, see Michael Williams (ed.), *Wetlands: A Threatened Landscape* (New York: Basil Blackwell, 1991).
49. Barry Meier, "Fight Looming in Congress over Panels that Regulate Commercial Fishing," *New York Times*, September 19, 1994.
50. John Cushmann, "Commercial Fishing Halt is Urged for Georges Bank," *New York Times*, October 27, 1994.
51. Cochrane and Runge, *Reforming Farm Policy*, pp. 21, 5, 96. Critics deride the BLM as the "Bureau of Livestock and Mining."
52. Ibid., p. 62.
53. Ibid., p. 117.

Notes to Chapter 2: Forests, Parks, and Wilderness

1. Roger Sedjo, "Forest Resources: Resilient and Serviceable," in K. D. Frederick and R. A. Sedjo (eds), *America's Renewable Resources: Historical Trends and Current Challenges* (Washington, DC: Resources for the Future, 1991), pp. 84–5.
2. George Catlin, *North American Indians: Letters and Notes on Their Manners, Customs, and Conditions, Written during Eight Years Travel among the Wildest Tribes in North America, 1832–39*, vol. I (London: George Catlin, 1880), pp. 292–3.
3. Quoted in Noble, *Cole*, p. 299.
4. Henry David Thoreau, "Maine Woods" in *Walden and Other Writings* (New York: Barnes and Noble, 1991), 3, p. 208.
5. Torrey and Allen (ed.), *Journal*, 14, p. 305.
6. Congressional Globe, 42nd Cong., 2nd Sess. I (January 30, 1872), p. 697.
7. US, *Statutes at Large*, XVII, p. 32.
8. All the quotes from this and the following paragraph are from Roderick Nash, *Wilderness and the American Mind* (New Haven, CT: Yale University Press, 1982), pp. 114–15.
9. Kenneth D. Frederick and Roger A. Sedjo, "Overview: Renewable Resource Trends," in Frederick and Sedjo, *America's Renewable Resources: Historical Trends and Current Challenges* (Washington, DC: Resources for the Future, 1991), p. 8.
10. Quoted in Sedjo, "Forest Resources," p. 89.
11. Carl Schurz, *Annual Report of the Secretary of the Interior on the Operations of the Department for the Fiscal Year ended June 30, 1877* (Washington, DC: US Government Printing Office, 1877).
12. Commissioners of State Parks of the State of New York, *First Annual Report*, New York Senate Doc. 102 (May 15, 1873), pp. 3, 10.

13. "The Adirondack Park," *Forest and Stream*, I (1873), p. 73.
14. New York Laws, 1892, chap. 709, p. 1459.
15. See Gifford Pinchot, *The Fight for Conservation* (Garden City, NY: Harcourt, Brace, 1910); Gifford Pinchot, *Breaking New Ground* (New York: Harcourt, Brace, and Jovanovich, 1947).
16. Bernard Fernow, "Letter to the Editor," *The Forester*, 2 (1896), p. 45.
17. W. J. McGee, "The Conservation of Natural Resources," *Proceedings of the Mississippi Valley Historical Association*, III (1908–10).
18. Theodore Roosevelt, "The Forest Problem," *Works*, vol. 18, p. 127.
19. Theodore Roosevelt, "First Annual Message," *Works*, vol. 17, pp. 118–19.
20. See Donald C. Swain, *Federal Conservation Policy, 1921–1933* (Berkeley: University of California Publications in History, LXXVI, 1963).
21. Quoted in George Marshall, "Robert Marshall as a Writer," *Living Wilderness*, 19.
22. Nash, *Wilderness and the American Mind*, p. 105.
23. Quoted in Elizabeth C. Flint, "Robert Marshall, the Man and his Aims," *Sunday* [Montana] *Missoulian*, November 19, 1939.
24. Robert Marshall, "The Problem of the Wilderness," *Scientific Monthly*, 30 (1930), pp. 144–5.
25. Robert Marshall to Harold Ickes, February 27, 1934, Record Group 79, National Park Service (Washington, DC: National Archives, 1934).
26. Harold C. Anderson, et al., *The Wilderness Society* (Washington, DC: 1935), p. 4.
27. Sedjo, "Forest Resources," p. 99.
28. Nash, *Wilderness and the American Mind*, p. 222.
29. US Congress, Senate, Committee on Interior and Insular Affairs, Hearings, *National Wilderness Preservation Act*, 85th Cong., 2nd Sess. (November 7, 10, 13, 1958), p. 573.
30. Wallace Stegner, "The Wilderness Idea," in David Brower (ed.), *Wilderness: America's Living Heritage* (San Francisco: Sierra Club, 1961), pp. 97–102.
31. Gary Snyder, "The Wilderness," from Snyder's *Turtle Island* (New York: New Directions, 1974), pp. 106–10.
32. Quoted in *Voices for Wilderness*, ed. William Schwartz (New York: 1969), p. xvi.
33. Roderick Nash, "Why Wilderness?" in *For the Conservation of the Earth*, ed. *Vance Martin* (Golden, CO: Fulcrum, 1988), p. 194.
34. Nash, *Wilderness and the American Mind*, p. 295.
35. Edward Abbey, *Desert Solitaire*, pp. 148–9.
36. Keith Schneider, "U.S. Would End Cutting of Trees in Many Forests," *New York Times*, April 30, 1993.
37. Eliot Norse, *Ancient Forests of the Pacific Northwest* (Washington, DC: The Wilderness Society, 1990), pp. 138–9.
38. "Owls, Trees and Jobs: The Timber Conference," *New York Times*, April 3, 1993, p. A22.
39. Tim Hermach, "The Great Tree Robbery," *New York Times*, September 17, 1991.
40. John Holusha, "Clinton Held Ready to Order Standard on Recycled

Paper," *New York Times*, September 30, 1993, p. A1.
41. Ibid.
42. Jacqueline Switzer, *Environmental Politics*, p. 79.
43. Tim Hermach, "The Great Tree Robbery," *New York Times*, September 17, 1991.
44. Norse, *Ancient Forests of the Pacific Northwest*, p. 162.
45. Switzer, *Environmental Politics*, p. 79.
46. Paul Schneider, "When a Whistle Blows in the Forest," *Audubon*, 7 (July 1990), p. 46.
47. Donald G. McNeil, "How Most of the Public Forests are Sold to Loggers at a Loss," *New York Times*, November 3, 1991.
48. Reuters, "Study Says U.S. Fails to Replant its Forests," *New York Times*, June 15, 1992.
49. Sedjo, "Forest Resources," p. 104.
50. McNeil, "How Most of the Public Forests Are Sold to Loggers at a Loss," *New York Times*, November 3, 1991.
51. Norse, *Ancient Forests of the Pacific Northwest*, p. 265.
52. Dale Bumpers, "Profit from the Parks," *National Parks*, 65, nos 3–4 (March–April 1991), pp. 16–17.
53. Edward O. Wilson, "Million-Year Histories: Species Diversity as an Ethical Goal," *Wilderness*, 47 (Summer 1984), p. 14.

Notes to Chapter 3: Mines, Drills, and Energy

1. Timothy Egan, "Billions at Stake in Debate on Gold Rush," *New York Times*, August 14, 1994.
2. John Cushman, "Forced, U.S. Sells Gold Land for Trifle," *New York Times*, May 17, 1994.
3. Ibid.
4. Egan, "Billions at Stake in Debate on Gold Rush," *New York Times*, August 14, 1994.
5. Ibid.
6. Ibid.
7. Of all sources consulted for this section, the most useful was David Howard Davies, *Energy Politics* (New York: St Martin's Press, 1993).
8. Richard Ottinger, "Introduction: The Tragedy of U.S. Energy R&D Policy," in *The Politics of Research and Development*, ed. John Byrne and Daniel Rich (New Brunswick, NJ: Transaction Books, 1986), p. 2.
9. Energy Information Administration, *Annual Energy Review*, 1990.
10. Jacqueline Switzer, *Environmental Politics*, p. 126.
11. Keith Schneider, "Clinton to Revamp Energy Department Role," *New York Times*, November 22, 1993.
12. Unless otherwise noted, all the following statistics come from Davies, *Energy Politics*, pp. 26–62.
13. Bernard Shanks, *This Land Is Your Land* (San Francisco: Sierra Club Books, 1984), pp. 124–3.
14. Walter Rosenbaum, *Energy Politics and Public Policy* (Washington, DC:

Congressional Quarterly Press, 1987) p. 176; Keith Schneider, "U.S. Mine Inspectors Charge Interference by Agency Director," *New York Times*, November 22, 1992.

15. Rosenbaum, *Energy Politics*, p. 165.
16. Quoted in Harry Caudil, *My Land Is Dying* (New York: E. P. Dutton, 1973), p. 85.
17. Unless otherwise indicated, all information has been gleaned from Davies, *Energy Politics*, pp. 63–131.
18. Shanks, *This Land Is Your Land*, p. 122.
19. Executive Office of the President, Energy Policy and Planning, *The National Energy Plan* (Washington, DC: Government Printing Office, 1977), p. vii.
20. Charles O. Jones and Randall Strahan, "The Effects of Energy Politics on Congressional and Executive Organizations in the 1970s," *Legislative Studies Quarterly*, 10, 2 (May 1985), p. 161.
21. Rosenbaum, *Energy Politics*, p. 50.
22. Ibid., p. 8
23. US Congress, House of Representatives, *National Energy Policy Plan: Message from the President of the United States*, H. Doc. 97–77, 97th Cong., 1st sess., 1981, p. 1.
24. Shanks, *This Land Is Your Land*, p. 125.
25. Quoted in James Everett Katz, *Congress and National Energy Policy* (New Brunswick, NJ: Transaction Books, 1984), p. 165.
26. Department of Energy, *The National Energy Policy Plan* (Washington, DC: Government Printing Office, 1983), p. 1.
27. Quoted in Rosenbaum, *Energy Politics*, p. 133.
28. Edward Byers and Thomas B. Fitzpatrick, "American and Oil Companies: Tentative Tolerance in a Time of Plenty," *Public Opinion*, vol. 8, no. 6 (December/January 1986), p. 43.
29. US Department of Energy, Energy Information Administration, *Monthly Energy Review*, May 1992, Table 9.1.
30. Switzer, *Environmental Politics*, p. 146.
31. Unless otherwise indicated, the statistics for this section come from Davies, *Energy Politics*, pp. 132–62.
32. Rosenbaum, *Energy Politics*, p. 87.
33. Quoted in US House of Representatives, Committee on Interior and Insular Affairs, Subcommittee on Oversight and Investigations, *Oversight Hearing: Emergency Preparedness and the Licensing Process for Commercial Nuclear Power Reactors*, April 18, 1983, serial no. 98–52, pt 1 (Washington, DC: Government Printing Office, 1984), p. 4.
34. Unless otherwise noted, all statistics in this section come from Davies, *Energy Politics*, pp. 163–205.
35. Davies, *Energy Politics*, pp. 192–3.
36. Rosenbaum, *Energy Politics*, p. 191.
37. Ibid., p. 89.
38. Ibid., p. 200.
39. Ibid., p. 90.
40. Cited in Christopher Flavin, *Electricity's Future: The Shift to Efficiency and Small-Scale Power* (Washington, DC: Worldwatch Institute, 1984), p. 40.

41. General Services Administration, National Archives, *Presidential Documents*, 13, 17 (April 25, 1977), p. 573.
42. Keith Schneider, "Clinton to Revamp Energy Department Role," *New York Times*, November 22, 1993.
43. Peter Passell, "Cheapest Protection of Nature May Lie in Texas, Not Laws," *New York Times*, November 24, 1992.
44. Matthew Wald, "Efficient Power from Fuel Gases," *New York Times*, June 10, 1992.
45. Lily Whiteman, "Recent Efforts to Stop Abuse of SMCRA: Have They Gone Far Enough?" *Environmental Law*, 20 (Fall 1990), p. 167.
46. Lawrence MacDonnell, "Mineral Law in the United States: A Study in Legal Change," in L. MacDonnell and P. Bates (eds), *Natural Resources, Policy, and Law* (Washington, DC: Island Press, 1994), p. 79.
47. John Young, *Mining the Earth*, Worldwatch Paper 109, July 1992, pp. 16–18.
48. Thomas Watkins, *Gold and Silver in the West* (Palo Alto, CA: American West Publishing, 1971), p. 277.

Notes to Chapter 4: Dams, Irrigation, and Faucets

1. William Ashworth, *Nor Any Drop to Drink* (New York: Summit Books, 1982), pp. 19–21.
2. Kenneth Frederick, "Water Resources: Increasing Demand and Scarce Supplies," in K. Frederick and R. Sedjo (eds), *America's Renewable Resources: Historical Trends and Current Challenges* (Washington, DC: Resources for the Future, 1991), pp. 25–6.
3. Ibid., p. 26.
4. Marc Reisner, *Cadillac Desert: The American West and its Disappearing Water* (New York: Penguin Books, 1993), p. 6.
5. Ibid., p. 12.
6. Ibid., p. 3.
7. Ibid., p. 308.
8. Ibid., p. 310.
9. Frederick, "Water Resources," p. 29.
10 Ibid., p. 31.
11. Quoted in Reisner, *Cadillac Desert*, p. 112.
12. John Muir, *The Yosemite* (New York, 1912), pp. 261–2.
13. Theodore Roosevelt, "Annual Message," *Works*, vol. 17, p. 618.
14. Quoted in Nash, *Wilderness and the American Mind*, 171.
15. Roderick Nash, *Wilderness and the American Mind* (New Haven, CT: Yale University Press, 1982), p. 181.
16. Reisner, *Cadillac Desert*, p. 62.
17. Ibid., p. 84.
18. Ibid., pp. 116–17.
19. Ibid., p. 183.
20. Frederick, "Water Resources," p. 38.
21. Bernard Shanks, *This Land Is Your Land* (San Francisco: Sierra Club Books, 1984), p. 142.

22. Reisner, *Cadillac Desert*, p. 186.
23. Ibid., p. 162.
24. John Ferejohn, *Pork Barrel Politics: Rivers and Harbors Legislation, 1947–68* (Stanford: Stanford University Press, 1974).
25. Frederick, "Water Resources," p. 39.
26. E. Arnold Hansen and C. W. Mattison, *The Nation's Interest in Conservation in 1905 and 1955* (Washington, DC: 1955), p. 1.
27. Howard C. Zahniser, "Our Wilderness Need," *Living Wilderness*, 20 (1955), p. 1.
28. US Congress, Senate, Committee on Interior and Insular Affairs, Subcommittee on Irrigation and Reclamation, Hearings, *Colorado River Storage Project*, 84th Cong., 1st Sess. (February 28, March 1–5, 1955), pp. 696, 679–84.
29. Wallace Stegner, *This Is Dinosaur: Echo Park Country and its Magical Rivers* (New York: Alfred A. Knopf, 1955).
30. US Congress, House, Committee on Interior and Insular Affairs, *Supplemental Report on HR 3383*, 84th Cong., 2nd Sess., House Rpt 1087, pt 2 (February 14, 1956).
31. David Brower, *The Land No One Knew* (San Francisco: Sierra Club, 1964), p. 3.
32. Quoted in François Leydet, *Time and the River Flowing: Grand Canyon* (San Francisco: Sierra Club, 1964).
33. Lawrence Mosher, "The Corps Adapts, the Bureau Founders," in *Western Water Made Simple* (Washington, DC: Island Press, 1987), p. 16.
34. Reisner, *Cadillac Desert*, pp. 324–9.
35. Frederick, "Water Resources," p. 49.
36. Reisner, *Cadillac Desert*, p. 482.
37. Benedykt Dziegielewski and Duane D. Baumann, "Tapping Alternatives: The Benefits of Managing Urban Water Demands," *Environment*, 34, no. 9 (November 1991), pp. 6–11.
38. Ed Marston, "When Water Kingdoms Clash," in *Western Water Made Simple* (Washington, DC: Island Press, 1987), p. 36.
39. Charles Wilkinson and Daniel Conner, "A Great Loneliness of Spirit," in *Western Water Made Simple* (Washington, DC: Island Press, 1987), p. 59.
40. Cynthia D. Stowell, "Salmon: Continuity for a Culture," in *Western Water Made Simple* (Washington, DC: Island Press, 1987), p. 77.
41. Pat Ford, "The View from the Upper Basin," in *Western Water Made Simple* (Washington, DC: Island Press, 1987), p. 88.
42. Ed Marston, "Reworking the Colorado River Basin," in *Western Water Made Simple* (Washington, DC: Island Press, 1987), p. 202.
43. Paul Krza, "The Bureau's Rube Goldberg Machines," in *Western Water Made Simple* (Washington, DC: Island Press, 1987), p. 184.
44. Jose Trava, "Sharing Water with the Colossus of the North," in *Western Water Made Simple* (Washington, DC: Island Press, 1987), p. 178.
45. Quoted in Ibid., pp. 179–80.
46. Lawrence Mosher, "The Corps Adapts, the Bureau Founders," p. 25.
47. Ed Marston, "Reworking the Colorado River Basin," p. 203.
48. Reisner, *Cadillac Desert*, pp. 484–5.

49. Ibid., p. 485.
50. Ed Quillen, "What Size Shoe does an Acre-foot Wear?" In *Western Water Made Simple* (Washington, DC: Island Press, 1987), p. 190.
51. Reisner, *Cadillac Desert*, p. 201.
52. Ibid., p. 510.
53. Ibid., p. 227.
54. Quoted in ibid., p. 221.

Notes to Chapter 5: Natural Resource Policy in the Twenty-first Century

1. Roderick Nash, *Wilderness and the American Mind*, p. 38.
2. Lester R. Brown and Sandra Postel, "Thresholds of Change," *The Futurist*, **21** (September/October 1987), p. 11.
3. Lawrence MacDonnell and Sarah Bates, "Rethinking Resources," in MacDonnell and Bates (eds), *National Resource Policy and Law* (Washington, DC: Island Press, 1994), p. 16.
4. Shanks, *This Land is your Land*, p. 288.
5. Cochrane and Runge, *Reforming Farm Policy*, p. 19.
6. David Howard Davies, *Energy Politics* (New York: St Martin's, 1993), p. 149.
7. World Commission on Environment and Development, *Our Common Future* (Oxford: Oxford University Press, 1987), p. xi.
8. William Stevens, "New Studies Predict Profits in Heading off Warming," *New York Times*, March 17, 1992.
9. Zaslowsky and Watkins, *These American Lands*, p. 2.
10. Quoted in ibid., p. 57.
11. William K. Stevens, "Study Finds Scores of Ailing US Ecosystems," *International Herald-Tribune*, February 16, 1995.
12. John Cushman, "GOP's Plan for Environment is Facing Big Test in Congress," *New York Times*, July 17, 1995.

Bibliography

Abbey, Edward, *Desert Solitaire: A Season in the Wilderness* (New York: 1968).

Abbey, Edward, and Dave Foreman, *A Field Guide to Monkeywrenching* (Tuscon: Ned Ludd, 1987).

Allison, Graham, *Essence of Decision* (Boston, MA: Little, Brown, 1971).

Ashworth, William, *Nor any Drop to Drink* (New York: Summit Books, 1982).

Bates, J. Bates, "Fulfilling American Democracy: The Conservation Movement, 1907–1921," *Mississippi Valley Historical Review*, XLIV (1957) pp. 29–57.

Bell, R. W. *et al.*, *The 1990 Toronto Personal Exposure Pilot Study* (Toronto: Ontario Ministry of the Environment, 1991).

Bennett, Hugh Hammond, *Soil Conservation* (New York: McGraw-Hill, 1939).

Billington, Ray A. (ed.), *Frontier and Section: Selected Essays of Frederick Jackson* (Madison: University of Wisconsin Press, 1961).

Blanpied, Nancy A., *Farm Policy: The Politics of Soil, Surpluses, and Subsidies* (Washington, DC: Congressional Quarterly, 1984).

Blumberg, Louis and Robert Gottlieb, *War on Waste: Can America Win its Battle with Garbage* (Washington, DC: Island Press, 1989).

Bookchin, Murray, *Toward an Ecological Society* (Montreal: Black Rose, 1980).

Boyle, Robert H., "Activists at Risk of Being SLAPPed," *Sports Illustrated* (March 25, 1991) pp. 20–3.

Brower, David, *The Land No One Knew* (San Francisco: Sierra Club, 1964).

Brower, David (ed.), *Gentle Wilderness: The Sierra Nevada* (San Francisco: Sierra Club Books, 1967).

Brown, Lester R. and Sandra L. Postel, "Thresholds of Change," *The Futurist*, 21 (September/October 1987).

Bumpers, Dale, "Profit from the Parks," *National Parks*, 65, nos 3–4 (March–April 1991) pp. 16–17.

Byers, Edward and Thomas B. Fitzpatrick, "American and Oil Companies: Tentative Tolerance in a Time of Plenty," *Public Opinion*, 8: 6 (December/January 1986).

Calabrese, Edward and Charles E. Gilbert, "Drinking Water Quality and Water Treatment Practices: Charting the Future," in *Safe Drinking Water Act: Amendments, Regulations, and Standards*, ed. Edward J. Calabrese, Charles E. Gilbert, and Harris Pastides (Chelsea, MI: Lewis Publishers, 1989).

Carson, Rachel, *Silent Spring* (Boston, MA: Houghton Mifflin, 1962).

Castleman, Barry I., *Asbestos: Medical and Legal Aspects* (Englewood Cliffs, NJ: Prentice Hall Law and Business, 1990).

Caudil, Harry, *My Land is Dying* (New York: E. P. Dutton, 1973).

Cochrance, Willard W. and C. Ford Runge, *Reforming Farm Policy: Toward a National Agenda* (Ames: Iowa State University Press, 1992).

Commissioners of State Parks of the State of New York, *First Annual Report*, New York Senate Doc. 102 (May 15, 1873).

Council on Environmental Quality, *Environmental Quality: The First Annual Report of the Council on Environmental Quality* (Washington, DC: US Government Printing Office, 1970).

Crosson, Pierre, "Cropland and Soils: Past Performance and Policy Changes," in Kenneth Frederick and Roger Sedjo (eds), *America's Renewable Resource: Historical Trends and Current Challenges* (Washington, DC: Resources for the Future, 1991).

Dana, Samuel and Sally Fairfax, *Forest and Range Policy: Its Development in the United States* (New York: McGraw-Hill, 1980).

Davies, Howard, *Energy Politics* (New York: St Martin's Press, 1993).

de Tocqueville, Alexis, *Democracy in America*, ed. Phillips Bradley, 2 vols (New York, 1945).

Dubos, Rene, *A God Within* (New York, 1972).

Dubos, Rene, "Symbiosis Between the Earth and Mankind," *Science*, **193** (1976).

Dubos, Rene, *The Resilience of Ecosystems* (Boulder, CO: Westview Press, 1978).

Dubos, Rene, *The Wooing of Earth* (New York, 1980).

Dunlap, Riley E., "Public Opinion and Environmental Policy," in *Environmental Politics and Policy: Theories and Evidence*, ed. James P. Lester (Durham, NC: Duke University Press, 1989) pp. 87–134.

Dziegielewski, Benedykt and Duane D. Baumann, "Tapping Alternatives: The Benefits of Managing Urban Water Demands," *Environment*, **34**: 9 (November 1991) pp. 6–11.

Edwards, George C. and Ira Sharkansky, *The Policy Predicament* (San Franciso: W.H. Freeman, 1978).

Elmer, Fred, "Saving the Economy by Saving the Environment," *Sierra Atlantic*, **20**: 1, p. 15.

Emerson, Ralph Waldo, *Self-Reliance* (New York: Bell Tower, 1991).

Environmental Pollution Panel, President's Science Advisory Committee, *Restoring the Quality of our Environment* (Washington, DC: US Government Printing Office, 1965).

Erlich, Paul and Anne, *Extinction: The Cause and Consequences of the Disappearing Species* (New York, 1981).

Executive Office of the President, Energy Policy and Planning, *The National Energy Plan* (Washington, DC: GPO, 1977).

Faragher, John Mack, *Daniel Boone: The Life and Legend of an American Pioneer* (New York: Henry Holt, 1992).

Ferejohn, John, *Pork Barrel Politics: Rivers and Harbors Legislation, 1947–68* (Stanford: Stanford University Press, 1974).

Flavin, Christopher, *Electricity's Future: The Shift to Efficiency and Small-Scale Power* (Washington, DC: Worldwatch Institute, 1984).

Ford, Pat, "The View from the Upper Basin," in *Western Water Made Simple* (Washington, DC: Island Press, 1987).

Fortuna, Richard C. and David J. Lennett, *Hazardous Waste Regulation, The New Era: An Analysis and Guide to RCRA and the 1984 Amendments* (New York: McGraw-Hill, 1987).

Frederick, Kenneth D. and Roger A. Sedjo, "Overview: Renewable Resource Trends," in Frederick and Sedjo, *America's Renewable Resources: Historical Trends and Current Challenges* (Washington, DC: Resources for the Future, 1991).

Frederick, Kenneth, "Water Resources: Increasing Demand and Scarce Supplies," in Frederick and Sedjo (eds), *America's Renewable Resources: Historical Trends and Current Challenges* (Washington, DC: Resources for the Future, 1991).

Gardner, B. Delworth, "Rangeland Resources: Changing Uses and Productivity," in Frederick and Sedjo (eds), *America's Renewable Resources* (Washington, DC: Resources for the Future, 1991).

Garrison, John, "Will the New Law Protect Public Health," *EPA Journal* 17: 1 (January–February 1991).

Gore, Al, *Earth in the Balance: Ecology and the Human Spirit* (New York: Plume, 1993).

Gottlieb, Robert, *A Life of its Own: The Politics and Power of Water* (New York: Harcourt, Brace, and Jovanovich, 1988).

Greve, Michael S., "Environmentalism and Bounty Hunting," *Public Interest*, **97** (Fall 1989).

Hansen, E. Arnold and C. W. Mattison, *The Nation's Interest in Conservation in 1905 and 1955* (Washington, DC, 1955).

Hansen, Shirley J., *Managing Indoor Air Quality* (Lilburn, GA: Fairmont Press, 1991).

Harris, Christopher, William L. Want, and Morris A. Ward, *Hazardous Waste: Confronting the Challenge* (New York: Quorum Books, 1987).

Harris, Richard A. and Sidney M. Milkis, *The Politics of Regulatory Change* (New York: Oxford University Press, 1989).

Hays, Samuel P., *Conservation and the Gospel of Efficiency: The Progressive Conservation Movement, 1890–1920* (Cambridge, MA: Harvard University Press, 1959).

Heclo, Hugh, "Issue Networks and the Executive Establishment," in *The New American Political System*, ed. Anthony King (Washington, DC: American Enterprise Institute, 1979).

Hembra, Richard L., director, Environmental Protection Issues, Resources, Community, and Economic Development Division, US General Accounting Office, in "Observations on the Environmental Protection Agency's Budget and Public Works," US Senate, March 7, 1990.

Hoffer, Eric, *The Temper of Time* (New York, 1967).

Holloway, Marguerite, "High and Dry," *Scientific American*, **265** (December 1991) pp. 16–17.

Jacobs, Wilbur R., "The Great Despoilation: Environmental Themes in American Frontier History," *Pacific Historical Review*, **47** (1978).

Johnson, Lyndon B., "Natural Beauty – Message from the President of the United States," *Congressional Record*, 89th Congress, 1st Session, vol. 111, pt 2 (February 8, 1965) p. 2086.

Jones, Charles O. and Randall Strahan, "The Effects of Energy Politics on Congressional and Executive Organizations in the 1970s," *Legislative Studies Quarterly*, **10**: 2 (May 1985).

Julber, Eric, "Let's Open up our Wilderness Areas," *Reader's Digest*, **100** (1972) pp. 125–8.

Julber, Eric, "The Wilderness: Just How Wild Should It Be?," *Trends*, **9** (1972) pp. 15–18.

Katz, James Everett, *Congress and National Energy Policy* (New Brunswick, NJ: Transaction Books, 1984).

Kingdom, John, *Agendas, Alternatives, and Public Policy* (Boston, MA: Little, Brown, 1984).

Kreiger, Martin, "What's Wrong with Plastic Trees?," *Science,* **179** (1973).

Kriz, Margaret E., "Pesticidal Pressures," *National Journal,* December 12, 1988, pp. 3125–6.

Krza, Paul, "The Bureau's Rube Goldberg Machines," in *Western Water Made Simple* (Washington, DC: Island Press, 1987).

Lavelle, Mariane, "Talking about Air," *The National Law Journal,* June 10, 1991.

Lavelle, Mariane and Marcia Coyle, "Unequal Protection: The Racial Divide in Environmental Law," *National Law Journal,* September 21, 1992, p. S–2.

Leopold, Aldo, "The Green Lagoon," *American Forests,* **51** (1945).

Leopold, Aldo, *A Sand Country Almanac and Sketches Here and There* (New York: Oxford University Press, 1949).

Lester, James, "A New Federalism?," in *Environmental Policy in the 1990,* ed. Norman J. Vig and Michael E. Kraft (Washington, DC: Congressional Quarterly Press, 1990) pp. 59–79.

Lewis, Jack, "Superfund, RCRA, and UST: The Clean-up Threesome," *EPA Journal,* **17**: 3 (July–August 1991) pp. 7–14.

Leydet, François, *Time and the River Flowing: Grand Canyon* (San Francisco: Sierra Club, 1964).

Lowi, Theodore W., *The End of Liberalism* (New York: W.W. Norton, 1969).

MacDonnell, Lawrence and Sarah Bates, "Rethinking Resources," in MacDonnell and Bates (eds), *National Resource Policy and Law* (Washington, DC: Island Press, 1994).

MacDonnell, Lawrence, "Mineral Law in the United States: A Study in Legal Change," in MacDonnell and Bates (eds), *Natural Resources, Policy and Law* (Washington, DC: Island Press, 1994).

Malin, James, *The Grassland of North America* (Lawrence: University of Kansas Press, 1947).

Malone, Charles R., "National Energy Strategy and High-Level Nuclear Waste," *Bioscience,* **41**: 11 (December 1991).

Marsh, George P., *Man and Nature, or Physical Geography as Modified by Human Action* (New York: Charles Scribner, 1864).

Marshall, Eliot, "The Geopolitics of Nuclear Waste," *Science,* February 22, 1991, pp. 864–7.

Marshall, Robert, "The Problem of the Wilderness," *Scientific Monthly,* **30** (1930) pp. 144–5.

Marston, Ed, "When Water Kingdoms Clash," in *Western Water Made Simple* (Washington, DC: Island Press, 1987).

Marston, Ed, "Reworking the Colorado River Basin," in *Western Water Made Simple* (Washington, DC: Island Press, 1987).

McGee, W. J., "The Conservation of Natural Resources," *Proceedings of the Mississippi Valley Historical Association,* III (1908–10).

Melnick, R. Shep, *Regulation and the Courts* (Washington, DC: Brookings Institute, 1983).

Meyer, Stephen M., "Ain't Necessarily So: The Myth of Jobs Versus the Environment," *Sierra,* March/April 1993, p. 45.

Mosher, Lawrence, "The Corps Adapts, the Bureau Founders," in *Western Water Made Simple* (Washington, DC: Island Press, 1987).

Mossman, Brooke T. *et al.*, "Asbestos: Scientific Developments and Implications for Public Policy," *Science*, **247** (January 19, 1990).

Muir, John, "The Wild Parks and Forest Reservations of the West," *Atlantic Monthly*, **81** (1898).

Myers, Norman, *The Sinking Ark: A New Look at the Problem of Disappearing Species* (Oxford: Oxford University Press, 1979).

Nash, Roderick, *Wilderness and the American Mind*, 3rd edn (New Haven, CT: Yale University Press, 1982).

Nash, Roderick, "Why Wilderness?" in *For the Conservation of the Earth*, ed. Vance Martin (Golden, CO: Fulcrum, 1988).

Nash, Roderick (ed.), *American Environmentalis: Readings in Conservation History* (New York: McGraw-Hill, 1990).

National Research Council, *Acid Deposition Atmospheric Processes in Eastern North America: A Review of Current Scientific Understanding* (Washington, DC: National Academy Press, 1983).

Norse, Elliot, *Ancient Forests of the Pacific Northwest* (Washington, DC: The Wilderness Society, 1990).

Oelschlaeger, Max, *The Idea of Wilderness* (New Haven, CT: Yale University Press, 1991).

Ophulus, William, *Ecology and the Politics of Scarcity* (San Francisco: W. H. Freeman, 1977).

Ottinger, Richard, "Introduction: The Tragedy of US Energy R & D Policy," in *The Politics of Research and Development*, ed. John Byrne and Daniel Rich (New Brunswick, NJ: Transaction Books, 1986).

Pinchott, Gifford, *The Fight for Conservation* (Garden City, NY: Harcourt, Brace, 1910).

Pinchott, Gifford, *Breaking New Ground* (New York: Harcourt, Brace and Jovanovich, 1947).

Pollock, Cynthia, *Mining Urban Wastes: The Potential for Recycling* (Washington, DC: Worldwatch Institute, April 1987).

Portney, Paul, "EPA and the Evolution of Federal Regulation," in *Public Policies for Environmental Protection*, ed. Paul R. Portney (Washington, DC: Resources for the Future, 1990).

Postel, Sandra, *Altering the Earth's Chemistry: Assessing the Risks* (Washington, DC: Worldwatch Institute, 1986).

Powell, John Wesley, *Report on the Lands of the Arid Regions of the United States*, US House of Representatives, Executive Document 73, 45th Congress, 2nd Session, Washington, DC: US Government Printing Office, April 3, 1878.

President's Council on Environmental Quality and US Department of State, *The Global 2000 Report*, vol. 1: *Summary* (Washington, DC: GPO, 1980).

Quillen, Ed, "What Size Shoe Does an Acre-foot Wear?," in *Western Water Made Simple* (Washington, DC: Island Press, 1987).

Reich, Charles, *The Greening of America* (New York, 1971).

Reiger, John F., *American Sportsmen and the Origins of Conservation* (Norman: University of Oklahoma Press, 1986).

Reisner, Marc, *Cadillac Desert: The American West and its Disappearing Water* (New York: Penguin Books, 1993).

Ridgeway, James, *The Politics of Ecology* (New York: E.P. Dutton, 1970).

Roosevelt, Theodore, "Opening Address by the President," in Newton C. Blanchard (ed.), *Proceedings of a Conference of Governors in the White House* (Washington, DC: US Government Printing Office, 1909).

Roosevelt, Theodore, *African Game-Trails: An Account of the African Wanderings of an American Hunter-Naturalist* (New York, 1910).

Rosenbaum, Walter A., *Environmental Politics and Policy* (Washington, DC: Congressional Quarterly, 1991).

Rowley, William D., *US Forest Service Grazing and Rangelands* (College Station, TX: Texas A&M Press, 1985).

Russell, Milton, E. William Colglazier, and Bruce E. Tonn, "The US Hazardous Waste Legacy," *Environment*, **34**: 6 (July–August 1992) pp. 12–15.

Sale, Kirkpatrick, "The Forest for the Trees: Can Today's Environmentalists Tell the Difference?," *Mother Jones*, **11** (November 1986) pp. 25–6, 28–9, 32–3, 58.

Schneider, Paul, "When a Whistle Blows in the Forest," *Audubon* 7 (July 1990).

Schurz, Carl, *Annual Report of the Secretary of the Interior on the Operations of the Department for the Fiscal Year Ended June 30, 1877* (Washington, DC: US Government Printing Office, 1877).

Schwartz, William (ed.), *Voices for Wilderness* (New York, 1969).

Sedjo, Roger, "Forest Resources: Resilient and Serviceable," in Frederick and Sedjo (eds), *America's Renewable Resources: Historical Trends and Current Challenges* (Washington, DC: Resources for the Future, 1991) pp. 84–5.

Seredich, John, *Your Resource Guide to Environmental Organizations* (Irvine: Smiling Dolphins Press, 1991).

Sessions, George, and Bill Devall, *Deep Ecology* (Layton, UT: Peregrine Smith, 1985).

Shabecoff, Philip, *A Fierce Green Fire: The American Environmental Movement* (New York: Hill and Wang, 1993).

Shank, Bernard, *This Land is your Land* (San Francisco: Sierra Club Books, 1984).

Shea, Cynthea Pollock, *Protecting Life on Earth: Steps to Save the Ozone Layer* (Washington, DC: Worldwatch Institute, 1988).

Shearer, C. Russell, "Comparative Analysis of the Basel and Bamako Conventions on Hazardous Waste," *Environmental Law*, **23**: 1 (1993).

Slovic, Paul, Mark Layman, and James H. Flynn, "Risk Perception, Trust, and Nuclear Waste: Lessons from Yucca Mountain," *Environment*, **33**: 3 (April 1991).

Smith, Henry Nash, *Virgin Land: The American West as Symbol and Myth* (Cambridge: Harvard University Press, 1950).

Standing Bear, *Land of the Spotted Eagle* (Boston, MA: Houghton Mifflin, 1933).

Stegner, Wallace, *Beyond the Hundredth Meridian: John Wesley Powell and the Second Coming of the West* (Boston, MA: Houghton Mifflin, 1954).

Stegner, Wallace, "The Wilderness Idea," in David Brower (ed.), *Wilderness: America's Living Heritage* (San Francisco: Sierra Club, 1961) pp. 97–102.

Stegner, Wallace, *This is Dinosaur: Echo Park Country and its Magical Rivers* (New York: Alfred A. Knopf, 1955).

Stegner, Wallace, *The Sound of Mountain Water* (Garden City, NY: Doubleday, 1969).

Stowell, Cynthia D., "Salmon: Continuity for a Culture," in *Western Water Made Simple* (Washington, DC: Island Press, 1987).

Synder, Gary, *Earth House Hold* (New York: New Directions, 1969).

Snyder, Gary, *Turtle Island* (New York: New Directions, 1974).

Snyder, Gary, *The Real Work: Interviews and Talks, 1964–1979* (New York, 1980).

Swain, Donald C., *Federal Conservation Policy, 1921–1933*, LXXVI (Berkeley, CA: University of California Publications in History, 1963).

Thoreau, Henry David, *Walden and Other Writings* (New York: Barnes and Noble Books, 1993).

Trava, Jose, "Sharing Water with the Colossus of the North," in *Western Water Made Simple* (Washington, DC: Island Press, 1987).

Tucker, William, "Is Nature too Good for Us?," *Harper's* (March 1982) pp. 27–35.

Tufte, Edward R., *Political Control of the Economy* (Princeton, NJ: Princeton University Press, 1978).

Turnage, Robert, "Ansel Adams: the Role of the Artist in the Environmental Movement," *Living Wilderness*, **43** (1980) pp. 8–9.

Turner, Frederick Jackson, *The Frontier in American History* (New York: Holt, Rinehart, and Winston, 1920).

US Congress, Senate, Committee on Interior and Insular Affairs, Subcommittee on Irrigation and Reclamation, Hearings, *Colorado River Storage Project*, 84th Congress, 1st Session (Feb. 28, March 1–5, 1955) pp. 696, 679–84.

US Congress, House, Committee on Interior and Insular Affairs, *Supplemental Report on HR 3383*, 84th Congress, 2nd Session, House Rpt 1087, pt 2 (Feb. 14, 1956).

US Congress, Senate, Committee on Interior and Insular Affairs, Hearings, *National Wilderness Preservation Act*, 85th Congress, 2nd Session (Nov. 7, 10, 13, 1958) p. 573.

US Congress, House of Representatives, *National Energy Policy Plan: Message from the President of the United States*, H. Doc. 97–77, 97th Congress, 1st Session, 1981.

US Department of Commerce, Bureau of the Census, *Statistical Abstract of the United States* (Washington, DC: GPO, 1989), Table 353.

US Department of the Interior, US Fish and Wildlife Service, *Wetlands Status and Trends* (Washington, DC: US Government Printing Office, 1991).

US Environmental Protection Agency, *A Citizen's Guide to Radon: What it Is and What to do about It*, Pamphlet no. OPA 86–004 (Washington, DC: GPO, August 1986).

US Environmental Protection Agency, *Environmental Progress and Policies: EPA's Update* (Washington, DC: EPA, August 1988).

US Environmental Protection Agency, *Characterization of Municipal Solid Waste in the United States: 1990 Update*, EPA/530–SW-90-042 (Washington, DC: GPO, June 1990) ES-3.

US General Accounting Office, "Ground Water Overdrafting Must Be Controlled," Report no. CED-80-96 (September 12, 1980).

US General Accounting Office, "The Debate over Acid Precipation: Opposing Views, Status of Research," Report no. EMD-81-131 (September 1981).

US General Accounting Office, "Efforts to Clean-up DOD-Owned Inactive Hazardous Waste Disposal Sites," Report no. GAO/NSIAD-85-41 (April 12, 1985).

US House of Representatives, Committee on Interior and Insular Affairs, Subcommittee on Oversight and Investigations, *Oversight Hearing: Emergency Preparedness and the Licensing Process for Commercial Nuclear Power Reactors,* April 18, 1983, serial no. 98–52, pt 1 (Washington, DC: GPO, 1984).

US General Accounting Office, "Cost-Benefit Analysis Can Be Useful in Assessing Environmental Regulations, Despite Limitations," Report no. GAO/RCED 84–62 (April 1984).

US General Accounting Office, "Toxic Substances: EPA Has Made Limited Progress in Identifying PCB Users," Report no. GAO/RCED 88–127 (April 1988), 3; Council on Environmental Quality, *Environmental Quality* (1986) Tables 9–9, 9–6.

US Public Health Service, "The Health Consequences of Involuntary Smoking," *Surgeon General's Report* (Washington, DC: GPO, 1986).

United Steelworkers of America, *Poison in our Air* (Washington, DC: United Steelworkers of America, 1969).

Vogt, William, *Road to Survival* (New York: William Sloane Associates, 1948).

Watkins, Thomas, *Gold and Silver in the West* (Palo Alto, CA: American West, 1971).

Waxman, Henry, "Quailing over Clean Air," *Environment,* **33**: 6 (July–August 1991).

Webb, Walter Prescott, *The Great Plains* (Boston, MA: Grosset & Dunlap, 1931).

Webb, Walter Prescott, *The Great Frontier* (Austin: University of Texas, 1952).

Wegman, Lydia, "Air Toxics: The Strategy," *EPA Journal,* **17**: 1 (January–February 1991) pp. 32–33.

Wernick, Robert, "Speaking Out: Let's Spoil the Wilderness," *Saturday Evening Post,* **238** (November 6, 1965).

Whitaker, John C., *Striking a Balance: Environment and Natural Resources Policy in the Nixon–Ford Years* (Washington, DC: American Enterprise Institute, 1976).

Whiteman, Lily, "Recent Efforts to Stop Abuse of SMCRA: Have They Gone Far Enough?," *Environmental Law,* **20** (Fall 1990).

Wilkinson, Charles, and Daniel Conner, "A Great Loneliness of Spirit," in *Western Water Made Simple* (Washington, DC: Island Press, 1987).

Williams, Michael (ed.), *Wetlands: A Threatened Landscape* (New York: Basil Blackwell, 1991).

Wilson, Edward O., *Sociobiology: The New Synthesis* (Cambridge, MA: Harvard University Press, 1975).

Wilson, Edward O., "Million-Year Histories: Species Diversity as an Ethical Goal," *Wilderness*, **47** (Summer 1984).

World Commission on Environment and Development, *Our Common Future* (Oxford University Press, 1987).

Worobec, Mary Devine, *Toxic Substances Controls Guide* (Washington, DC: Bureau of National Affairs, 1989).

Wuerthner, George, "The Price is Wrong," *Sierra*, **75**: 5 (September–October, 1990).

Wuerthner, George, "How the West Was Eaten," *Wilderness*, **54**: 192 (Spring 1991) p. 36.

Young, John, *Mining the Earth*, Worldwatch Paper 109, July 1992, pp. 16–18.

Zahniser, Howard, "The Second Wilderness Conference," *Living Wilderness*, **16** (1951).

Zahniser, Howard C. "Our Wilderness Need," *Living Wilderness*, **20** (1955).

Zaslowsky, Dyan and T. H. Watkins, *These American Lands: Parks, Wilderness, and the Public Lands* (Washington, DC: Island Press, 1994).

Index